W9-BDR-818

Picture Yourself Shooting Pool

Matthew Sherman

Course Technology PTR
A part of Cengage Learning

COURSE TECHNOLOGY
CENGAGE Learning

Australia • Brazil • Japan • Korea • Mexico • Singapore • Spain • United Kingdom • United States

Picture Yourself Shooting Pool

Matthew Sherman

**Publisher and General Manager,
Course Technology PTR:**
Stacy L. Hiquet

Associate Director of Marketing:
Sarah Panella

Manager of Editorial Services:
Heather Talbot

Marketing Manager: Jordan Casey

Acquisitions Editor: Megan Belanger

Project Editor: Jenny Davidson

Technical Reviewer: Carl Oswald

PTR Editorial Services Coordinator:
Erin Johnson

Interior Layout: Jill Flores

Cover Designer: Mike Tanamachi

DVD-ROM Producer:
Jaime Sherman

Indexer: Kevin Broccoli

Proofreader: Kim Benbow

© 2009 Matthew Sherman

ALL RIGHTS RESERVED. No part of this work covered by the copyright herein may be reproduced, transmitted, stored, or used in any form or by any means graphic, electronic, or mechanical, including but not limited to photocopying, recording, scanning, digitizing, taping, Web distribution, information networks, or information storage and retrieval systems, except as permitted under Section 107 or 108 of the 1976 United States Copyright Act, without the prior written permission of the publisher.

For product information and technology assistance, contact us at
Cengage Learning Academic Resource Center, 1-800-354-9706

For permission to use material from this text or product,
submit all requests online at **cengage.com/permissions**

Further permissions questions can be emailed to
permissionrequest@cengage.com

Library of Congress Control Number: 2008902393

ISBN-13: 978-1-59863-519-5

ISBN-10: 1-59863-519-0

Course Technology
25 Thomson Place
Boston, MA 02210
USA

Cengage Learning is a leading provider of customized learning solutions with office locations around the globe, including Singapore, the United Kingdom, Australia, Mexico, Brazil, and Japan. Locate your local office at:
international.cengage.com/region.

Cengage Learning products are represented in Canada by
Nelson Education, Ltd.

For your lifelong learning solutions, visit **courseptr.com**.

Visit our corporate website at **cengage.com**.

Printed in the United States of America
1 2 3 4 5 6 7 11 10 09

With appreciation to my lovely wife, Janine Marie Sherman,
who has been my cheerleading support,
giving me the will to work toward my dreams.

Acknowledgments

I AM GRATEFUL TO Art and Dana Rogers and their lovely Art of Billiards facility in Gainesville, Florida. I was privileged to prepare this book and DVD using their Diamond ProAm Tables, especially their finals table from an IPT King of the Hill Shootout, autographed by 22 of the world's top professionals who have enjoyed its playing surface. Art and Dana patiently worked with our crew and me as we prepared hours of instructional video and over 1,500 photos. They are always gracious people and run a great pool hall.

Thanks go to Jenny Davidson and Megan Belanger for their editing and continual encouragement, helping ensure the success of this project. They truly made the work of this book a pleasure. I am also indebted to BCA Master Instructor Carl Oswald, one of America's finest and in demand pool teachers, for taking time to review the manuscript and for tirelessly working to clarify terms and ideas.

Thank you to my friend, Don "Wisconsin Skinny" Lutz, known in many circles as "The Grumpy Old Coach." Donny, a Certified Bowling Instructor in the 1960s and a Certified Billiards Instructor since 1993, has also been a playing team member or coach of over 40 championship pool teams since 1966, besides the winner of numerous individual Eight-Ball and Nine-Ball titles. Don's passion for coaching pool inspires me to be exacting with my students. As my teammate or my opponent, Don's skills and knowledge inspires me to practice pool more!

Thank you to Course Technology PTR and Cengage Learning for believing in this book and bringing it to a wide audience to enjoy.

A "shout out" of thanks goes to the good people at About.com and my kind Sports Editor, Fred Meyer.

To the Sherman family, the Steinbergs, and the Lauricellas, I say a hearty thank you for your unwavering faith in me to be a better citizen, dad, and family man.

I appreciate the crew who worked many hours to create a quality book and DVD companion. Thank you to Kristen Lacoste and Victor Bard for your help with photo and DVD production, and to Jaime, Alex, and Ben Sherman for their kind support and many hours of assistance with each aspect of production. Jaime and I worked particularly closely and had a chance to deepen our friendship and mutual respect as one happy result. Thanks, brother. I am grateful to God for the freedom and pleasure of playing the sport of pool, and freedom of spirit since I trusted His Son for salvation in August 1990.

About the Author

MATTHEW "QUICK DRAW" SHERMAN, who was born in New York City, directs the University of Florida's Pool League, which has produced five national collegiate champions. Matt is the Guide to Pool & Billiards at About.com, a top five website with over 53 million visitors a month.

Matt has appeared internationally on television and in print, hosting and emceeing celebrities from the James Bond series and also real world intelligence officers from the KGB and CIA, Dr. Michael Behe of *Darwin's Black Box*, and Oscar and Tony award winners. He has appeared on NBC, CBS, ABC, Discovery, HGTV, VH-1, TNN, C-SPAN, and on the radio, and has been quoted in the *L.A. Times*, *Washington Post*, *Chicago Tribune*, *Las Vegas Sun*, *New Orleans Times-Picayune*, *Time*, and *Time Europe*, and in numerous other publications.

Matt and Janine Sherman reside in Gainesville, Florida, with their children, Alexandria and Benjamin. Matt is editor of a number of books in print and a regular contributor to several publications. *Picture Yourself Shooting Pool* is his first book.

Table of Contents

Chapter 6   Simple and Straight: Stroking Your Cue .. 125

Chapter 9   Master Moves: Guiding Your Cue Ball 203

Chapter 10 Tools of the Trade: Key Shots 227

Introduction

WRITING IS FAR DIFFERENT from lecturing, speaking, or preaching on any given subject. Word choices must be economical and precise to be effective. Writing for sport, however, requires in-depth explanation to translate how actions *feel* and the semantics of how to, where to, and what to do with stick and ball. Explaining the accurate racking of a set of pool balls takes mere moments to perform at a poolroom exhibition as on the companion DVD. In written form, it required seven photos and nearly 2,000 words for this book. But tighter racks on the pool tables of the world are worth the effort.

Also worth effort is most anything I can do to further pool. This great sport once was crowned king by daily appearances on *The New York Times*' front page, when flappers flapped, speakeasies poured, and legends of the felt Willie Mosconi and Ralph Greenleaf vied for headlines with Babe Ruth and Red Grange.

In the 1950s as the world war had ended, servicemen and women left military base tables in Europe and Asia behind for children and white picket fences stateside. Pool nearly died until reviving with Paul Newman as "Fast Eddie" and Jackie Gleason as "Minnesota Fats" in 1961's *The Hustler*. That pool boom and happy memories led my grandfather to get a table for his basement, which I long felt was destined for my enjoyment even before I was born.

It was October 1986 and Paul Newman, after personal and enthusiastic tinkering on the script, resumed as Fast Eddie for *The Color of Money* with help from acting colleagues, Tom Cruise, John Turturro, and Mary Elizabeth Mastrantonio, and a certain Martin Scorsese as director. Boom! While purists regard *The Hustler* as the superior film, *Money* put pool's money where its mouth was (hustlers and tournaments, action and drama) and racked a Best Actor Oscar for Paul Newman and nominations for Mastrantonio, art direction, and screenwriting. Watching in the theater with interest, I was a high school senior at Stuyvesant in New York, and Julian's, Manhattan's last great holdout, was the *only* pool hall to be found. It sat grandly just two blocks from school, but I was off to college just as pool's second revival would take wings.

Through the early 1990s, upwards of 40 to 50 regular players would congregate at the University of Florida's Game Room, whose pool hall boasted nearly 20 nine-foot pool tables, and Snooker, Cushion Billiards, and Bumper Pool tables. I was happy attending my chosen university. The action was wild and everybody thought they were Fast Eddie, Vincent Lauria, or Eddie or Vinnie's newest girlfriend. Pool hustlers descended on the students like flies, New York sprouted fabulous new halls like comedian David "Sticks" Brenner's Amsterdam Billiards, and pool was growing once again.

James Bond, Indiana Jones, and Batman soon were to replace pool's golden boys in the public mind, however. Heroes are fleeting and movie audiences are fickle. We hung on at the pool hall until everyone graduated. I planted roots in town and stayed long enough to run the leagues I used to win, and waited.

Pool now is going great guns with new tours and leagues, including the glamorous International Pool Tour (IPT), sponsored by infomercial giant Kevin Trudeau—I prepared this book and DVD using the IPT finals table Efren "The Magician" Reyes played on to defeat Mike "Captain Hook" Sigel for a $200,000 first prize. Sigel's second place award of $100,000 was more than he had earned for several entire *years* in the '80s when he was known as "Mr. Final" due to his success at the top levels of the game—winning approximately 85 of 95 tournaments where he reached the final match.

Pool appears today constantly on ESPN, including Speed Pool, Artistic Billiards, and trick shot tournaments, and in other media, especially advertisements and commercials where a youthful spirit of excitement is projected. A who's who of Hollywood have appeared in pool projects for TV and movies, including Famke Janssen, Omar Sharif, Rod Steiger, Christopher Walken, Johnny and June Carter Cash, Whoopi Goldberg, Rip Torn, James Coburn, Bruce Boxleitner, and more. Yet pool may slip back quite a bit again without its lifeblood maintained, players who know one end of the cue from the other.

"Let's do a pool book and DVD!" thus became an epic quest to bring you more enjoyment and more knowledge from pool than you've had before. Equipment, english, speed control, and lots of little and big secrets on stance and stroke. And you, the reader, and the sport of pool are worth all the effort and more.

Thanks for joining me at the table. Here's to another century or two of pool, some of the most fun you can have indoors.

1

Why a New Take on Learning
Pool?

How this Picture Yourself *book cried to be written*

PICTURE YOURSELF SHOOTING POOL like a champ. Picture yourself shooting stellar pool, balls rushing to pockets at your command, blazing a path across the table with mind and body as the white cue ball humbles itself to your whim. You smile as you spin balls, directing their motions with gentle movements of the small muscles in your hands, now and then smashing a rack to powder instead, the full weight of your body behind the stroke. What are the elements of terrific pool, and can anyone learn to become great at this colorful and magnificent table sport?

Pool Is Popular, Though Not Always Played Well

THERE ARE 30 MILLION casual and frequent pool players in the U.S. alone. Several million participate weekly in leagues and tournaments. American pool has experienced revival since *The Color of Money* starred Tom Cruise and Paul Newman in 1986. Thousands of new, chic pool halls cover the U.S., and a half-dozen more pool movies have since been produced. But among the hype, why aren't most people playing better pool?

I remember lively debates with pool friends (who could have easily ended as enemies as our talks burned). Is there one and only one correct way to make the balls do what you wish? Is the most efficient pool stroke a pull or push movement, or is the cue stick gently *tossed* into the white cue ball? Should I pause at the end of my backswing for a long moment or go through to the forward stroke without hesitating? Why do some pros bend low,

their chins nearly scraping the cue stick, while other great players stand nearly erect, their heads two feet above the table?

Figure 1.1
Rack and roll.

A Better Way?

MY OBSESSION FOR MANY YEARS, a quest of discovery, has been the search for a unified field theory applied to pool, a set of correct mechanics for stroke and stance combined with ultimate knowledge of pool physics. I've also sought a simple, elegant way of teaching what I've learned, to change my students' games for the better (and help me win more also, of course).

To my joy, I've found rock-solid principles for this game underlying the different styles pros use to get the job done. Along the way, I've kept notes of key shots and concepts to help you win more, even as you learn pool fundamentals.

I get a kick watching my students' games improve just as if my own game grows. The pool shooters I mentor improve fast as I make complex pool theory simple and approachable for new and intermediate players. In *Picture Yourself Shooting Pool,* I bring you the billiards key ideas I've shared with national pool champions. Learn correct methods for mind and body at pool and get more enjoyment out of the game soon. Dazzle your friends with your new and improved skills!

Figure 1.2
Quest for the best.

A New Method

I'VE WORKED TO SHED FRESH LIGHT not addressed elsewhere in print or on pool websites. Other concepts have been only touched on before and sparked more detail for this book. Most teachers do not explain avoiding the double hit foul (see Chapter 12), for example, and most pool books have a few scant paragraphs on stance and stroke, perhaps even one sentence like,

"Most players should balance their body weight between both feet and hold the cue lightly," the equivalent of telling a golfer, "Hold the club loosely with the hands then swing hard; that's all you need to know." There is more to pool, including different ways a cue may be stroked to produce special effects (see Chapter 7), with most pool books lackluster in this area, too.

I will use difficult-to-refute principles, physics, and geometry made simple to help you understand why the right moves are right for you:

▶ Why does standing as I recommend provide correct balance and head alignment?

▶ Why does gripping the cue stick lightly lead to heightened accuracy, and why do 90% of players use a tight grip in error instead?

▶ How can the player bend over the table correctly while keeping pressure off his lower back, even strengthening his core muscles while playing pool?

▶ What wrist motion(s) does the professional pool player use, and how can the more casual player incorporate pro techniques for added power and feel at the table?

The goal was simple but challenging: create one of the better books on pool instruction ever for the beginner and intermediate player. To do so, I've recorded intriguing details on aim and stroke and other critical points, but also produced for you (hopefully) clearer and simpler (if glossier) presentation than has been shared elsewhere.

It can be trying to work from typical vague instructions like "hold the cue however you are comfortable." You and I are on a journey together now, as we compare loose and tight grips on the stick, correct and incorrect body stance, different stroke methods, and more, all which may make your holding the cue *uncomfortable* for a short while until things click in and your pool game suddenly improves. Embrace change at the table, and you'll soon overcome your initial discomfort.

Get More from the Book and DVD: Using *Picture Yourself Shooting Pool*

THIS BOOK'S FORMULA STATES that by adding the following:

1. Using the right equipment and stroke motion **and**

2. Understanding how to read the shot at hand **and**

3. Setting your body correctly to the stick and table

Your game will progress quickly. You will shoot ten in a row and be the life of the party.

PLEASE BEWARE

Overcoming the errors that hold most players' games in check requires commitment to having body, stroke, and a good read of the table in place before any and every shot.

The book is to be studied sequentially, each new concept building upon those given before. Read the whole book through, watch the DVD, then return to those book and DVD chapters you find most helpful.

I want to emphasize to you also to actually prepare and *play the shots as diagrammed* on your local table. Your skills will increase much faster than if you read without physical practice.

Going from Basics and Beyond to Expert Play

AUTHOR ROBERT BYRNE has quoted a pool hustler who said once of a sitting U.S. President, "...That guy can't run six balls." Ten in a row or more without a miss is considered a basic skill set for Straight Pool (see Chapter 14), but fewer than 1 in 100 pool players have ever strung ten shots together in one turn. With some practice applied to the concepts in this book, you will be hitting that mark quite soon and often. Enjoy!

Figure 1.3
Pool is true cool.

Why Is Pool Cool?

BEFORE WE JUMP IN, I consider it my duty to mention reasons why pool is such an amazing sport. You are in good company reading this book.

Pool Is the Game Where You Can Be Successful for a Lifetime

You need not be athletic or have marvelous hand-eye coordination to play pool well. Good reasoning and logic abilities are two plusses; only legal blindness can end your career permanently. Great pool is less about scoring spectacular trick shots than knowing how to guide the white cue ball where you want and make shots (as explained within). The fact is, women often surpass the opposite gender at the game (staying coolly logical, playing heads above hearts), trumping the macho men who smash away without care. You can be thin or heavy, tall or short, otherwise coordinated (or klutzy), and still excel at pool.

As in most other stick-and-ball sports, you apply a basic set of similar movements to any shot to win at pool. Pool's basics as taught within adjust to the many possibilities on the felt. I'll show you also any tweaks needed for especially challenging shots, added stroke power, defensive play, and more.

Figure 1.4
A smashing good time.

There is much to learn in pool, and new worlds to explore at every turn. One researcher has calculated **54 quadrillion** different pool shots available to any pool table. This startling number was mentioned in Ray "Cool Cat" Martin's *99 Critical Shots*, but the actual number may be greater still. We'll organize the quadrillions down to basic, repeating principles. Even if you learn new moves 50 years from now, though, you're in good company.

Most pool pros peak in their late thirties, before the strain of competition weakens their nerve and weakened eyesight sours their game, but the average Joe improves and learns continually until the end, having more plateaus to reach toward. Young people tend to shoot strong in general but fall to those with more experience. There are plenty of 75-year-olds who can thrash the young whippersnappers (and my wallet is emptier for it, believe me). You can enjoy pool lifelong, so start now.

Pool Has Had the Worst Reputation of Any American Sport, but Is Chic Now

In the Depression, through World War II, then into the 1950s, poolrooms were a misogynist wonderland for men behaving badly, and having fun doing so. Child runaways transformed in pool halls to become misspent youth guzzling booze and smoking cigarettes, who later graduated to tobacco-spittin' genuine pool bums. Today, however, women shooters are allowed in the hall without frowns and often can whip the fellows, too. You can drop $20 an hour to play pool with local celebrities dressed to the nines, while you sip a latté and watch ESPN on a giant plasma screen. Go figure. Poolrooms have evolved to sporting dream centers. Mix, mingle, and Perrier the night away.

Are there still pool hustlers, sharks who prey on "pool fish" at the local dive? Certainly! Money changes hands in most pool halls nightly around the globe. Although 21st-century pool features on TV and in print constantly, featuring beautiful, glamorous models enjoying a cool time without gambling.

Figure 1.5
The sport has advanced beyond pool's "glory days."

Pool Gets You Closer to the Action

I've enjoyed playing at the table adjacent to Hall of Fame stars, and at times, they've even asked me to join them on their table (not that I was anyone special). We pool fans can live closer to the limelight than football or basketball fans at the stadium. On TV, the cameras close in on action so tight, you can see the sweat on the pool shooters' faces.

Pool pros usually are blue-collar folk (a famous exception being rich kid Irving "The Deacon" Crane), so they can be easygoing and welcoming to fans. Since they make far less money than their athlete counterparts in golf or tennis (and often Table Tennis or chess!), they appreciate their fans who are appreciative of their skill.

Pool Has a Rich, Lengthy History

As spoken a long time ago in a palace far, far away…

Cleopatra

"Let it alone; let's to billiards: come, Charmian."

Charmian

"My arm is sore; best play with Mardian."

—*Antony and Cleopatra,* Act II, Scene V, William Shakespeare

Pool may not be quite as old as the Roman Empire, but its history will give us fascinating insight as we pick up our modern cues and learn the game together, starting with the next chapter.

How to Learn Any Sport: Imitating

2

Models

The imitative mind is the mightiest pool tool

I'M GOING TO REVEAL to you a secret from the world of sport. Great athletes rarely learn their craft from books and instructional materials (making writing this book an added challenge). They learn primarily by modeling, by imitating the performances of other fine athletes. There are countless stories in pool history of Young Guy X or Gal X watching Old Master Y shoot pool, and then going forward to create outstanding skills by imitation.

The ability to recall a particular body action from memory is called *procedural memory*.

Pool Procedural Memory

PROCEDURAL MEMORIES are already in our brain's recall banks for everything from tying a shoe or walking down the street to shooting pool. Such tasks are learned by mimicry by and for the right brain, the visual and *feel* side of the brain. When we over-think procedural tasks rather than visualize them or "just do them," we hamper our natural ability.

Thinking or saying aloud the specific instructions for walking while crossing the road, for example, from the left side of the brain, the articulating or "word" brain, would slow you down, as you can imagine. You might be slow enough to be hit by oncoming traffic! Likewise, Tiger Woods' fluid golf swing would slow or stop entirely if he placed it into spoken words during performance.

Tiger watched his dad swinging in the garage at age two, picked up a small club and mimicked while he watched, and was off to the golf races. I will likewise coach you within this book and companion DVD to make your good pool stroke a procedural memory or feeling, an automatic tool for you to use, your right brain seeing and feeling good pool with few mental words (though I will give you many words ahead to *learn how to feel* great pool).

Know What Feels Right

Procedural memory is huge in pool (and any stick-and-ball sport) since without it, you are reduced to a bowl of jelly quivering over the next shot. If you "left brain" comprehend that the next shot should be struck with "medium speed, a dash of draw spin, and two tips of left english," but you do not know how medium left english with draw *feels*, how can you be relaxed and confident to perform?

If you are like me and of average coordination, you may be thinking, "So, I am not Tiger Woods. I don't have his phenomenal athleticism, genius for sport, and thousands of hours to devote to practice. Can I be great at golf or pool?" Fortunately, this is not a tome on golf!

Tiger can swing a one-pound golf club around his body at 150 miles per hour, a senior golfer might be able to swing 75 to 100 m.p.h., but on few pool shots does the ball need to exceed 20 miles per hour on the table. You can do pool right, and this book even shows you plenty of strokes you can do as well as any pool pro. So, why don't most people play better than they do? Most amateurs don't know the pro pool moves or can't see the rich possibilities at the table.

Best Athlete Might Not Be Best Teacher

AS GOOD AS TIGER IS at golf, I wouldn't want him to teach me to play. Instead, I would have the best golf coach in the world to learn from instead of the best golfer. Over the long haul, would you like Tiger Woods teaching *you* to play golf or would you prefer the best golf *coach* in the world? Think about that for a moment.

This is my saving grace for *Picture Yourself Playing Pool*, for while I have no claim on being the best pool player in the world, I do teach my students effectively, and I will teach you what to think about and feel at the table (procedural learning) so you can progress faster.

You will read many words on how to hold the cue stick and how not to hold it, the motions of the wrist, where to aim, what to think about, and more. No matter your present skill level, this book will take your game to the next level.

PLEASE BEWARE

Don't skim this book, and resist the temptation to jump ahead. This book is designed to be read sequentially. In-depth instruction on the cue stick grip, for example, may take you 20 or 30 minutes to read and understand, including hands-on examples, but the correct grip will take seconds at the pool table once your mind (left brain) and body (right brain) grasp the complete picture of right and wrong procedure.

Figure 2.1
At play.

How Does It Feel?

SO, HOW DOES IT *FEEL* to smash a rack of Nine-Ball to powder or jump a cue ball high into the air over trouble? It feels lovely to me, but I am of course referring to the mental and physical sensations I can model for you to play great pool. My goal is to give you the all-important athletic "body knowledge" in addition to the left-brained stuff, including angles, speeds, and directions.

Fortunately, shooting pool is mostly small motion made with the smaller muscles of the body. Grandma can play as well as the young, macho kid next door, and she often plays far better because she is calmer in mind.

Including procedural feel or "athletic touch," there are three types of recall brainpower you can apply to pool as in life:

- ▶ **Procedural learning.** The feel and touch anticipated for the upcoming shot at the table—learning from and understanding correct motion and sensation during play.

- ▶ **Semantic learning.** The facts and figures, the how, what, and why of pool.

- ▶ **Episodic learning.** Remembering a list short-term or recalling a past occurrence, planning pool goals, and absorbing scoring and strategy concepts.

Many Players, Few Models

I WANTED TO WRITE THIS BOOK because pool players who enjoy the game acquire episodic learning on their own but need far more in-depth coaching and modeling. I don't fancy myself the Stephen Hawking of pool, but my personal *A Brief History of Pool* would include that our sport has long lacked enough teachers and coaches (their acceptance as professionals among the public has been difficult) to help the pool masses. Plenty of shooters like to "help," but their assistance can do more harm than good. I've seen players insist that no one can predict where a cue

ball will come to rest, for example, and recommend their fellow players trust to Zen more than physics and geometry.

Pool is in a rut regarding models to imitate for several reasons. First, great players tend to congregate in certain rooms on certain days and times in each town and city around the world (a sort of top-dog regular gathering at the local hotspot). If you are in the wrong room on the wrong days or learned pool from a poorly playing mom or dad on the family table, you are without a solid model.

Second, would you know a great pool player worth imitating if you saw one? This *Picture Yourself* volume was written to show you how a good player thinks and moves at the table. After a while, you learn to scent the fine and thoughtful player, the hustler, the tournament pro—a need as the best pool players often seek anonymity to hustle money by disguising their skill. They would rather you not watch them too closely and imitate their moves. You can hardly learn from things hidden from view.

Besides hustlers, the pros often don't want personal pool secrets out for other pros to improve their games or even criticize their "secrets." As one pro put it succinctly, "I'd give lessons but I'm a natural pool player and I don't know what I'm doing at the table." Plus, money on tour is hard fought for and scant, so often pool teaching becomes a chore for the pro to make a few bucks fast.

At times, however, a truly fine shooter is one table adjacent, three feet away, and you don't even realize it. Most casual players are wrapped in their own game and wouldn't know the hall-of-fame player next door on sight. Top hustlers and pros aren't household names as in other sports. You've heard of pool greats "Minnesota Fats" and probably Willie Mosconi, but both men have since passed on.

The pro ballplayer can hit a ball 500 feet or sink a basket from across the court, but the pro pool player makes very few spectacular shots; they are simply consistent to make many of the basic shots I will demonstrate in this book. *If you can pocket an easy shot as you make the white cue ball go where you need for the subsequent shot most of the time, you would be a pool pro, too.*

You would need to sit and study how the pro moves *in between* shots taken to see their total fluid rhythm, their determination to have the right fundaments in place *before* taking the stroke. That's great pool, and you need a pro or teacher to model it for your benefit.

Those Who Can Play Don't Teach

Other pool pros who might teach, can't teach. Toiling ten hours a day since their youth in the pool hall, and as implied by their appearances in poolrooms, not schoolrooms, they aren't articulate people or able to teach (with some notable exceptions). It takes a giving, patient person to make a great pool teacher. Besides this fact, the world of pool lacks certified and willing pro instructors. Every golf and tennis club in America has a resident teaching professional and perhaps several assistant pros. Sadly, few poolrooms have a teaching pro in-house. An added shame because those that employ a teaching pro are far busier and more profitable establishments year-round.

Figure 2.2
I am passionate (crazy?) about teaching pool.

Due to a quirk of TV entertainment, great pool players are limited in appearances on television and the media for you to watch and imitate. A good procedural learning opportunity is missed. Matches may be found online but get references or reviews for purchases, as at times lighting and camera work are inadequate.

Heavily edited TV segments are used to show tournament highlights, emphasizing simple-to-follow action like the explosive (but bad for the beginner and intermediate) game of Nine-Ball. "Billy will sink the 4-ball, folks, then try to sink the 5-ball, then the 6- and the 7-balls after" is understood by anyone watching.

What I would consider dramatic defensive and strategic shots are left on cutting room floors. Subtle cue ball control games like Straight Pool and Carom Pool are off screen almost entirely today. The casual viewing audience would be lost with these clever games (or so the TV producers believe, but skilled commentators can bring these games to life).

Classic Games Build Skills Overseas

Not coincidentally, in places like the Philippines, where players are devoted to more strategic games than Nine-Ball, top pool shooters are developed at a per capita rate much greater than here in America. Filipinos are crushing Americans at pool, yet watching American television, amateurs are led to believe they must play pool in a much more offensive, attacking style than the classic strategy style the Filipinos use. Nine-Ball on TV encourages the novice to become a spectacular shot maker rather than precisely guide the cue ball (the fast track to pool skill in this book).

4339055

What Happened to TV Pool?

Years ago, pool on TV featured more classic tests of skill than now. One year the bottom fell out as a large number of sleepy defensive pool battles were played poorly; the little screen moved to much more action-packed formats soon after. This disturbing trend continues today, with the surge of trick shot competitions aired on TV. As much as I enjoy watching trick shots like pool balls shot into plastic bottles or over physical obstacles or to topple dominoes, how does that help the average player's game?

In any case, Chapters 13, 14, and 15 will mix it up for you with popular games such as Eight-Ball, more classic skill tests, and some fun trick shots that are all illustrative of basic pool principles. All work and no fun burns out the pool shooter, especially if he is purely a student, never ceasing practice and study enough to enter the flow of true play.

Figure 2.3
Pool offers endless varieties of fun.

Semantic Knowledge and Pool

I AM FASCINATED BY the art and science of teaching and by semiotics in general (how meaning is communicated and symbolized or made concrete to our understanding). Such stuff has come in handy for pool teaching for me and now for you as my reader. For example, researchers have classified two other base types of memory adding to the procedural memories we've discussed for pool: semantic memory and episodic memory.

Semantic memories are facts and figures—what is a key, and what is a lock? How many quarters are in a U.S. dollar? I will provide you with pool's finest semantic knowledge, facts to answer the different shades of pool questions the table asks of you—which ball to shoot at first, or should I play to miss instead? What choices does a pool pro consider, and what do they focus on during the stroke? Although this book is written for pool beginners and intermediates, we are going in-depth together on stance and stroke, and the logic of pool, so even longtime fans can learn much about their own game.

Losing My Mind

THE THIRD TYPE OF MEMORY, *episodic memory*, is the first to degenerate noticeably as we age. Episodes or memory flashes seem to be held in the brain's frontal lobes, whose small surfaces show the effects first of losing brainpower as we age.

Episodes flash away at times, don't they? "Where are my keys?" "I found my keys, but which lock does this key fit inside?" The loss of episodic memory on a great player, whose brain is strong with pool procedures and semantics, fills the old yet true tale of the fellow who can win the game with ease, but can't remember if he is solids or stripes in

Eight-Ball and starts sinking his opponents' balls by mistake! Lost episodes affect me on occasion, too, though I've just a bit of white in my hair.

PLEASE BEWARE

It's not enough to have great hand-eye coordination or feel at the table (procedural memory). You'll need the facts and figures (semantic memory) of pool to succeed. Feel and facts are the focus of this book, so if you can remember whether you are stripes or solids (episodic memory), you will be well on your way!

Join the Grand Adventure

IT TAKES IMAGINATION and creativity to conceive and make outstanding pool shots. Billiards fans extend through history. Creative types historically have been devoted to pool and billiards.

Especially avid fans through history include Mark Twain (six hours a day of Cushion Billiards [no pockets] at times), Lewis Carroll, Jackie Gleason, and Jerry Orbach (who tangled with top players and hustlers when off stage or TV), Presidents George Washington and Abraham Lincoln, Napoleon Bonaparte and Marie Antoinette, Frank Sinatra and his Rat Pack, Woody Allen (whose giant billiards table dominates one room of his Central

Park digs), Buck Henry and Mel Brooks (who played at a table in their office while they scripted *Get Smart*), Charles Dickens, Mozart, Van Gogh, Peter Falk, Fred Astaire, Humphrey Bogart, Paul Newman and Tom Cruise as seen in *The Color of Money*, and many more who have relished the game and brought creativity and timing to sinking pool balls.

You are in good company enjoying pool, and not all devoted pool aficionados are pool bums or pool hustlers. If you can dance, sing, or simply toss a ball straight ahead of you, you probably have all the rhythm and touch you need to play great pool. Study with me what to study and feel while at the table.

"Experteering"

A CHARMING TERM coming into vogue for the science of developing people into subject experts is *experteering*. An experteering seminar comes down to two facts—pick something you are interested in then study continually, and you can become an expert in pool or anything catching your fancy.

A year as a paralegal or accountant's assistant working fulltime will teach you much about those fields. You would learn still faster if you enjoyed those subjects. In the same way, you can slowly but surely become an expert in almost any area of your choice.

Searching the Internet, poring through books, visiting sites in person, and speaking to other fans and experts—an hour a day for five years, devoted to studying any area of interest that stimulates you, will bring you 1,500 hours of knowledge, making you an expert in that endeavor, be it how to operate a nuclear power plant or collecting stamps or Bible preaching.

Most pool players, however, are not much more skilled after five years' devoted play than before they started—because they have no accurate model and no one is telling them *what* to learn in pool. 1,500 hours of pool with bad habits cannot make an expert of the amateur. I know from experience; I could write a book filled with the *bad* pool advice I've received or tested in my career. You might not want to become a total pool expert, but you pur-chased or received this book to become more skilled at playing the game. It won't take you 1,500 or even 100 hours to read and apply the concepts within. Read each shot or concept and then *actual-ly perform it at the table*. Drop me a note or e-mail if you have questions. I derive more knowledge from my students' thoughtful questions than in answering the questions.

You Can Learn Pool

WE ARE GOING TO journey through the procedures (feel) of pool, and the tools, tactics, and techniques to tackle most pool situations that arise (the logic and sci-ence and semantics of pool). Anyone who applies his energy can learn the simplified physics and geometry of pool as presented here, and the proce-dures as shown on the companion DVD will add to your game style. You may vary in your body shape and size from me (I stand to the table and shoot pool like other people over six feet tall), but the concepts presented will transfer to you regardless of your idiosyncrasies.

To sum up Chapter 2, you can and will learn pool reading through this book sequentially. What good pool *feels* like I will demonstrate to your under-standing; we'll also explore the fun and varied pos-sibilities that present themselves as mysteries of the table awaiting your pool detective skills. I can teach you about thinking through pool and feeling what the pro is trying to think and feel at the table, and you take it from there.

Next, we'll step inside a truly beautiful pool hall and grab the equipment we need. The *right* equipment.

3

Find What Works: Selecting
Equipment

What are they talking about?

As Rᴉᴄᴋʏ ᴛʜᴇ Sʜᴀʀᴋ complained to Johnny Brooklyn, *"The fish cased the match with a slop four-railer 9-ball in the side pocket."*

We will learn fun pool slang as we study pool, so you'll understand why Johnny was shocked at Ricky's tale (and so you'll sound hip the next time you linger at your local poolroom). Yes, it's time we hit the table, choosing the best equipment to learn with, and then we'll shoot a few shots.

What's in a Name?

THE FORMAL NAME for our sport is "pocket billiards," more commonly known as "pool" after the betting rooms that accompanied gamblers, the bookmaking rooms of a bygone era. Let's examine a typical pool table together.

Regulation Tables?

Any size or shape pool table may sadly be called "regulation" due to a lack of consensus and pool world politics, concerning which governing body should superintend table manufacturing and pool tournaments. Imagine three organizations running major league baseball instead of one and different teams and cities playing with different baseball rules as one result.

Pool tables are typically rectangular and about half as wide as they are long. Tables with about eight feet of playing surface in length are commonly called "eight-footers," and near-seven-feet tables are called "seven-footers," and so on. It is arguable whether a triangle or octagonal experimental table is still a pool table.

Nine-Footers Are Best

I heartily recommend play on nine-foot tables. You will have more shot room to stretch out your *stroke*, the full back and forth movement of the cue to apply power. The longer shots on the big table will help you will feel like a champ, too, when you are invited to play on a modest-sized eight-footer or a seven-foot mini-table.

All the small-sized tables use smaller balls, too, but they still rest up to 16 balls on their surface for play. The balls tend to pack together in tight clusters more often on the smaller tables, making roadblocks to smooth shooting.

You may find the nine-foot table a challenge at first, but stay with it. You'll be glad you did. As an aside, if you should find an antique ten-foot table, one of the monster tables from the early days of the 20th century, let me know! They are rare tables indeed.

What Size Is the Table?

BRING A MEASURING TAPE to the pool-room, and you'll get strange looks. In Figure 3.1, I am measuring the table more conveniently with my personal cue. A typical cue of 58 inches will go from the narrow end of the table to just past a side pocket (58 inches is a bit more than half the playing surface length) on the nine-foot table, as illustrated in Figure 3.1.

TAKE A TIP

Most cues are around 58 inches in length. Start by using this length until you develop a personal preference.

Figure 3.1
Measuring the table.

Table Name Conventions

WE'LL START LOOKING at the table more closely with components of play on the table surface, as in Figure 3.2. Keep in mind that the subsequent diagrams are not precisely to scale, but are meant to be a basic trip through the parts of the table to know for competition or practicing basic pool games.

The next two diagrams illustrate the top surfaces of a pool table from a perspective above. The same angle is often used to televise the full playing surface for pool on television.

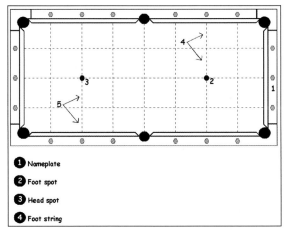

Figure 3.2
Points of interest.

The Strings and Nameplate

The Nameplate: Somewhere along this section of table we often find the manufacturer's brand or mark, and perhaps some type of *counter dials*, numbered wheels to help keep score during a match. You may want to take note of the nameplates on tables you enjoy the most and least for future reference.

The Foot Spot: An imaginary point on the pool table at the intersection of imaginary lines (dashed lines shown in Figure 3.2) stemming from midway between corner and side pockets along the width

of the table. Many pool tables, including the ones in this book's photos, have this spot marked with a small adhesive sticker. The balls will be racked for play with the foremost ball's bottom set on the foot spot. The section of the table containing the rack to start play is called the *foot* of the table.

The Head Spot: A point at the end of the table symmetrical to and opposite the foot spot; the white cue ball's bottom (the part of the sphere that rests on the table's surface) goes here for certain shots in certain pool games and, more rarely, an *object ball*, any colored ball that is not the cue ball. The head spot is not typically marked on the table but is found by intersecting lines. Note that both the head and foot spots are in the middle of table width-wise, opposite a middle pair of diamond-shaped markers, as counted from side or corner pockets.

The Foot String: An imaginary line (here marked with a dashed vertical line through the foot spot) dividing the foot quarter of the table (to the right of the line in the diagram) as the foot of the table. In most games, balls returned to the table after sinking go onto this section of the table.

The Head String: An imaginary line symmetrical to the foot string, it sections off the *head* of the table, the quarter of the table left of the dashed vertical line through the head spot in the diagram. In most pool games, when the cue ball enters the table for play, it must go within the head of the table, the bottom of the cue ball not closer to the head of the table than the head string. Think of the head string as an imaginary wall beyond which the cue ball may not pass when placed by hand.

Rails and Diamonds

Top of Short Rail: The playing surface sides are enclosed by three-dimensional low walls or cushions known in pool slang as *rails*. As we will see in Chapter 4, the rail tops are handy for resting or cupping a hand upon during play. The typical table is approximately twice as long as it is wide, and the cushions fixed along the two shorter sides are called *short rails*.

Top of Long Rail: The rails containing the side pockets, called *long rails*, come into play more often than the short rails. The opening shot of most pool games is played somewhat parallel to these rails, from the head toward the foot of the table.

Cushion: Cushions are often called *rails* in pool slang (a "three rail shot" actually strikes three cushions) though strictly speaking, a rail is the section

of table where the cushion is attached. The sides of the cushion touching the table's cloth are made with a synthetic (inexpensive) or vulcanized (more expensive but preferred) rubber to make them elastic. Every pool player loves springy, resilient cushions, though balls return to play with only about one-third of their energy following impact.

Diamond: Begun in pool history as decorative inlays of wood or semiprecious materials, these traditionally diamond-shape markers progressed to a series of points by which the table may be measured and shots calculated by the player. Standard layout is as shown in Figure 3.3, three diamonds between each two adjacent pockets around the circumference of the table.

Through the Point: There are diverse *diamond systems* proselytized in pool, measures of calculation for predicting the paths of balls striking the rails around the table. Fewer pool issues are touched by more controversy and confusion than diamond systems, some pros advocating them, some saying to play by feel and intuition instead. I will clear up some of these issues later; for now it is sufficient to note that any diamond system telling the player to aim at a particular diamond refers to aiming through the *point atop the rail where the actual diamond sits*, not the rail adjacent the diamond. In Figure 3.3 a player has shot correctly the maroon 7-ball from the area marked "10" straight through the diamond marked "9." The ball has hit the rail correctly as it was aimed on the *shortest line straight from the ball through the diamond*, in this case Diamond 9. Many players shoot in error to hit along the dashed line running between Diamond 9 and the opposite long rail instead. The second, wrong aim is the closest point on the rail to the diamond *adjacent* to the diamond. The correct way is to shoot *through* the diamond or point.

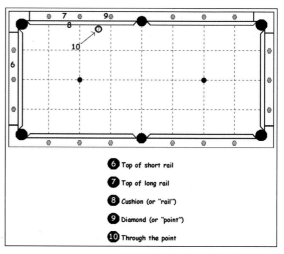

Figure 3.3
Highlighting the table's sides.

Pockets and You

Side Pocket: The pool table, of course, has six pockets. The two bisecting the long rails are called *side pockets*. They are slightly wider than the corner pockets, to compensate for the added difficulty of sinking a ball within.

Corner Pocket: The four pockets at the four corners of the table rectangle are *corner pockets*. Look closer at the pocket openings in Figure 3.4. You can see a shot not straight into the corner may

require some clever calculations to sink accurately. More on adjusting aim to ease shots later in Chapter 8.

Jaw Point: The angle where the long or side cushion turns into the pocket is called the *point* of the pocket. Each pocket has two such points, together forming a mouth or *jaw* opening into the pocket. At the risk of oversimplifying, if the edge of the ball goes inside the point, the ball will sink into the pocket at most speeds. If the ball hits the point itself or the far side of the jaw, it bounces away from the rail and misses the pocket.

The Rack: Typically triangular in shape, the rack holds up to 15 balls for placement to start the game. A diamond shape rack used for Nine-Ball, holding the number 1- through 9-balls, is an example of a *specialty rack*.

Pool Fan: The only thing missing from the diagram is you, the pool player! Let's step into the pool hall and start selecting the best equipment.

Arty Billiards

MANY OF THE SUBSEQUENT illustrations were prepared at the beautiful *Art of Billiards* facility in Gainesville, Florida. At this fine poolroom I had the privilege of preparing this book and DVD on two storied Diamond brand pool tables used by Karen "The Irish Invader" Corr, Ray "Cool Cat" Martin, Efren "The Magician" Reyes, Mike "Captain Hook" Sigel, and more, some of the greatest ever to wield a cue, in the World Straight Pool Championship and other classic battles.

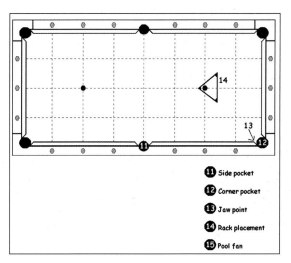

Figure 3.4
The pockets differ in width.

Off the Rack

IDN'T BRING YOUR personal cue to the hall? Select one from the poolroom, called a *house cue*, as it remains permanently housed in the local hall. The key is to select is a house cue with a great cue tip. Everything else is secondary. (See Chapter 16 for more on selecting a personal cue stick instead.)

House cues are usually racked conveniently around the poolroom on walls or columns nearby the pool tables. Certainly, the Art of Billiards house cues I am examining bear quality tips, a good indicator.

I haven't cared to examine the length or weights on the cues but am pointing toward the most important part of any cue stick, a clean, rounded tip.

I have a good leather tip on all my personal cues. I'll demonstrate a variety of pool techniques with a personal cue or two, but first I'll walk you through the same critical steps I use to appraise an unfamiliar house cue when I'm on the road.

A Hot Tip

The small, black tip on the edge of the cue is the business end of your cue stick. Round and true, it's all a pro needs to dazzle you at the game. It's been said of all-time great Willie Mosconi that given a mere broomstick with a good leather tip on the handle end, he could wipe everybody out in the poolroom and then sweep the place clean after. Friends and I have proven the point by winning many games with crooked cue sticks with decent tips, and not often the other way round.

A tip whose flattened edge spills past the white *ferrule* area of the cue beneath it (the ferrules are the white sections of the sticks in Figure 3.5) is said to have *mushroomed*. Mushrooms are a huge problem for your game. The mushroomed part of the tip that contacts the ball will have no weight behind it, and slide right off the white cue ball with disastrous results, called a *miscue*.

You should be able to find a few cues with decent leather tips inside even the meanest pool hall. If you can't find tips in decent shape, the very heart of the game, it's time to play somewhere else. The proprietor is surely careless with his tables also.

Figure 3.5
Reaching for a house cue.

Going Round

You will want a rounded tip on your cue stick. The tip should be substantial enough in length (see the black section visible from the chalk blue tip to the place it meets the white *ferrule*—the composite material serving as a go-between joining leather tip to wood cue shaft) to best cushion and spring again forward with the force of the stroke. The older the tip, the more it is worn small from use.

The blue, chalked top needs to be round. A flat tip may cause all sorts of miscues. Avoiding miscues with correct playing procedures is covered throughout this book, but why add to the issue with a poorly shaped tip?

A coin placed behind the tip will show you its top edge's degree of roundness. In God We Trust, but don't use a penny as I have in Figure 3.6 to check the edge of the tip. Trim your tip to the roundness of a nickel's edge instead (most players) or perhaps a dime, as some players use a dime's edge shape for added spin on the balls but with a possible loss of ball control due to the steeper curved edge. Most poolroom cue tips are set to a nickel rather than a dime, so start at a nickel before you experiment.

Trimming the leather tip to shape as desired is done with care and a bit of sandpaper, or one of the tools we will explore in Chapter 16, but a cue craftsman can shape one for you in minutes, and their services are available at many poolrooms.

Figure 3.6
Checking the tip's roundness and thickness.

A tip of 13 millimeters in thickness is standard for most house cues, for ease of use, while some prefer a narrower tip closer to 12 mm. for their game requirements. Most players find 13 mm. the simplest to aim and play.

A Matching Set

FIGURE 3.7 HIGHLIGHTS the first things we need to enjoy pool—a good table, a set of clean pool balls and a designated spot to rest them upon, and what I am pointing toward for emphasis, a cue stick's tip in rounded, decent condition.

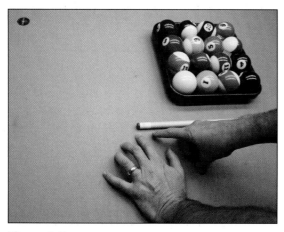

Figure 3.7
Balls on a plastic tray, a head spot, and the front of a cue stick.

Clean and Go

The set of balls resting in the black plastic tray in Figure 3.7 are clean, having been wiped briskly with a cotton towel before play. Any unwanted dirt or chalk on the balls will mar the true roll of the balls. Take the set for a dry towel rub or a little water with soap and dry before any serious play or practice.

A clean table, vacuumed free of chalk and dirt, helps during play also. Don't use a home vacuum on your table, it will pill and tear the cloth surface. Try a gentle handheld dustbuster mini-vac or pool brush instead.

The black circular marker on the cloth in the top left of Figure 3.7 is where the balls will be *racked*, set for the start of play, as soon as we check the rest of the equipment together.

Spheres of Joy

A typical set of pool balls (also called *billiard balls* for the hits they make against one another called *caroms* or *billiards*) is comprised of the solid white *cue ball* (perhaps with a red dot on its surface for practice or training use) and 15 additional balls, banded or solid in color, which the cue ball will strike to set in motion.

See the pattern in color and name conventions below?

▶ Primary Yellow: 1-ball (solid) and 9-ball (striped with color)

▶ Primary Blue: 2-ball (solid) and 10-ball (striped with color)

▶ Primary Red: 3-ball (solid) and 11-ball (striped with color)

▶ Dark Purple: 4-ball (solid) and 12-ball (striped with color)

▶ Bright Orange: 5-ball (solid) and 13-ball (striped with color)

▶ Dark Green: 6-ball (solid) and 14-ball (striped with color)

▶ Maroon: 7-ball (solid) and 15-ball (striped with color)

▶ Black: The 8-ball

The pattern is to add or subtract eight from the number of ball to find the match in color in set, for example, the 9-ball is yellow, $9 - 8 = 1$ and the 1-ball is the same yellow color. The 8-ball is solid black and by itself as the last ball in the game of Eight-Ball.

The lower seven are often called *lows* or *little ones* for their lower numbers or *solids* for their almost complete color coverage, and the highest seven numbers above the 8-ball are *stripes*, *highs* or *big ones*. The 8-ball is called all manner of things in poolrooms, some of them not repeatable here.

Cue Ball and Object Balls

The white cue ball, by the way, needs to be especially distinct from the colored balls, because it is hit first, and so the other 15 balls are called *object balls*, the objects the cue ball will strike.

TAKE A TIP

Colorblind people might have trouble aiming at the surfaces of the balls, and full-sighted folks find certain colors (especially the purple and green balls) sometimes challenging to aim at during a long play session. I'll provide tips to solve these problems in Chapter 8.

"Regulation Balls"

I'm frequently asked about "regulation sized" pool balls. Pool can be somewhat lax compared to golf and other sports with exacting standards. In most regulated golf tournaments, players may carry up to but not more than 14 clubs in their golf bag. There are likewise regulations for ball size in tennis, baseball, golf, basketball, and softball, but pool allows for a tremendous variety of equipment, because it may be played at times in confined spaces and the ball size may be adjusted *relative to the table size* being used. Most poolrooms use 2.25" balls, however.

A typical set of pool balls has all 16, including the white cue ball, at the same size and weight. Smaller balls are usually for smaller-sized tables like those sold cheaply by retail department stores. If the set feels and weighs alike, it may be sold as "regulation balls" by its seller even though the term carries little meaning except as an advertising ploy. Whose regulations or specifications were used to manufacture the pool balls?

Oversized and Magnetic Balls

Coin-operated tables, the type commonly used in bars as pay-per-game income, rely on either a magnetic cue ball or oversized cue ball to govern the *ball returns*, channels beneath the surface of the table, along which sunk balls roll toward the head of the table for convenient return to play.

The other-sized white ball comes out a slot instead, so it may be returned for play while colored balls that sink are paid for to start a new game. The object balls' different size or non-magnetic action keeps them out of play until the next game session is paid for in advance.

Each concept presented in this book is based on same-sized, same weight cue balls. Excellent direction for accommodating outsized or large-weight cue balls is found in R. Givens' excellent work, *The Eight Ball Bible*. Most pool halls and home tables use same-sized cue balls, however. If you plan to purchase a used table that was formerly coin operated, ask so that you get the equipment you want.

Explosive Pool

Modern ball sets include glow-in-the-dark colors, logo balls with favorite sports team designs, exotic stripe patterns, and much more. I prefer the traditional set, but I'm grateful that whatever the colors, we may enjoy modern *phenolic resin* pool balls, noted for their playability and durability.

Years ago, clay balls (which are not very durable) were standard in pool halls. I've split one in half during a forcible stroke, sinking only *half* a ball with my shot. I couldn't figure whose turn was next!

In pool's distant past, balls were made of wood, which presented incredible trouble in creating a set of consistent pool balls. A later innovation, ivory balls, retained their shape better, but they yellowed and sometimes chipped with age. When they came into vogue in the 1800s, they caused African elephants to be hunted to near extinction.

In the search for a replacement to ivory, a clever chemist named John Wesley Hyatt mixed camphor with nitrocellulose to create his "collodion balls."

Winning a $10,000 purse for the discovery was dulled when his collodions were found to become *flammable* in play, or even *explode* powerfully during the manufacturing process!

Hyatt later crafted a celluloid coating, providing the modern resin billiard ball, the first plastic product ever. In one fell stroke Mr. Hyatt revolutionized modern life with plastics, saved elephants worldwide, and inadvertently created untold non-biodegradable waste.

All Sticks Are Not Created Equal

AS I EXAMINE THIS cue stick, the front section seems clean and smooth with a quality, rounded cue tip attached. Next, I will heft the cue in my hands to determine its weight or check the midsection, as many cues have a stamped weight in ounces there.

In Figure 3.8, it seems I've chosen an 18-ounce cue from the rack on the hall wall. It's true, the tip is more important to me than the weight or length of the cue, so only now do I care to note the weight on the stick.

We also see the attractive triangular *forearm points* where the cue stick color changes between light and dark color, where wood sections have been fitted together (as on most quality house cues). To an extent, fitting two woods together will yield different play qualities through the stroke in the rear or *butt section* of the cue (heavy, durable) and for the *shaft* or top section (flexibility, feel).

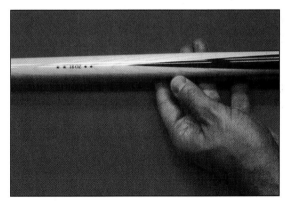

Figure 3.8
The cue stick's midsection.

What Am I Weighting For?

Every pool student asks me, "What are the pros and cons of different cue stick weights?" One answer is personal freedom of choice, but a heavier cue provides more force and roll (spin) to the cue ball, while a relatively lighter cue is easier to manipulate gently with the hands.

A heavyweight cue keeps to the straight line of the shot longer with an imperfect stroke due to sheer momentum, which means it will add more unwanted spin to a miscue, as well. A lighter cue will provide more accurate cue ball speed control.

In other words, the light cue takes a bit of touch to master, and the heavier cue is easier for beginners but makes any bad shot come out still worse.

Most novice players will want the heft of a 20- to 21-ounce cue in their hands until they are more comfortable in play. The intermediate to advanced player will want an 18-ounce or 19-ounce cue instead. Cues run in half and quarter ounces also.

I'll demonstrate in Chapters 4, 5, and 6 how to manipulate the lighter cue, but if you are a novice, start with a heavyweight stick for now until you feel ready for the next level of play.

The Rear of the Cue Stick

THE MAJORITY OF THE WEIGHT is at the back of the pool cue, tapering in width as it does back to front. The rubber *bumper* as seen in Figure 3.9 just above the heel of my thumb has two shock absorbing purposes. First, it dampens unwanted vibration caused by the cue stick's impact with the heavy cue ball. Second, the bumper prevents injury to the cue should it strike the floor or wall.

Be Bumper Savvy

Pool purists know the traditional way to salute a teammate's or an opponent's exceptional play is to thump the bumper of their stick onto the floor. The gesture is ample recognition without being as distracting as applause or cheers.

Figure 3.9
The butt end of the stick.

Looks Aren't Everything

F IGURE 3.10 HAS ME smoothly rolling the 18-ounce house cue along the table to check for any undue wobbling in the movement. A wobble would mean the cue is not straight but warped, right? You will see something similar at your local pool hall once in a while, but the roll technique does not always work accurately!

The concept is that any wobbling movement indicates the cue has a bump, bend, or warp somewhere along its wooden length. The trouble is that a mushroomed tip (see "A Hot Tip" above) will cause a bit of shimmy in the roll anyway. So will a table that is less than perfectly level; if the table isn't level or has dents, even the straight cue may show some wobble to it. There's a better way to examine your cue for warping.

Figure 3.10
Rolling looks cool but is the wrong idea.

Looks Cool and Works

I'VE DEVISED A FASTER, better way to check an unfamiliar cue. Simply hold the butt end of the cue under an eye and turn the tip end to a tilt approximately 45 degrees above the floor. Close the other eye so you see one cue stick in your line of vision, peering down the length of the stick. Turn the cue around and even a subtle warp will show as a glaring bump along the cylinder of the cue stick.

Turn any large bump you find to face upward to the ceiling (the top of the cue from your perspective) and then you may set the tip end on the floor, then press down hard with the palm of your hand, removing the warp and bending the cue straight once again. Take care not to break the cue.

Any repairs to a cue beyond light pressure and any extensive tip work should be done by a cue repair professional. Most pool halls will recommend a local craftsman they already deliver work to or are at contract with, but be sure to get references from individual satisfied customers, too.

Figure 3.11
Sight down the cue stick for warp.

Brush It On

THE *CHALK CUBE,* paper wrapped around chalk you will powder the cue tip with between shots, comes new with a concave depression at its center where the chalk has been exposed. Master brand is best and the most used internationally, blue the most common and pre-ferred color for pool. Some players swear Master blue even plays better than Master chalk dyed in other colors.

Lightly glide or scrape the *edge* of the chalk cube along the *edge* of the cue tip as in Figure 3.12. Continually turn the cue with one hand beneath the chalk while you are raking back and forth with the other hand.

For a heavy coating, you might lightly grind the cue stick into the cube straight on. This practice is frowned on by most, however, as it wears down the cube fast and tends to waste excess chalk dust onto the floor or the table surface. Chalking is of vital importance, though, and for games requiring intense precision with the cue ball, the pros will grind the chalk a bit, though a heavy coating is less effective than an even, light coating.

Do not use a chalk cube you find to have been deeply worn in this manner; the sides of the chalk bowl will scrape at the edges of your white cue stick ferrule, making an ugly blue ring around its white surface and permanently scraping the surface.

Figure 3.12
Chalking the cue tip after ensuring it is round.

Chalk, Chalk, Chalk, and Chalk!

AFTER A FEW MOMENTS' application, your tip should be evenly coated with chalk as seen here in Figure 3.13. Do you know the history of pool chalk and its extreme importance to your game?

Captain Mingaud's Holiday

The short version of the story is of a fellow named Francois Mingaud, who became a political prisoner in early 19th-century France. Capt. Mingaud used personal connections to procure a billiards table to keep him happily occupied during his sentence, where he both practiced for countless hours and perfected a refined leather tip for his cue. Excited beyond measure by his innovation, a *rounded* leather tip, this giant of billiards history requested a longer prison stay to further refine his research!

Mingaud later published a book on billiards, astonishing the pool world with his proven theories. He had brought the game fully from a mace-like pounding of balls short distances across a table to shots that could spin and curve about the table so wondrously that there were accusations of witchcraft leveled at the good Captain's table magic.

Point of Contact

By adding a rounded, filed leather tip to the flattened leather atop the cue stick, Mingaud could meet his goal of more consistent point-to-point

contact between cue stick and cue ball. Not the first to try leather as a cue tip, Mingaud was certainly the first to round the tip's leading edge.

Pool chalk, a white carbonate of lime, came into vogue in the early 1800s when it was discovered that it would cause Mingaud's round leather or composite tip to adhere better to the cue ball, providing extra friction between tip and ball and thus added ball spin and velocity with ease. With the rounded tip and chalk, pool shooters could now perform legendary feats.

Figure 3.13
True blue.

Chalk Becomes Indispensable

In 1897, a new chalk mix was patented, providing a composite of materials including rock quartz silica, dyed green to better keep the table's appearance. The grit and firm packaging of the chalk cube guaranteed durability and performance for the pool player.

Great players soon went on record that the new chalk improved their billiards game more than anything else and the best chalk progressed to blue from green, with blue marks being essentially invisible where they stray. Players swear by blue and even believe it is superior to other colors in its friction properties. Pool had gone from a green surface game, green to resemble lawn billiards, to its own sport on the cloth.

Chalk Every Shot

Despite advanced, modern equipment, shots are not easily made without chalk. The chalk adheres the tip to the cue ball far better than leather alone. At impact, however, chalk flakes from the tip and needs to be replaced again for the next stroke. This replacing the chalk between shots is known in pool slang as *chalking up.*

You should seek an even application of chalk across the whole stick tip before taking any pool shot. Chalking is so important it could deserve an entire book chapter—that chapter would read, "Chalk completely before each shot… chalk completely before each shot… chalk **completely** before each shot…!"

Figure 3.14
Chalk is a beautiful thing.

Miscue a shot or have a poor result on a stroke that felt good otherwise? Look at the tip for the telltale black spot that chalk was missing or poorly applied before impact.

The Macho Miss

I've seen it happen many times—shooters work for three or four successful shots in a row without chalking before a tragic miss. The few shots made reinforce the player's bad habit of not chalking. I've seen macho players even show off this way— "Watch me shoot without chalking up!"

There is a logical explanation for the good shots before the miss:

1. The first shot included a chalk application and was well made.

2. The next shot had a different *portion* of the tip hit the ball than the one before. With a spherical edge, different parts of the tip strike the ball from different angles at times. Not all the chalk is rubbed from the tip each stroke.

3. Perhaps the third shot had the dead center of the tip contacting the center of the white ball, a shot requiring forward, level movement and not much chalk. (It's tougher than you think to hit dead center tip to dead center ball, as two spherical objects may touch each other at one and only one spot at one time.)

4. Mr. Macho misses the fourth shot as his chalk luck runs dry.

It's not hard to string together several simple shots without chalk, but it's a foolish thing to attempt on purpose, because you never know when the miscue will occur. I smile privately if my opponent doesn't reach for chalk between shots. He or she *will* miss soon.

Watch the pros model chalk behavior instead—the more important the shot, the longer they pause to dress the cue tip carefully with an even chalk coating. Many pros carry a personal cue holder for play, so vital is this facet of the game.

I will not start a pool session without at least two cubes of chalk in good condition at hand. I bring chalk with me to any pool hall in case the owners are out of chalk or simply chintzy, leaving poor cubes in play. Old, dry cubes or worn cubes should be discarded, room owners!

It's Not All Wonderful

In one of pool's great ironies, chalk occasionally *hurts* the player if it transfers at impact to the cue ball, leaving a telltale blue mark. As the cue ball hits another ball exactly on that blue spot the balls cling together unnaturally for an extended time at impact, ruining the shot (at least, that is the best way to think of throw, although the physical reality is different). See Figure 3.15 for an extreme example of chalk transfer to an object ball. See Chapter 8 for more on the "cling effect" called *ball throw*.

Figure 3.15
Blue chalk mars the red 3-ball.

Overall, despite the occasional misstep, chalk often and between each stroke taken. Clean the balls with a cloth or towel, in a severe case with some water before drying them thoroughly with paper towels or cloth, if you see stray chalk or dirt marks.

Touch the Table and Learn

YOU CAN LEARN MUCH about pool by stroking and handling the table with your bare hands. A few quick checks at a strange poolroom are a need if you want the chance to play on the best equipment available.

I am handling the plastic pocket insert in Figure 3.16 to check for any telltale gaps between the pocket and the top of the rail or its cushion. A wobbly pocket might reject a ball, and pocketing balls is enough of a challenge in itself.

The smaller the pocket or pocket jaw (pocket opening) in relation to the size of the balls being used, the *tighter* the pocket is said to be. *Loose pockets* are easier targets for those attacking them with relish.

Go Ahead, It Won't Bite

Go further and grip the edges of the pocket as I am doing in Figure 3.17. Cloth around the table's surface should be clean and adhere tightly to the rails and table slate beneath it.

Figure 3.16
Examining a pocket closely.

Figure 3.17
Checking the rails.

TAKE A TIP

The best table(s) in many cases is reserved for the best regular players the room enjoys. Look for these "head tables" at a poolroom near you and carefully compare the size of the pockets, the clean newness of the table's cloth, and other table aspects to the table you are offered when you visit. You can learn much from the comparison and watching the better competitors on these tables.

Search for Pills and Tracks

Loose ends of fiber surfaces pill after a while, especially on a pool table. Room owners who care change the felt on each table at least biannually if not quarterly.

In Figure 3.18, I am searching for the little fuzzy balls that tell me the felt is worn and pilling. Right beneath the rails along the cushions is a great place to look for worn grooves in the felt also, since balls travel the line along the rail quite a bit. A worn groove means the table's felt is badly in need of freshening. Hustlers might appreciate them, however, as grooves beneath the long rails may provide tracks to pocket more balls in the corners!

The Nap of the Felt

The nap of pool cloth is the direction in which it tends to run the fastest, much like the slope or grain on the grass of a golf course.

Figure 3.18
Seeking a non-groovy surface.

Naps are properly installed in one direction toward the head of the table, to make for the fastest possible *break shot* or opening shot of most pool games, though they add little for most breaks. In Figure 3.19, I am examining the nap near the foot spot. The cloth is tight, fast, clean, and the nap is evenly installed—it's difficult to discern a nap at all because the cloth's so tight and finely woven, but it's there.

Figure 3.19
A fast cloth indeed.

Table Speed

YOU MIGHT DEVELOP a preference for a *fast* or *slow* pool table. The terms fast table and slow table are relative and somewhat subjective. The pros shoot certain games demanding long distance shots (such as Nine-Ball) preferably on fast tables. Games of precision like Straight Pool could go well on slower cloth and a slower underlying *slate*, the rock beneath that table that provides durability and a level surface.

You don't want to play on a table that was formerly fast but has slowed due to poor maintenance. That's just not fun. The cloth (players call the cloth *felt* in pool slang) in Figure 3.19 is Simonis 860 brand, known for fast speed and high-quality manufacturing, a pleasure to play on.

I also haunt certain slower tables for fun. Adjusting to different speeds and local conditions is part of the champion's arsenal. And any kind of pool, even slow play, is better than jacks or pick-up-sticks if you ask me!

Corner Pocket Width

You can examine the size of the table you play on with its ball set to check the relative difficulty ahead.

Let's look at a standard or typical setup for a nine-foot table. Just about 2 1/4 balls wide, as shown in Figure 3.20, this corner pocket will pose a base level of difficulty, not terribly difficult or simple.

Figure 3.20
The 9- and 15-balls, and a bit of the 6-ball all fit.

Side Pocket Width

Figure 3.21 shows a side pocket on a typical nine-foot table. Just about 2 1/2 balls will cover the width of this pocket. The wider side pocket partially compensates for its added difficulty. I will give you tools to solve this difficulty with ease in Chapter 8.

A pocket width of 2 1/4 balls in the corner and 2 1/2 in the side is average, so we're ready to complete our table tour. Let's set the cue and balls for play next.

Figure 3.21
The side pocket is blocked with stripes.

Handy Cue Cleaner

WE WILL LOOK AT CUE maintenance in depth in Chapter 16. Detail cleaning a cue is accomplished easily, but for now, we'll wipe the cue fast with a towel before starting play. The ordinary soft towel I am using in Figure 3.22 removes dirt, chalk, and accumulated oils in seconds, providing a smooth feel to the stick in my hands without abrading and weakening its playing surface.

Figure 3.22
Making a clean slate of the cue.

Racking the Balls for Play

I WILL DEMONSTRATE in detail preparing a tight racking of the balls to start your game. We will go in-depth in sequential order so that you get consistently racked games, but the steps below as outlined may all be accomplished in just a few seconds with a little practice.

Let Your Fingers Do the Tightening

The triangle rack, an aid to preparing the balls for the start of play (shown in Figure 3.23) is made of wood, more costly than the plastic racks seen here and there but providing better results on average. The wood surface is clean and free of nicks or notches that would pill or tear the cloth of the table.

I am standing behind the short rail at the foot of the table, ready to push the rack onto the marked foot spot for play. I've separated the solids and stripes a bit for a game of Eight-Ball (see Chapter 13 for more on Eight-Ball racking) and placed the yellow 1-ball at the front of the pack. Most players are used to seeing the 1 there, and I am a courteous fellow. They can tell the 1-ball by its yellow color, though, so there is no need to have any ball number facing any particular direction or even visible as with the 1-ball now.

The first key to racking tightly and accurately is to place your fingers inside the bottom of the triangle and facing you (to the rear of the pack) to press the balls firmly against the front point of the triangle.

I am seeking to really wedge the 1-ball immovably within the rack. As I glide the rack along the felt into final position, I want to see the balls slide rather than roll in place. I do not want the balls to spin in place more than a little. Any rolling would indicate that the balls or the rack itself is not a tight triangle.

Figure 3.23
Fingers go behind the pool balls.

Note the discoloration of some of my fingers near the knuckles. I am stretching my fingers wide to touch each of the five balls to the rear of the pack and pressing hard into the balls, wanting each of the 15 balls to touch all the balls adjacent, one solid mass.

We want really tight racks for practice purposes and to thwart our opponents. Loose racks yield unpredictable results with one exception—balls are much easier to sink on the break out of a loose rack.

Checking the Rack's Alignment

Figure 3.24 is a check against a sloppy rack. Not only should the rack be tight, it should be symmetrically aligned to the sides of the table. I am in the process of lifting my cue stick above the 1-ball and atop the diamond marker on the rail.

You can use a straight pool cue to ensure the top center of the 1-ball as seen from above, and beneath, the bottommost point where it rests on the cloth, is set directly on the head spot aligned with the middle diamond (the second marker from the corner pocket) along the long rail.

A cue held above the last row of five balls would also demonstrate that the rack is perfectly parallel to the short rail.

After some time, you will no longer need a cue for a visual aid to check rack alignment. Yet even the pro will work on alignment occasionally in this fashion as a quick refresher. Again, a symmetrically aligned rack is the first defense against the breaking opponent.

Figure 3.24
Lining for the second diamond.

Aligning to the Short Rail

Figure 3.25 is the first cousin of 3.24. With the same rack, I am shown lifting my cue across the precise middle of the side rail, again at the middle or second diamond between the two corner pockets. The diamonds are cunningly placed for our pool calculations.

If the rack is even horizontally at its base, the cue will be seen directly over the center of the middle balls in the third and fifth rows, right? Review the placement of the 8-ball and 3-ball in Figure 3.23 for more.

Figure 3.25
Checking against the rail's middle.

Revisit Figure 3.1 at the beginning of the chapter if you want to review the location of the foot spot for racking.

Tap If You Need

A quick tap directly atop a ball's center with another ball will set it firmly in place if felt is worn or giving you trouble. Trick shot experts tap each ball of every shot to ensure the balls don't turn and wobble away from their place.

Use a ball from the back of the rack, in the case of Figure 3.26, the purple 12-ball, to do the work. Balls from the rack's rear row (the one that is five balls across and closest to my hands) may be removed and placed again tightly without disturbing the rest of the pack.

Figure 3.26
I tap the 5-ball firmly in place.

You can see my left hand's fingers are still firming the rack, as well. There is space left over in a pool rack behind the set of balls, space we will use to our advantage as seen in the next illustration.

Gently tapping a ball in a loose rack is benign and understood by pool purists. But dropping the balls from a height to the table or rapping hard, not tapping, is a foul habit indeed. Hard raps create microscopic dents on the table's slate beneath the felt, which over time develop into *wobble spots*, small cracks, or dents that befoul play and make the balls turn off straight paths to the pain of pool shooters. Gently does it, please.

Move Forward, Not Back

Occasionally you will be plagued by a table with its foot spot in awful condition, a wobble spot of grief. You can use a ball to try to press out dimple damage on the spot or simply move the whole rack a bit ahead of the spot and away from you (fractions of an inch) to a smoother area on the felt.

Don't worry about the legality of this move forward past the foot spot, it's common courtesy among pool players and accepted under challenging field conditions.

PLEASE BEWARE

Never under any circumstances bring the rack any distance toward the foot of the table instead by racking below the head spot. Such a rack is quite vulnerable to balls sinking on the break against you. Only rack below the spot when showing off your break shot for friends! Outcast of pool that I am, nobody bothered to grant me the forward, not back, tidbit until Hall-of-Fame great Mike "Captain Hook" Sigel told me himself as we played, when he watched me struggle over a wobble spot. Thanks, Mike. (Sigel won the game anyway despite the tight rack.)

If you are still having difficulty racking on the spot or just past it, you might switch the foot and head spots in your mind and rack on the far side of the table instead. You will lose any nap in your favor on the break, though, and the far side of the table might pose a hazard to passersby as balls leap off the table on the break sometimes.

No need to cheat the spot when you play pool on TV. The cloth and foot spot marker will be new and adequate for racking the world championship, I promise.

Push the Rack Forward

Our rack on the head spot has the balls tightly aligned to each other and the diamonds on the table, along the head string and *center string* (lengthwise imaginary line dividing the table in half) of the table. Now we simply lift the wood rack away and play, right?

Lifting now will probably disturb the balls and force a re-rack to take place. Your opponent may call for a re-rack, and you should offer one as a courtesy if they even *suspect* a loose rack has been set.

Instead of lifting, gently push the rack forward fractions of an inch so the triangle leaves the 1-ball behind as in Figure 3.27. Note my thumb and fingers are gently pushing forward from the ends of the triangle to provide a balanced press on the wood rack.

Figure 3.27
The pro rack move.

Leaving Space

In Figure 3.28, note pushing the rack gently forward has moved the empty space on the felt *behind* the balls in Figure 3.26 to the *front* of the rack. Now I can lift the wood rack away entirely without banging the balls apart again out of place.

Figure 3.28
Note the adequate space between wood and ball.

Lifting the Rack

Figure 3.29 has me gently and carefully removing the rack from the table, leaving the balls neatly in place. This is no time to rush. I am gently holding the rack at its rear.

Here is where a lot of otherwise careful racks are ruined by a flourish or sudden move. Lift the rack away carefully, and then spin it over your forearm or something else in dramatic fashion away from the table as you wish.

Figure 3.29
Lift the rack carefully.

Let's review the correct racking procedure:

1. Place the object balls as needed in the rack for the game of choice.

2. Place your hands to the rear of the rack against the balls, sliding, not rolling, the balls into place as one pack.

3. Set the triangle of balls to rest along the vertical center of the table and horizontally also in symmetry, with the bottom of the front ball squarely on the head spot.

4. Tap the front few balls if needed, all 15 of them if you are playing a life-or-death game

of pool. (Hey, it could happen. Remember *The Twilight Zone* with Jack Klugman and Jonathan Winters, the episode called "A Game of Pool"?)

5. Push the rack a bit forward from the rear, then lift it from the rear forward and up carefully from the table.

Again, it will take you far less time to rack accurately than to read these instructions, but most players need to learn correct racking procedure. Learn it well, and use it going forward!

Looking Back

IN SUM, we've discussed plenty about basic equipment needs in this chapter:

▶ table components

▶ the set of cue and object balls

▶ identifying a good house cue by tip, weight, and straightness

▶ the significance of chalking carefully before every shot

▶ table options, including fast or slow cloth, relative difficulty posed by tight or loose pockets, and table condition

▶ racking the balls with flair and accuracy

By pursuing the best available stick and ball conditions, you and I gain a leg up on the competition.

Avid players even use a bit of chalk or tape at times, marking their favorite house cue to find it on a repeat visit to the same hall. I've seen players work to hide a favorite cue in the room somewhere for their use! Equipment is that important. If your local hall's equipment is in shoddy condition, find another spot to play.

Summing Up

W E'VE GONE A GOOD DEAL toward completing the formula for success outlined in Chapter 1 by understanding the equipment facts of good pool. We now move on to setting our body to the cue and table accurately and the correct stroking motion(s) before we delve into strategy, tactics, and simple and clever shot making.

We start by learning to hold the cue stick correctly, and how to stand and bend to the table without any muscle pain or strain. You will quickly discover the secrets of pool and how to apply them to sink more shots faster than you've dreamed.

4

On Being Handy: Gripping a
Cue Stick

How to build this game right

T HERE WAS A TIME when I would have given anything to have the information I'll share with you over the next two chapters. I see players standing every way imaginable at the table and holding their cue sticks a dozen different ways in pool, let alone its sister sports, *Snooker* and *Cushion Billiards* (played without pockets on the table). Why would I play so well one day and then so poorly the next?

I determined to resolve my confusion over holding the cue and standing to the table by creating a set of fundamentals, to give myself a fighting chance *before* taking any pool shot.

Finding Universals

AFTER MUCH PATIENT study and experimentation, and many observations in the field, I built a body of knowledge for you and me to find a great hold on the cue stick and set the body comfortably to the line of the shot.

You might adjust slightly based on the length and thickness of your fingers, your playing temperament, or your physical comfort at the table. Please try my way as suggested, though, before any experimenting. In my experience, it is far simpler to set you on the right path than have you try to unlearn bad habits.

The first fundamental is this—we're going to pursue a *gentle clasp* on the cue to ease the silky, flowing stick movement most great players share.

A Tale of Two Hands

WE'RE GOING TO DISCUSS both hands' role in the pool stroke throughout this chapter. Let's begin by making distinctions between the use of the *shooting hand*, your dominant hand, which you will use to bring the cue backward and forward during the stroke, and the *bridge hand*, your non-dominant hand, which serves more passively as a guide or channel for the cue stick to pass along during the shot.

Pool players basically use the one shooting hand to bring the cue back and forth through the shot while the bridge hand helps gauge the cue stick's distance to the table and ball, and holds it for a precise strike.

What if you are a disabled pool player? No worries, I've seen excellent players adapt to a prosthetic limb or hook. In fact, they play marvelous pool, their artificial limb especially immobile as a bridge hand during the stroke. I've been beaten before literally "one handed" in this manner and enjoyed watching the win, too!

What if you are ambidextrous? That's terrific; you can reverse shooting and bridge hands anytime and avoid using the rake (see "The Mechanical Bridge" later in this chapter) on many shots.

There's the old but true tale of the ambidextrous pool hustler walking into a poolroom one day for a game. This shark beats on his *mark*, his betting patsy, playing right-handed. He offers to triple the bet and play left-handed instead "just to keep things interesting." You can guess the end of the story!

Figure 4.1
Feeling for the balance point.

Balancing Act

THE HOUSE CUE I've pulled from Art of Billiards' rack in Chapter 3 will be like any other in its tapering cylinder, thicker at the rear or butt end (the dark section of the cue as shown in Figure 4.1) and narrowing to its tip end with the chalked, blue tip, its black base atop the white cue ferrule. The majority of the tapering cue's weight, therefore, will be to the rear of the cue.

The *balance point* is the exact spot where half of the cue's weight sits to either side. The balance would make a natural fulcrum if the cue were to become a seesaw. We need to identify the balance point on any cue, as it is incredibly difficult to shoot with the shooting hand gripping the cue

ahead of this point toward the tip, the weight pulling down and threatening to yank the front of the cue into the air. We want to hold the cue somewhere back of the balance, so let me give you a fun way to find it fast without using a scale.

Grasp the cue with both hands, one near each end of the cue lengthwise. In this example, I'll place the tip end along the left hand. Let the cue rest upon an upturned finger or two in each hand before bringing the hands toward one another, sliding along the cue's length, as I am doing in Figure 4.2. The cue will naturally move more in my left hand (the longer, thinner weight) than in my right hand at the meaty end of the cue.

Figure 4.2
The balance discovered.

After a moment or two, the right hand meets the left. This place of togetherness is the actual cue balance point. See Figure 4.2. You can let go with one hand if you like and dazzle your audience as you balance the cue on a single finger.

Behind the Balance

Most players do best holding the cue during play three inches to a foot to the rear of the balance point, where I am setting my shooting hand, my right hand, in Figure 4.3. The precise position depends upon your physical attributes and the requirements of the shot at hand.

There are fine players who hold the cue back near the rubber bumper, and I will explain in Chapter 5 when you might move the shooting hand with specific reason, but the less you vary from the norm for now, the better.

Figure 4.3
I know where to hold this cue.

If you are an intermediate player as many of my students are (intermediates bring all their bad habits), I can tell you from experience that trying to hold the cue close to the balance as suggested feels awkward and new at first but will yield pleasant results. It may take a week or two to get adjusted if you play somewhat frequently.

I hold the cue farther back than six inches from the balance point on a number of shots, but I am over 6'2" in height and need to adjust to the table and my own wingspan.

PLEASE BEWARE

It bears repetition—I am serious in suggesting that you change your grip to a new spot on the cue near the balance if you're accustomed to holding your shooting hand farther back. It's going to help you apply the concepts in the next chapter far better.

Where Is the Action?

MY DOMINANT HAND, my right or shooting hand, is outlined in the next illustration. Study Figure 4.4 and see the parts of my hand that do the lion's share in holding and manipulating the cue stick.

The forefinger or the first two or three fingers of my hand below the first knuckle, and the padded areas beneath them on the top of the palm (inside the blue semi-circle) caress, cradle, and stroke the cue stick, with occasional help or incidental contact from the rest of the hand. The fewer fingers touching the stick, the fewer points of contact the unconscious mind can employ to manipulate the cue off line when the player is under stress.

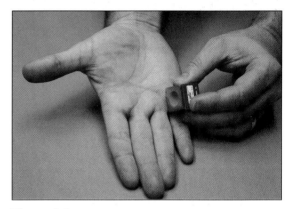

Figure 4.4
I use chalk just like most teachers, but my hand serves as a blackboard.

Now Pay Attention, 007

WHAT I'LL TELL YOU NEXT about the fingers and wrist of the shooting hand is a bit controversial; there are many diverse opinions in our sport. There are pool greats who are exceptions to the following rules. Pool pros put in thousands of hours of practice, however, and overcome any awkwardness that deviates from what I am outlining here.

Where Do I Begin?

SIMPLY LET YOUR ARM REST along your side, fingers pointing to the ground, as if you are starting on a walk. I hold the cue with my left (bridge) hand and place it in my shooting hand (right hand), along the areas of that hand outlined in Figure 4.4.

I then close or curl the fingers around the cue gently, wrapping them far enough around the stick to cradle it from below so it won't drop to the floor. The thumb might touch the cue or not, it need not play a large role in the stroke.

PLEASE BEWARE

The grip on the cue I advocate, the wrists movements you should do (or not do), and the way to stand at the table, and more, all are designed for you to stroke the cue back and forth, straight along your side on most shots. If the cue stick moves a bit up and down as it shuttles back and forth, it's not the worst thing for your stroke, but unplanned side-to-side, left and right movement, is a disaster.

When a Teacup Is a Sledgehammer

LOOK AT THE GENTEEL GRIP in Figure 4.5. Grip doesn't seem quite the right word, does it? A better word for the gripping action on the stick might be *clasp* or *cradle*. Unfortunately, "grip" is the commonly accepted term in the sport. Do you cradle a small baby or grip it? Do you clasp a lover's hand in your own or grip it?

In this photo I am holding the cue so lightly it is just short of dropping from my hand and clattering to the table. The fourth and pinky fingers are held away from touching the cue stick at all.

You won't see this grip often at your local pool hall—unless some truly stellar players are there. Quite a few topnotch pool artists who use this grip on the cue still deliver crushing force to the cue ball when needed.

Figure 4.5
Easy is fine.

Gentle Is Good

TO PARAPHRASE AUTHOR George Fels' comments on pool equipment, the cue ball weighs nearly the same as a regulation baseball, and a cue stick, a baseball bat. Rather than smash the cue ball into air for a home run 450 feet over centerfield, however, pool players slide the cue ball a few inches to a few feet over a glass-smooth surface, level to thousandths of an inch.

The history of pool is a history of subtle, gentle motion, and with a few exceptions like *open breaks* (anything goes breaks) to start certain games, gentle movements are all you need.

I fondly recall legend Willie Mosconi's answer when asked how hard to hit the ball on most shots. His reply? "I use three main ball speeds,

slow, slower, and slowest." Willie understood a slowly moving, rolling object ball has the best chance of sinking when it reaches the pocket.

I am exaggerating just a bit in the Figure 4.5 illustration. Most fine players using a thumb and two fingers will hold the cue a tad higher within their fingers, but still not touching the palm or that semi-circle of flesh between thumb and forefinger in any way. The point is this photo is easier to see and if you can't *see* the grip, how will you imitate a player model using a soft grip?

Again, even with the grip of Figure 4.5, I know players who can do it all at the table.

Rocky's Fist Is for Fights, Not Pool

The other extreme, the death grip, is what we wish to avoid, as pictured in Figure 4.6. Note the discoloration around and above my knuckles.

Most people throttle the cue stick like an errant schoolboy, a wasted effort to provide a perfectly obedient straight stroke. There is a far easier way to shoot straight and with power by *allowing your muscles to move with fluidity, not in rigidity.* The first fundamental to achieve this is a gentle clasp on the cue.

Again, you will see players grip a cue this way (too many players in my opinion) and succeed somewhat, but without convoluted arm motions it becomes difficult to perform many shots.

Figure 4.6
We can't squeeze blood from a turnip or a cue stick.

Typical Light Grip (as Used by Experts)

Figure 4.7 shows my usual hold on the cue. It may look somewhere between the death throttle squeeze and the teacup hold, but it is quite close to the teacup hold in pressure applied, though the hand wraps about the cue for a guide.

When preparing to shoot, I hold the cue with scarce more effort than you would use to pick up a set of car keys from a table. Pick up keys now if you would, or a pen or pencil, to see and feel what I mean and to store this tip in your procedural memory, our friend from Chapter 2.

The cue stick weighs a bit more than a pound but is beautifully balanced in its length. You should sense only the weight of the few ounces of that part of the cue resting in your clasp.

My palm is not touching the cue stick at all. I can look back to my shooting hand and see a bit of space between the top of the stick and the fleshy skin flap just above, connecting thumb and forefinger.

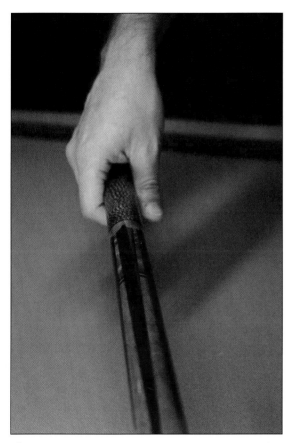

Figure 4.7
A happy medium.

No Squeeze Play

Here is correct grip pressure explained from another perspective. In Figure 4.8 I am demonstrating a teaching technique I use in all my cue grip seminars.

I ask a volunteer with a visibly tight pool grip to step forward, and then I clasp one of their forearms with my own hand. The forearm is somewhat cylindrical like a cue stick and makes for a good demonstration.

I then tightly squeeze as I see them doing on the pool cue. They realize the amount of pressure they are squeezing onto their cue during play. Such pressure restricts the fluid, easy movement you want your cue stick to have in pool.

A natural athlete is said to make their equipment flow as if it is part of their body. What does making the cue stick a mere *extension of your hand* imply about the grip? Would it be an easy grip or a throttle? Do you consciously clench your hand tightly when throwing a ball, turning a key, or performing small, subtle ranges of motion with the wrists?

Figure 4.8
I'm hurting your arm.

Lighten Up!

Next, I invite them to *feel* the minimal pressure I exert on the cue, so they have a model grip to imitate, one sensible for procedural memory.

Figure 4.9 shows my gentle clasp on another's forearm. I hold the arm lightly, as if I were directing this fellow in a gentlemanly fashion on a walk together.

I also have the player re-grip his cue, directing him to take his regular hold, then drop the pressure by half, then half again. One-quarter of the old pressure is still a bit much, but it's a start. I have also asked players to show me what a "ten" grip looks like, ten being the maximum pressure they can muster, and "zero" a dropping of the cue stick with no grip at all. Near "one" or "two" is where most pros hold their stick for most strokes.

In Figure 4.9, you can better view how my palm is not holding the cue (forearm). Your palm can touch the cue anytime you wish, mine does too at times, but I want you to build the gentlest possible grip and motion, and then experiment from there if you need.

As Above, So Below

Here is a unique perspective on grip from beneath the cue. The cue is gently cradled by three or four fingers (or even two as shown in Figure 4.5).

The cue is held lightly enough so that it is just short of falling from my grasp. There is no conscious pressure at the bottom of the fingers; they are there for convenience to prevent the cue from falling to the floor.

Your hand already "knows" (procedural memory) how to carry an object of a few ounces' weight, so why add tension to playing the game? Holding the cue lightly during and between shots reduces fatigue at the tables besides yielding smooth, fluid movement.

You might tighten the grip a bit on certain shots. I'll discuss this in more detail in Chapters 6 and 7.

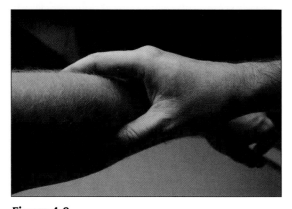

Figure 4.9
I'm holding your arm.

Figure 4.10
Seen from beneath.

Next we'll examine the role the shooting hand's wrist plays for most strokes, combining wrist facts with holding the cue gently with the fingers.

PLEASE BEWARE

If you are a devoted member of the strong grip club, I urge you to try a walk on the other side. Many of the stroking motions I advocate in upcoming chapters are difficult to perform with a death grip. If you think it looks macho to squeeze the cue and smash the shots, it's much more flashy to gently cradle the cue and make light motions to yield amazing results. Pool beginners are amazed at how much more action pros get from the same equipment amateurs use, yet with less physical strength applied to the stick.

It's All in the Wrist

AH, THE BONES and hands of the wrists! So much controversy in pool about how they can work actively or else remain passive during the stroke. Let's clear up the confusion together.

There are six basic movements or directions you can make with the wrists, separated into three pairs by type:

1. *flexion*, either palmar (flex wrist straight forward) or dorsal (flex straight back)

2. *roll*, either pronative (rolling inward) or supinative (rolling outward)

3. *deviation*, either radial (inward deviation) or ulnar (outward deviation)

You have many small bones in the wrists, which make them flexible. You can, therefore, combine several of these wrist motions at once, which can make teaching stick and ball sports quite the challenge. If you've taught multiple sports as I have, you realize various games require different wrist motions at times.

Let's look at each motion uniquely on its own merits for pool. Hang in with me for a bit; we're going to simplify wrist motion in the stroke for you and change your pool game for the better.

Start from the Grip (Neutral Position)

THE SIMPLEST WAY to prepare the wrist for the start of the stroke play is hanging freely at the end of your arm, as shown in Figure 4.11 and discussed above in "Where Do I Begin?"

I am not moving my wrists consciously in any of the six directions yet.

Each of the subsequent figures shows both right and left hands for your convenience, though only one (the dominant hand, usually) will shoot the cue stick.

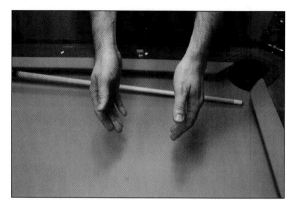

Figure 4.11
Wrists held in natural position.

Scared Straight

MOST POOL STROKES are to go straight back and through. You place your cue on the shot line and go back and forth, back and forth.

Sounds easy, doesn't it? You might be surprised how many players doubt their ability to stroke the cue. They really are torn over their seeming inability to stroke the cue straight. I'll show you how to alleviate this fear.

We begin by looking at the wrist movements we need to make or avoid to bring the cue straight back and forward again every time.

Palmar Flexion (Fingertips In)

SIT IN A COMFORTABLE CHAIR with the palms of your hands resting upon your thighs, your knees pointed straight in front of you. Lift your wrists up and forward without moving your fingertips off your legs. Your thumb and base of your hand will lift up and forward from your thighs, until the backs of your wrists face forward past your knees.

That's *palmar flexion* at the wrists, as in Figure 4.12, the wrist move the basketball player uses to bring a last caress of spin to the big orange ball as it leaves his hand.

Palmar flexion is sometimes known as *plantar flexion*.

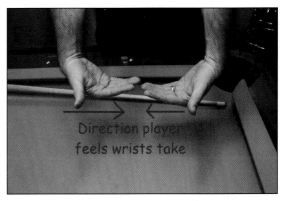

Figure 4.12
Wrists crooked using palmar flexion.

Dorsal Flexion (Fingertips Out)

RETURN YOUR HANDS to their starting position and curl the hand and palm up from the wrist as if you wish to drive the tops of your fingers into the topside of your forearm to make *dorsal flexion*.

The basketball player cradles the ball in his dominant hand during a foul shot with dorsal flexion. This is also the wrist set of a waiter creating a hand tray to hoist a box of pizza or tray of dishes above his head.

Can you imagine how palmar or dorsal flexion can break down an otherwise good pool stroke, taking it from a straight movement to a crooked stroke?

Figure 4.13
Dorsal flexion.

Pronative Roll (Turning Palms Over)

HANDS ON THIGHS AGAIN, this time let's roll the hands inside toward one another, rolling the thumbs and thumb pads along the thigh and lifting the pinkies and palms beneath into the air. See Figure 4.14.

Your elbows should have lifted up and out, away from your body. From the elbow down, the forearm performs this pronation. You don't really roll your wrists at all but rather the arms. The wrist changes location during the pool stroke if you roll, and not in a good way on most shots.

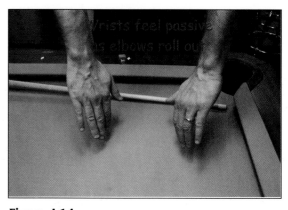

Figure 4.14
Wrists pronated.

Supinative Roll (Turning Palms Up)

IN FIGURE 4.15, we've rolled our forearms outward, flipping the hands over and ending with our palms toward the sky to *supinate* the wrists.

Golfing legend Ben Hogan realized he could smash a golf ball still farther by winding both arms back and through the golf stroke with two-handed pronative and supinative motion, but complicating golf instruction for millions by sharing his revelation. It's not easy to combine roll with pulling and pushing the golf club around the body, and players hurt their game until they realize they roll the arms, not the hands, to pronate and supinate motion.

It's also difficult to time rolling forearm motion in a straight pool stroke, so leave aside roll where you can. It's easier to have the forearm do karate chopping motion through the stroke than to roll it over or under.

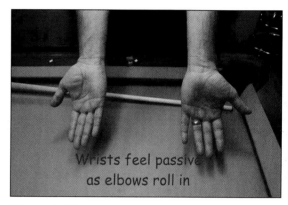

Figure 4.15
Wrists rolled over.

Radial Deviation (Wrist Bend Toward Thumb)

BACK TO PUTTING OUR HANDS on our thighs, but we're getting somewhere good now.

Radial deviation from the start position: wipe the palms of your hands along your thighs, the fingers

brushing the tops of your thighs as they begin to turn in, each hand pointing toward the other hand. If done while standing, bringing your hands up and inward from the base of the thumb and moving the thumb tops toward the forearm will provide the radial deviation shown in Figure 4.16. Note the creases at the wrists.

Radial deviation feels a bit strange to you, doesn't it? From the seated position, do you often turn your wrists inward to brush your hands in that manner? Try it standing. What circumstances would have you lift just your hand from the wrist upward?

You wouldn't feel comfortable lifting a package in this way. Radial deviation causes up to a 20% reduction in hand strength with just 25° of motion from a neutral position (from the relaxed position in Figure 4.11 to the awkward bend of Figure 4.16).

We are of course left with the last of our six ranges of wrist motion.

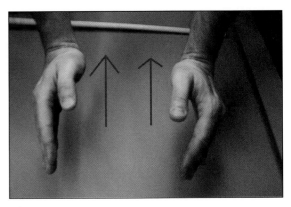

Figure 4.16
Wrists in toward thumbs.

Ulnar Deviation (Wrist Bend Away from Thumb)

ULNAR DEVIATION IS ALSO a side-to-side movement of the hand at the wrist, this time away from the thumb. Hands on thighs one more time, please, and pull your hand from the wrist so the pinkies of your hands stretch to the left and right of your seated position. Do this moving the forearms as little as possible.

In Figure 4.17, I have begun from a neutral position, hands along sides, palms turned in, and then turned at the wrists so that my pinkies point behind me. Fully extended in this way, I could strike an object with the forearm and hand and my arm's dorsal bone would hit first. The wrist is extended away near the ulna, the bone running from elbow to wrist on the forearm side opposite the thumb.

At a 40% wrist break angle, ulnar deviation sees a similar drop in available strength to radial deviation. But we need accuracy, not excessive strength, to play good pool. Nearly every pool shot is a straight shot, and we want to keep the cue moving *straight along the chosen line* of the stroke.

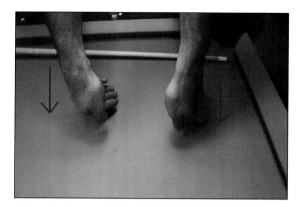

Figure 4.17
Wrists out toward pinkies.

TAKE A TIP

In a word, we've traveled through the possible wrist motions so you know ulnar or a bit of radial deviation or both (wrist moves as forearm pendulums or chops back and forth) occur in a good stroke. Avoid flipping, rolling, or twisting your hands as you play pool, with the infrequent but notable exceptions I'll mention in Chapter 9.

Not Really a Pendulum

THE HAND MOVES through the *correct* pool stroke rather simply. Pool teachers have been saying for nearly two centuries that what is needed is a pendulum-like action in your stroke from the forearm down. That's a close but imprecise picture of the true movement.

Imagine the upper arm parallel to the table and the lower arm hanging straight down from the elbow, swinging like the pendulum on a grandfather clock. Gripping the cue lightly in the fingers, you simply pendulum your lower arm back and forth in an arc. If it's so simple, why don't more pool players shoot better pool?

The pendulum sounds effective and is a good mental image, except for several points:

1. Pool teachers have used the analogy "*like* a pendulum" knowing that a true pendulum movement is not the total pool stroke.

2. If the shooting hand is the bob or the weight of the pendulum, remaining passive in the stroke, the wrist bones provide at times an added *hinge on the pendulum near its bottom* (radial and ulnar deviation). For a beginner, this could create a pendulum forearm that bends somewhere unwanted during the stroke.

3. The pendulum concept makes players think "up and down in a perfect arc," and then stroke up and down, trying to time the bottom of the arc at the cue ball, but the good stroke should go mostly straight back and forth and not up and down. While some up and down motion is unavoidable and even cultivated in some pros' backstrokes, it is slight near impact and the image of a grandfather clock's pendulum can harm a player's stroke unless it is placed in context, pendulum-like elbow motion blended with other motions that straighten the stroke, lengthening the arc and flattening it near its bottom.

Almost a Pendulum

TO CONSIDER A pendulum-*like* stroke let's hold the cue stick, forearm hanging down in a neutral position at our side. I maintain somewhat of a neutral wrist position, perhaps with a tad of ulnar or radial deviation, by swinging the cue stick like a pendulum back and forth from elbow down to the hand (to my rear and forward again facing the shot).

Indeed, to keep the cue relatively level through the stroke, at times I let the cue glide through (and along) my hand, as in Figure 4.18. Note the line of the knuckles has tilted in contrast to the line of the cue stick. I am drawing the cue back and building momentum for the forward stroke.

Figure 4.18
Bringing the cue stick back.

The Hand Opens Going Back

A simple way to handle the motion of the cue going back is to allow the shooting hand to butterfly open a bit on the backstroke. The relaxed hand allows the cue's momentum to spread the fingers open. This is not a conscious movement. See Figure 4.19.

A few fingers are cradling the moving cue and the thumb is gently touching the stick or off it entirely. If I kept the hand closed around the cue, I might arc the forearm higher or add a bit of radial wrist deviation instead, keeping the cue as level as possible.

Figure 4.19
The hand may open on the backstroke.

Moving Forward Again

I am rolling the cue along my hand and going forward in Figure 4.20. No worries, I will walk you through the stroke thoroughly in Chapter 6. We are simply discussing grip and wrist so you know what to do in a general way—a relaxed hold and a supple but non-turning, non-flipping wrist.

Again, to this point of the stroke, I have kept the wrist in a fairly neutral plane parallel to the walls of the room (no bend or twist).

Figure 4.20
Sending the stick forward through the cue ball.

The Hand May Pop Open

The cue is still going forward and my pendulum is running out of track fast, from the elbow. I only have so much forearm and upper arm flexibility to my body and so do you.

At some point as the rear end of the cue comes up in an arc, after impact with the cue ball, my wrist will *want* to make a radial deviation (bend up toward my right thumb), but the weight of the cue in my hands will preclude that movement. Instead, one possibility is the top of my hand will begin to open up and the bottom of my ring and pinky fingers will start to cradle the cue more so than the first two fingers. My first fingers are now loosening quickly on the cue stick. This motion is not consciously made. It is a consequence on certain strokes taken with a relaxed hand.

Imagine the bob on the pendulum is swinging freely when it is suddenly pulled by a hinge just above it (where the forearm meets the wrist).

In Figure 4.21, you can see my neutral wrist position (no radial deviation) has brought my hand up quick as if I am tossing a ball up rather than sending the stick forward.

Figure 4.21
One way to finish the stroke.

Ulnar's Where It's At!

THERE'S AN EASIER WAY than partially letting go of the cue on the forward stroke! Simply allow a relaxed wrist to incur some ulnar deviation on the forward stroke (Figure 4.22). The cue tip finishes low and level to the table.

PLEASE BEWARE

We've come far so don't give up now. Do you push or pull the cue stick? How fast, how far, the same grip on each shot? I will put wrist, hand, and arm position into context in subsequent chapters. For now, this quick look helps us understand we want either a neutral position or a bit of ulnar deviation on the forward stroke, with wrist positions *made easier with the light finger grip* under discussion.

Figure 4.22
One may bend the wrist opposite to that shown in Figure 4.21.

Why Not Roll the Hand?

POOL TEACHERS DISCOURAGE their students from any palmar or dorsal flexion, as in Figures 4.23 and 4.24.

First, I am holding my forearm straight up and down in Figure 4.23, but the wrist position means I must lose the simplicity of having the forearm in line with the shot. Most shots are all about building a straight-line movement. I can get my forearm atop the cue stick more but would need to set the wrist at a still more awkward angle. Figure 4.24 is worse than Figure 4.23, just an ugly mess. Awkward moves are wasted energy in pool.

Second, and this is key, any flexion or rolling of the wrist during the stroke will take the cue off line.

Figure 4.23
Palmar flexion on the cue stick.

Figure 4.24
Dorsal flexion on the cue stick.

TAKE A TIP

If I hold the cue loosely with the fingers, then suddenly clench or tighten on a nervous stroke, the cue stick goes up or down in a plane along the straight aim line. But if I clench or tighten while the cue stick is palmed or the wrist is twisted or rolled, I will miss the line of stroke to the right or left. *Up or down* hits on the cue ball affect the *distance* the cue ball travels, *side-to-side* misses affect the *direction* the cue balls travels. Distance versus direction is the difference between an object ball struck too hard or too softly versus one not even struck at all! There are many reasons to start the stroke with with a neutral wrist, cue held lightly in the fingers.

We will review wrist and hand action later as we study stance and stroke. First we must learn how to set the bridge hand and body in relation to the cue stick and table to line us straight on the shot every time.

A Bridge Not Too Far

TIME TO LEAVE the shooting hand alone for now and look at the role of the bridge hand in play. Your non-dominant hand is going to do some clever things to aid you in pool, and the more bridge variations you learn, the less you will need the mechanical bridge or *rake*.

Going forward, some of the pool instruction photos are seen from a rare perspective over one shoulder so you can *see what I see* at the table. Shadows touching those photos are my head or shoulder in the shot.

Photos that do not appear as center ball hits are mostly due to the illusion caused by camera placement. The cue stick seems to be pointed left to right while I have it straight ahead under my eyes, as the camera sits atop my left shoulder.

Most photos of hand bridges were taken while my cue was pointed *dead center* on the cue ball. Dead center means the intersection of the cue ball's vertical axis (midway between the ball resting on the cloth and the top of the ball) and its horizontal axis, from my perspective behind the ball in my stance at the table.

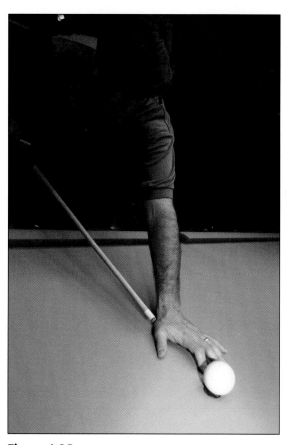

Figure 4.25
Moving to the open bridge.

TAKE A TIP

A dead-center hit can be a challenge, as you are seeking the exact middle of a plain white sphere viewed from an elevated perspective, your head somewhat above the ball and table. Many poolrooms use cue balls with handy red spots on their surface. The "red dot cue ball" may be turned to focus on one spot for cue ball aim practice. Touching the cue ball to manipulate it in place for most pool shots during the game incurs a penalty.

Why Cue with Both Hands?

WE'VE GRIPPED THE cue stick lightly in the fingers somewhere behind its balance point. We want the cue close to the table to strike level hits on the cue ball with more than half the cue weight forward of our shooting hand. The easiest way to balance the stick to the table is to use our non-dominant bridge hand, bridging the distance between shooting hand and cue ball.

Your other hand comes in "handy" too, as your arm length never changes lifelong (if you are an adult) granting you a consistent length bridge as you keep the bridging non-dominant arm consistent in position, relaxed yet straight in length and without much elbow bend.

Bridge Under Construction

CUE GRIPPED BY THE shooting hand, simply place your other hand palm down on the table near the cue ball and rest the cue stick upon it.

Interestingly, you will bridge atop the very part of the hand that I wrote should not touch the stick at the shooting hand, the fleshy palm fold between thumb and forefinger, as seen in Figure 4.26.

Figure 4.26
Beginning the open bridge.

The Bridge Is Open

L EAVE THE FINGERTIPS resting on the table, stretch your pinky finger out, and scrunch your fingers and thumb a bit toward one another as the cue rests atop the groove along the thumb. You will see what I mean in Figure 4.27, as I zero in on the red dot placed at center ball position.

The stroking movement will rub the flesh along the hand. Note the wrinkles adjacent to my thumb in Figure 4.27. Press the thumb into the forefinger so that the thumb will not float free.

Be sure, as with all pool shots, to set the cue's tip quite close to the ball before beginning the stroke or even any *practice strokes*, gentle rehearsal movements of the stroke to warm up in preparation to strike the cue ball.

This open bridge has appeal for pool beginners in its simple, two-step construction:

1. Extend the bridging arm comfortably and straight forward, resting the hand on the table so the groove along the thumb will line up to the stroke.

2. Bring the first three fingers and thumb in and stroke the cue along the thumb and forefinger.

There are pitfalls, however. The cue stick is vulnerable to leaving the bridge hand and springing into the air unchecked, ruining the beginner's stroke.

I will show you *the* bridge to use next. It takes just one more step to build than this one. You can do it!

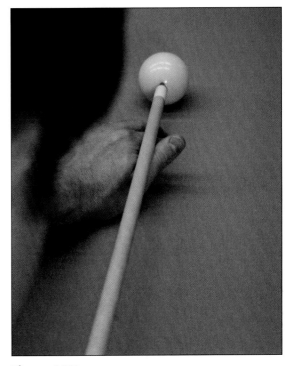

Figure 4.27
Completing the open bridge.

TAKE A TIP

Hitting in the center of the cue ball is lovely, but what about hitting the ball higher or lower, left or right? We will discuss the best way to play right and left spin (cue english) in Chapter 9; but to hit higher and lower on the cue ball for most shots, simply draw the fingers in tighter to the palm or else lower them, spreading them wide. Move the fingers *without* lifting or lowering the shooting hand. Yes, it's that simple.

The Closed Bridge, 1-2-3

THE CLOSED BRIDGE is a powerhouse of pool, adapting to almost any shot need. It's quite simple to make:

1. Extend the bridging arm (my left arm) comfortably and straight ahead, resting the hand on the table as a fist, palm side down on the table behind the ball (see Figure 4.28).

2. Spread out the first finger and thumb on the bridge hand, leaving the rest of the fist intact on the felt. See Figure 4.29.

Figure 4.29
Open the thumb and forefinger.

Figure 4.28
Start by making a fist.

3. Place the cue along the same channel you built with the open bridge and close the forefinger around the cue, pressing this finger loop into the middle finger with the thumb and making the cue a snug berth in the finger loop. Your bridge now resembles my left hand in Figure 4.30.

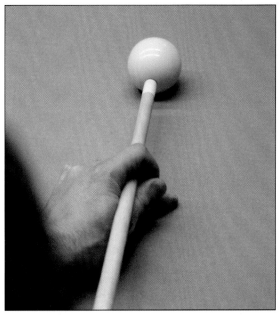

Figure 4.30
Make and close the loop.

Don't Resist the Switch

POOL STUDENTS CAN construct this bridge 1-2-3, but resist making it part of every shot, as it feels a tad uncomfortable at the beginning to push the cue through the loop. For the specialty shots we'll shoot later, you will certainly want this bridge. American pool professionals compete today mostly with the closed bridge.

Whether you rely on an open or closed bridge, you will want the bridge hand to remain immobile, unmoved throughout the stroke. It is the solid guide for the moving shooting arm and the gliding forward cue stick.

TAKE A TIP

Take a fist and point it palm toward your face. Bring just the forefinger up in a tight curl touching the middle finger. Squeeze the thumb against the forefinger into the side of the fist. Spread the last three fingers out in a fan. The closed bridge is easy to make, isn't it? As you stroll or walk anywhere for the next several weeks, form the closed bridge with one or both hands until it becomes second-nature, part of your pool procedural memory.

A Few Bridge Pointers

M ANY OF THE PROS maintain a *bridge distance*, the distance between the loop of the bridge hand and the cue ball at address, of ten inches or more for most shots. They also have the procedural memory of hitting the ball many, many times and a smooth, flowing stroke to avoid the errors beginners create with such a faraway stick fulcrum.

You may want a shorter bridge of five or six inches as you start to learn the open and closed bridges, until you are comfortable in your bridge and stroke. If you struggle to hit the balls accurately, you can use an open bridge of two inches and a closed bridge distance of just an inch or two, as I demonstrate in Figure 4.31.

Regardless of the bridge length, keep working the closed bridge until it is comfortable, or you will struggle to take your game to the next level.

Figure 4.31
Close up for accuracy.

Look through the Loop

A JEWELER USES a loupe to peer at gemstones, so let's see what we can learn looking through a bridge loop instead. Can you find the space between cue and fingers in my bridge?

Making too tight a loop around the cue causes a tight, jerky stroke movement, and tightly constructed closed bridges stop most amateurs from using this tool effectively. Too loose a closed bridge, in contrast, is just an open bridge that looks funny.

I want a flowing, not a rigid, motion of stroke. A bit of space within the loop itself won't hurt the stroke. Figure 4.32 shows space to the right of the cue stick as seen from my perspective.

Figure 4.32
Vantage close to the bridge hand.

Another View

I N FIGURE 4.33, we see the same bridge taken from another angle. My pinky points parallel to the direction of the stroke; you may also point ahead or a bit to either side.

You can just make out the fourth finger resting on the table from this perspective. Simply spread your fingers *without* lowering the shooting hand to hit lower on the cue ball or raise the fingers in place, drawing them by sliding the tips along the felt into your palm, to hit higher on the ball. Again, be certain to leave your relaxed shooting hand in place. It is the bridge alone that moves up or down as needed and not the grip hand.

Since the cue stick is near level to the table, the loop of the bridge will move a bit higher on a high shot, lower on a low shot. More on adjustments to follow in subsequent chapters.

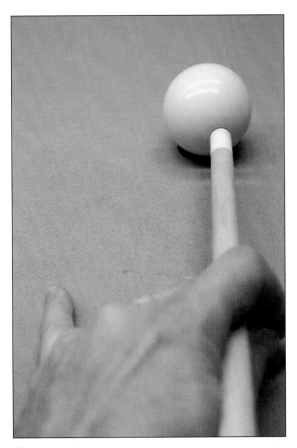

Figure 4.33
Overlooking the pinky finger.

Basic Rail Bridging

I N FIGURE 4.34, the cue ball is too close to the cushion for a simple open or closed bridge. There are great options along the rail, giving you the benefit of keeping both hands on the cue stick to sense its movement and build those important procedural memories, the remembrance of how a good or bad shot will *feel*.

This bridge is easy and a real eye-opener to even skilled players:

1. Start by placing the cue on the line of aim (straight ahead in this instance) and rest the bridge hand on the table. The hand's thumb will point parallel to the line of aim, and the cue will slide along its length. See Figure 4.34.

Figure 4.34
Setting up for the rail bridge.

2. In Figure 4.35, I have left my thumb in place and lifted my forefinger up and over the cue stick. Note that this bridge works best when the cue ball's distance from your hand allows the bridge hand to sit partially atop the polished wooden rail, partially atop the cushioned cloth itself. Where the blue and wood meet forms a small hill around the rails of the table. See Figure 4.36.

Figure 4.36
Tighten the hand.

3. Last, I bring the other fingers toward the thumb a bit, as I wish to tighten the bridge in place. The cue may be passed back and forth very vigorously through this snug loop now. Practice a bit, feeling the cue sliding along your thumb, and you will even be able to hit a hard, fast break shot using this basic rail bridge and a smooth stroke.

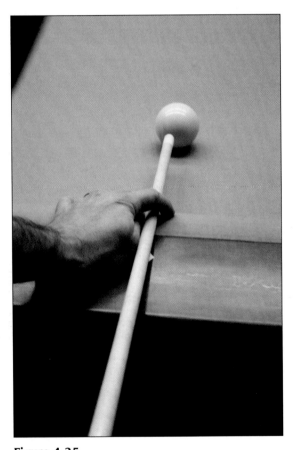

Figure 4.35
Loop one finger over the stick.

Over-the-Rail Bridge

T HE CUE BALL is still closer to the rail in Figure 4.37. A clever combination of rail and open bridge solves the problem as shown.

TAKE A TIP

For this over-the-rail bridge to work effectively, you must have the palm of your hand along the gentle downslope of the top of the rail as pictured. Note the heel of my hand is off the table completely, allowing the channel or action section of my bridge to be near level with the center of the cue ball. With the hand atop the rail instead, it would be difficult to take a level stroke, and I would need to shoot down at the ball.

Figure 4.37
Bridging in an unusual spot.

Closed Bridge at an Angle

FIGURE 4.38 is another hybrid. This time we have built a closed bridge and leaned it on the far side of the cushion to get the cue stick into a corner.

This bridge demands that somewhat less than a level stroke is made. For that reason, I have brought my bridge quite close to the ball to heighten accuracy. Any adjustment from a level stroking motion to one that is more up and down requires care.

Figure 4.38
An odd-looking bridge.

Open Bridge at an Angle

Y ET ANOTHER HYBRID concept building on earlier bridge ideas. In Figure 4.39, I am leaning an open bridge over a rail for a rare stroke demanding cue elevation.

Over the Wall

Figure 4.40 shows the same bridge with the photo taken from another angle. The bridge is still open but elevated steeply over the side of the cushion wall. The open bridge set at a height further leads to the next style of bridge, both attractive and functional in nature.

Figure 4.39
Open, sloping bridge.

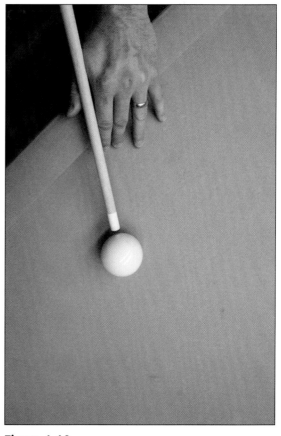

Figure 4.40
From another perspective.

Raising Your Bridge

PLANTING THREE OR MORE fingertips at the table to balance a bridge in the air is called a *tripod bridge* (see Figure 4.41). Make the tripod by setting the regular open bridge on the table before leaving the fingertips in position and bending the hand from the wrist up with our old acquaintance, dorsal wrist flexion. And you thought all that wrist information wouldn't come in *handy*.

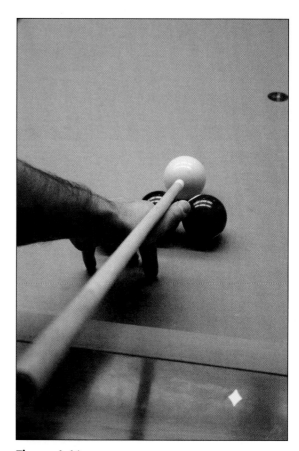

Figure 4.41
Tripod bridge.

Bridging Over Troubled Waters

F IGURE 4.42 IS THE SAME bridge from another angle, better illustrating why I raised my hand to begin the shot. I want to elevate the cue stick over the 8-ball and other obstacles to take a clean stroke on the white cue ball without touching another ball.

Remember to make each and any hand bridge firm and secure *before* you begin stroking the cue stick. This is even more important on a suspension bridge like this one. A great player leans down on unusual bridge shots, designing a custom bridge from a perspective near the table, before standing up again to assume their bridge and stance. It's an elegant procedure to watch.

Figure 4.42
Another look.

The Mechanical Bridge

THE FINAL BRIDGE TO CROSS (pun intended) is the mechanical bridge, known in pool slang as the *rake*. Mechanical bridges are available at poolrooms for your use free of charge.

Shown in Figure 4.43 is a clever rake with a wide variety of channels placed on its surface, for stroking the cue across the non-abrasive plastic smoothly and at different heights.

There are two correct methods for bridge use. With this first method, I hold the butt end of the cue just beneath my chin so I can sight down the cue stick easily. My thumb and a few fingers hold my cue near the rear (the bridge requires more of a shove than it does a balanced stroke).

Figure 4.43
Using the rake.

My elbow is turned horizontal to my shooting hand, forearm approximately parallel to the table surface. A bit of a sideways flick using palmar wrist flexion, a bit of thrust forward, and the cue ball will be struck forward.

Due to the precarious angle of the cue stick, I avoid hitting the cue ball other than on its vertical axis if at all possible. The mechanical bridge is best reserved for shots that cannot otherwise be reached with a human bridging arm.

Another Use of the Mechanical Bridge

FIGURE 4.44 IS the same shot, ball and rake in same position as before. The sole difference is I have turned my elbow to point straight down. The accordion of my upper and lower arm is now pointed up and down. Again, a bit of palmar flexion and a bit of shove from the shooting hand's fingers, and we can still hit that cue ball well.

Elbow under, or out to one side horizontally, take your pick. Next, I'll demonstrate the wrong way to use the rake.

Figure 4.44
Using the rake, Part II.

Raking Like an Amateur

Figure 4.45
Not this way!

THE CUE BALL HAS NOT MOVED since Figure 4.44. What is the difference in Figure 4.45?

While previous figures illustrated the rake held down along the table surface, here the rake handle is picked up into the air along with the cue stick. It's a common mistake I see often. The cue is in the air, so why not the rake?

The rake is to be anchored in place with moderate to firm pressure from the bridge hand, or it will slide along the smooth surface of the table. Any movement could wreck the shot!

A rake hoisted in the air is upsetting to see at a pool clinic, but brings a smile in competition. It means my opponent misses often with the mechanical bridge.

What Have We Learned?

THIS CHAPTER PLACES the game of pool and your success squarely in your two hands.

Your dominant or shooting hand:

- ▶ is placed a few inches to a foot (if you're taller) to the rear of the cue stick's balance point

- ▶ sets to the table in a relaxed, neutral wrist position

- ▶ clasps the cue lightly using the thumb and a finger or two

- ▶ moves through a pendulum-like arc (not a true pendulum but one blended with straight back and forth motion)

- ▶ may bend at the wrist using ulnar or radial deviation, but is not to be twisted or rolled off line

- ▶ may employ a bit of incidental up or down hand movement but not unwanted side-to-side movement

Your bridge hand:

- ▶ remains relaxed but immobile on the table

- ▶ can become any of a dozen shapes in two or three steps to rest the cue stick and guide direction

- ▶ is stretched to the table by a relaxed yet sturdy bridging arm

- ▶ can be supplemented by the mechanical bridge on a shot that cannot be otherwise bridged by the hand

Next Ahead

CHAPTER 5 WILL HELP you set your body in place precisely to the table. "Bend over the table and put your chin on the stick" is not the whole story. I'll show you how to avoid back pain and avoid muscle strain and fatigue, while teaching you to stand at the table like a pool pro.

You will then be able to aim and hit a variety of shots, speeds, and spins with ease and style. Let's go!

Stand and Deliver: Body
Alignment

Place for the win, not a show

*J*ERRY STROLLED INTO THE POOL HALL, *a happy tune playing about his lips. His gaze regarded Table 30 in the far corner, taking the measure of the long, skinny fellow who grimaced as the 9-ball slid into a corner pocket. The opponent, vigorous and burly but with a paunch, brushed aside an angry blond comma of hair that had fallen across his field of vision.*

"Another hundred bucks?" The table cleared of balls with the last shot, the man Jerry had mentally dubbed "Fats" smirked as his much taller adversary racked the balls again for punishment....

There is a look and feel to the correct pool stance granting a pro a huge edge *before* they shoot the stick. "Jerry" could see what made "Fats" so good even before he stroked the cue—an elegant, balanced billiards stance. I will pass that gift on to you in this chapter.

Fundamentals

WATCHING MAJOR LEAGUE ballplayers assume their stance at the plate, each one looks somewhat unique. Some hunch somewhat whereas others stand more upright. Some grip higher to "choke up" on one end but others hold their bat near its bottom. Despite variations, however, *all* ballplayers' stances accomplish two key purposes by keeping their eye on the ball throughout play and holding themselves comfortably to move with maximum power and finesse.

A correct stance is also key to fine pool shooting. Though the knock-kneed balance differently at the table than the bow-legged, and the tall, skinny player varies from the short or stout, the fundamentals most pros use I will teach you now. You might succeed holding your cue behind your back one-handed while hopping on one foot, but the fewer alterations you need to make from the norm, the better.

Pool players who throw away the fundamentals of stance fool themselves for the worse. To borrow another golf analogy for this book (pool and golf are alike in many ways besides being single-player sports), imagine a pro with a balanced, athletic stance and an excellent grip on the golf club—who stands to play with his club soled on the ground 15 feet away from the ball. If your pool game is stagnant, it's usually a poor stance that is to blame.

This Magic Moment

Pool cognoscenti refer to a period of outstanding play as "really stroking" or "dead stroke." The best players reach the top after they've discovered their best stroke and remain near their peak, ready to play great pool at any time. When the pro's game takes a downturn and slumps, however, they soon return to reviewing the fundamentals.

Your personal best stroke is a combination of stance, grip on the cue, arm movements, and timing, enabling you to shoot consistently every time you play. Players who discover the specific grip position that works best for them, for example, will probably hold the cue that way for their entire pool career.

Finding your stroke is different from merely having a good session or two at the tables. If you excel at "gripping it tight and hitting with all your might," you probably haven't found *it* yet. With few exceptions, the great ones stroke smoothly, gently, and with minimal effort.

Good pool shooters hold the cue stick nearly level, lightly cradling it in their fingers and usually near its balance point as discussed in Chapter 4, and use smooth, gentle strokes whenever possible.

Face your shots and bend to the table as outlined below, and practice, practice, practice. When your skills reach an intermediate level, you may wish to experiment, shifting a foot here or a finger there. Record your original stance first in photos or words so you can return safely from any false starts.

The directions below need to be reversed for left-handers (though the physics of english always remain the same—see Chapter 9). Remember, exceptions work for top players for each shooting "rule" presented here. There are also successful wheelchair players, and many fine players use an artificial limb to hold the cue or stand to the table. There are pros who hold the cue at its extreme end, use only an open bridge, etc. The greats also play and practice up to ten hours a day. Learning the fundamentals most use, however, and the theory supporting them, would undoubtedly improve most amateurs' skills.

Body Stance

TO THE UNINITIATED, a pool shooter merely bends over the table and fires away. In reality, a proper stance is a carefully laid, ideal platform to shoot from. The player aligns to the shot comfortably balanced to send the cue ball straight down the line of aim every time.

The body is placed out of the way of the right arm's movements. The trunk of the body is angled about 45 degrees to the table, except for shots when the player must stretch far across the table. Your personal girth may require some adjustment.

Three Stances

I learned pool the wrong way—I spent much time shooting the incorrect way and made the game much harder than it should have been. Reading this chapter carefully will save you much time and trouble.

There are three ways to take your stance at the pool table, and we will review all three, as beginners do the first, intermediates the second, and pros the third, with few exceptions.

I have never seen the following three stances reviewed in a pool book, but I see most of my students do their stance badly until corrected:

1. a dreadful way to stand is to "align the chin" with the cue ball then bend forward"

2. a second poor way to stand is to "line the stick to the shot line before bending over the stick"

3. less than 1 in 100 knows the secret—align stick to ball *and* balance the body separately

Big Mistake

Consider Figure 5.1 most carefully. You are going to see why most players miss constantly (and you may have stood to the table this way for years).

Figure 5.1
How a beginner stands.

We are going to use a green solid ball and two stripes as if they are all cue balls. The white cue ball as discussed in Chapter 3 is the only ball your cue tip will strike in most cue games.

I am standing behind the short rail of the table, belt buckle, chin, and more aligned with both the green 6-ball and the head spot in the middle of the table—the middle of my body is symmetrically aligned with the exact middle of the table equidistant from the long rails. The yellow striped 9-ball is opposite my *shooting hand* gripping the cue; my right hand, and the orange striped 13-ball is opposite my left hand.

I am illustrating one poor way to build stance, the interpretation most people take from "Bend over so your chin goes atop the cue stick."

I set my chin behind the green ball in the middle of the table, and we can see the problem already in Figure 5.1—*pool uses a hand from one side of the body, not our head in the middle of the body.*

Can you see how the cue stick is misaligned? If I thrust my right hand forward, the green ball will fail to roll straight down the middle of the table and over the foot spot. Instead, the ball is aimed to my left, the right side of the photo from this perspective.

Big Mistake, Continued

In Figure 5.2, I simply stepped forward with the left foot then bent over the ball from the position in Figure 5.1. I look determined and even resemble a skilled pool player, yet just as my left leg and left arm are to one side of my head, my all-important right hand and shooting arm are off to the other side!

Figure 5.2
Bad start, bad stance.

Starting with the chin over the ball is terrific if you shoot pool with your chin and not your hands, which were created on either side of your torso. A player can get some success with this stance with a last-minute swerve in their stroke, or making a ball not requiring extreme accuracy, etc. But the end result is, I am always slightly misaligned with my chin directly behind the ball but with my shooting hand off a bit to the side.

Players who stand chin first and then bend report that their shooting arm feels uncomfortably scrunched to their side and blocked by the body. If they twist their arm and hand unnaturally (and some-how keep their chest and leg from interfering also), the stick might feel as if it emanates from the center of their body so they can play a few good shots.

There's much more to a good stance than the old standby, "Comfortably bend so your head is over the stick," as many teachers suggest.

Still Not Fixed

Figures 5.3 and 5.4 somewhat improve on stance but are still not right. Were you taught to shoot pool this way?

Figure 5.3
How an intermediate stands.

I am smiling as most intermediates do when they discover their shooting arm must be considered *first* when approaching the stance. My head is over the green 6-ball still, but my shooting arm holding the cue stick is resting at my side comfortably and aligned to shoot the yellow 9-ball straight down the table. So far, so good, but the intermediate's mistake is coming.

Figure 5.4
In back pain and stroke trouble.

Still Not Fixed, Continued

I leave my cue arm behind the 9-ball and bring my head down and atop the stick to get from the upright stance of Figure 5.3 to the shooting posi-tion of Figure 5.4. Can you guess the problems I will encounter, before you read on?

Crumpled and Off Balance

If you said, "Matt's off balance and bent out of shape," then you are correct. The intermediate knows they shoot pool with an arm along their side and not their body center, so they set the cue stick down first, the same way the pro golfer places his club in position then later adjusts his body or as a pro baseball hitter plots the path for his bat with a few practice swings.

I am exaggerating slightly for the camera in Figure 5.4, but my weight is leaning strongly on my right side and my head is off kilter. Most of us with average eyesight want the head held level, not collapsed like we are playing the violin.

My shooting arm is bunched tightly, too, rather than relaxed in this awkward stance. All three factors of head tilt, collapsed left side, and restricted shooting arm make it difficult to shoot and might cause a cramp or kink in muscles, too.

Bingo!

Figure 5.5 has me wiser and well heeled. I am ready to shoot better pool.

Figure 5.5
How most pros stand.

Once again, I get behind the ball, in this case the 9-ball, so that my shooting arm is lined up to the ball but my feet and body are off to the side.

TAKE A TIP

I haven't made any awkward moves to get to the position in Figure 5.5. I clasped a gentle grip on the cue stick some inches behind the balance point (see Chapter 4) and then I walked up to place the cue tip behind the 9-ball, hand at my side as is comfortable, as if I were strolling down a sidewalk.

The Critical Move

I again leave the shooting hand straight on the line behind the ball where it was in Figure 5.5. I am shown bending down my head and torso to the table. This time, however, instead of forcing them over the cue, they are naturally coming down over the green 6-ball!

Figure 5.6
Begin the bend.

In other words, I leave the cue stick and the arm holding it in place and bring my body straight down. Sit in your favorite chair for a comparison. Did you naturally fold your hand in to beneath your chin (Figure 5.2) or collapse your body weight and head onto one of your hands where it sits on an armrest (Figure 5.4)? I took one step forward with my left foot to accommodate balance, and lowered my trunk down, not atop the stick.

The secret of stance involves leaving your shooting arm dangling in space while you wrap your body into position for the shot. For example, you can see in Figure 5.6 how my bridge arm, my left arm, has slid beneath my chin to position the cue stick.

I extend my bridge arm over to the cue stick to shoot. I do not stretch my body over my cue stick. The distinction is a critical one if you want to play stellar pool.

TAKE A TIP

Place the stick in *approximate* position behind the cue ball. It's not yet time to fuss over the exact aim. Focus on relaxed, comfortable arms. **Don't consciously hoist the right arm into the air in any way.**

Free the Shooting Arm

Figure 5.7 has me coming down still a bit more to firm the point. The position of my right arm may look bizarre to you. It seems as if the shooting arm is divorced from the rest of my body. That is precisely what good pool is about!

Figure 5.7
Still coming down.

Head and Eye Alignment

An ideally built pool robot would have its eyes mounted on top of its right shoulder. For human beings, an optical illusion can make the cue stick appear to be aimed a bit left or right instead of straight ahead. Now my eyes are to the left of my cue stick, but I can see the shot well enough to play.

Some players have two level eyes and cue beneath them, some have a bit of head tilt, and some have one eye or the other held directly over the stick. Many pool instructors advocate holding one's dominant eye above the cue. In my case, my left eye is dominant, but I feel I need to strain my neck and torso to place my left eye above the cue. I play well with my right eye or chin above the stick instead. The cue itself may waver a bit within my vision and appear slightly bent away from the target, but I can see the angles on the balls best this way.

TAKE A TIP

You will ultimately want to settle on a particular head position. Try all three settings— the left eye above the cue, the right eye above it, and a binocular look from a cue held beneath a level chin—yet you might find a fourth spot that works best for you. Your preference will be based on your eyesight and focus, but once you find the best spot for you to shoot straight, strive to place your head there in the same spot each time you shoot, to build your personal pool robot for the movements of the stroke.

The main thing is to avoid any neck strain or unusual tilt, while you put the head in the same place every time you shoot. My method of teaching stance involves setting the stick and then the body weight, rather than the old adage of placing one eye over the stick like shooting a rifle or bending so the chin goes over the stick.

Get your arm right and your body set. You would be amazed at how well you can then shoot pool, even with both eyes closed.

Take the Medicine

I can shoot most shots from the position of Figure 5.7 quite well. When I take my students through the three stances, however, showing them the two wrong ways and the one better way to stand, I hear similar complaints each time:

- ▶ "My body position feels strange...."
- ▶ "My shooting arm seems like it is all alone in space...."
- ▶ "I don't think I can control my shooting arm this way...."

- ▶ "I want to go back to the way I used to stand for pool...."

All the complaints end soon after they shoot a few balls with this new stance. I usually arrange a pool shot they would otherwise find challenging, and they make it in on the first try! Discomfort produces balls going into the pockets and comfort will follow soon with practice.

So much of stroking the cue stick well requires a freely flowing motion from a shooting arm along on the line, as we will see in Chapter 6. Take a close look at the next photo.

Locked In

Here in Figure 5.8, I am squared away to play pool. My legs, body trunk, and left arm are mostly away from the line of the shot. My head is over the shot line with the center of the head at the chin approximately over the cue stick. It need not be directly over the cue. My right eye is over the cue stick, not my chin. Your head position may be somewhat different than mine. Be consistent and return to the same head position once you are sighting your best.

Figure 5.8
Set to shoot!

My head is not awkwardly tilted as in Figure 5.4, though, and my shooting hand is basically where it began in Figure 5.5. The shooting hand is directly beneath the elbow or nearly so.

In reality, I make a blended move down and usually do not bring my head as far down as the last photo, Figure 5.7, before taking it over the cue stick during play. I strongly suggest, however, that you bring your body weight down to shoot, lowering before adjusting to set your head over the cue after you feel the difference caused by lowering the body straight down. Avoid crumpling over the cue as in Figures 5.2 and 5.4 at all costs.

My weight is now balanced between my feet and my body center is to the left of the shot, even as my head is comfortable and nearly over the cue.

TAKE A TIP

Perhaps the best part of the body-balanced stance I advocate is the hand is on line for any shot. At the risk of oversimplifying the stroke (see Chapter 6), my shooting hand is relaxed at my side and goes straight back and forth for play. I can execute most shots with both eyes closed after assuming this full, correct stance, tip ready near the cue ball.

A Closer Look

Figure 5.9 is the same in-balance stance as the previous photo, but with my head set quite low atop the cue stick for an illustration. I am squared away to play pool. My legs, body trunk, and left arm are mostly away from the line of the shot. My head is over the shot line with the center of the head at

the chin approximately over the cue stick. I don't stand this way usually with a greatly lowered head, but Figure 5.9 is a good representation of how many pros stand to the table.

Figure 5.9
Way down there.

This figure has been highlighted so you can best see how my head and the upper portion of the shooting arm are in line with the aim of the shot. Many pros stand this low to the stick for a better look at certain angles on the table. The restricted field of vision from close to the felt enhances concentration and minimizes distracting sights from outside the table.

Leaning down so far that the cue practically grazes your chin is fine, but don't go farther, with the cue passing along one cheek near the eye. You will not be able to discern the angles for shots.

I do find this low stance awkward for play, as do most shooters. You can do very well with your chin a foot or more above the stick for most shots.

More Stance Tips

I HAVE FURTHER encouragements for you on correct stance. You'll want to maximize your chances of success on every shot and win with these tips.

Bridge Arm Positioning

My non-shooting arm is never held rigid. It is relaxed and approximately straight. When I need to curl it around a rail or bend it from the elbow to get the cue tip into position, I do it. Tensing that arm leads quickly to soreness in that shoulder following play.

Don't worry too much about your bridge arm for now. Stick it out ahead of your shooting hand consistently, so that the bridge hand is the same distance from the cue ball for most shots.

Shooting Arm Hangs

There certainly is more than one way to swing a cue and succeed. For example, Willie Hoppe (rhymes with "poppy"), considered one of the greatest billiardists who ever wielded a stick, held his cue in a bizarre sideways fashion, his arm flung horizontally to one side from the elbow, not hanging down vertically as most players.

Pros sometimes use this bizarre hold on the cue, their shooting arm bent crooked to the shot, since they've been playing since they were toddlers and always needed to stretch their arms for shotmaking as best they could.

Most players who weren't born with cue stick in hand would do better to leave the lower half of the shooting arm hanging from the elbow down toward the table. We will revisit arm and wrist positions in Chapter 6 as we learn the makings of an excellent stroke.

TAKE A TIP

With the shooting forearm hanging roughly perpendicular to the floor and in the proper, balanced stance, the direction and movements of your shooting hand are quite similar to those when you walk down the street. Pool can be almost that simple!

Take a Leg

Just as we considered three body alignments to the table, there are three basic ways pool shooters position their feet and legs at the table. The first two are poor choices for most shooters:

1. Leave the feet together as at address, as though you are standing upright at the table (poor choice).

2. Turn both legs and feet sideways at a 90° angle to the shot (also not a good idea).

3. Step one foot forward and hold the body about 45° to the shot at hand (best).

While I love feedback from readers, please do not write to name those pool pros who stand squarely to the table or sidesaddle. There are exceptions, of course, and having thousands of hours to practice helps the pool professional get along. Most players I know will do best placed about 45 degrees to the shot, as in Figure 5.10.

Figure 5.10
One giant step for "poolkind."

Standing with both feet square to the shot is not ideal in my opinion as it forces the back to be bent from the waist to get close to the shot. I fear for back injuries for the player. The squared stance is

better for snooker, a pocket billiards game requiring little of the extreme spin or power needed for certain pool strokes.

Standing completely sidesaddle to the table is also dangerous as it makes the shooting arm scrape along the belly of the player rather than allowing freedom of motion. Over time, serious neck and back problems can occur with such a stance. Players have thanked me for adjusting their stance and reducing their chiropractor bills as an added benefit.

I take one step forward with my left foot instead, and allow my right foot to pivot into place a bit from the heel as shown in the illustration.

TAKE A TIP

I use the foot on my shooting side (my right foot) as height control for my head and torso. By pivoting the right foot so the meat of it ahead of the ankle rests beneath the cue (on the shot line), I am comfortably above the table. By getting the foot and thigh still more across that line, I will naturally stand higher to the table (on hard to see shots requiring a higher vantage point for my eyes). Keeping the right foot off the line mostly, as in Figure 5.10, I am instead lowered to the table with my body. The shooting foot is my height control at the table.

Well Balanced

Figure 5.11 is another look at the position of 5.10, albeit a strange one. My head is bent to look at the floor and my right arm is where it would be for the stroke (held without a cue stick) so you can better see my torso and legs.

Figure 5.11
Looks more comfortable from here.

The knees are comfortably bent, the right leg a tad straighter than the left, in the classic billiards stance. Again, there are players who stand with both legs rigidly straight or both knees very bent, but with both legs moderately bent. This is a comfortable stance for my height of 6'2" and for most other players as well.

The stance for an average stroke requires a balanced, comfortable body so the right arm can move all by itself without any disturbing movement elsewhere. For power and other shots, weight will shift to one foot or the other as needed. In Chapter 7, we will review "slip strokes"—one such example of moving parts adding to the stroke.

More on adjusting the legs and feet in Chapter 7 and elsewhere ahead; for most basic strokes you want to be balanced so that if someone gave you a push on one shoulder or the other, you would not move at all, without any conscious tensing of muscles to resist the shove.

My center of gravity has lowered and I am "settled in" to the carpeting on the floor, yet there is nothing rigid or firm in my body. I am balanced and comfortable.

Save Your Back

Does your back begin to ache after a long session shooting pool? For that matter, does it hurt all the time? If you learn how to bend to the table correctly, shooting pool can actually help limber your back.

The key is to bend from your hips, not your waist. Your waist includes part of your spine, which is only meant to take gradual curves, not the 80- or 90-degree angle of an intense pool stance.

Many players can't discern the difference between a waist bend or "shooting from the hips" (pun intended), so let me explain how to feel the difference. You don't need a cue or a table to practice:

1. First, stand upright and place one index finger on each hipbone.

2. Try to tilt forward while using your index fingers as axles to rotate around (waist bend).

3. Stand up and move one forefinger to your tailbone, the other to the top of your head and bend again (seated into hips).

The two fingers now at the small of your back and top of your head should form a straight line along your spine between them, a line that continues to be straight as you bend over. Your behind should stick out and not be tucked in.

If you still aren't sure you are getting it, watch a professional golfer from one side as he takes his stance. You will see how the golfer bends from the hips, almost as if there were an invisible chair to rest upon. The pool pro takes that bend even further. Your posture now resembles Groucho Marx's trademark slouch.

You might want to go down and perhaps a bit forward into place (rather than lean backward from the shot and miss). Avoid stretching too far forward (or too far back) to prevent pain and strain.

Stance Checkup

For most strokes (when I have freedom of movement at the table and adequate space to position the body), I take a few simple steps as pictured above. The stance is as follows:

1. Stand comfortably with the *cue stick* behind the line the ball will travel, not your head. Your head remains above body center, and your stick will be to one side.

2. Step toward the shot by placing the bridge side foot (the foot opposite your shooting hand) one natural step forward.

3. Drop your body weight *straight* down toward the table while leaving your shooting arm to hang freely.

4. After you are comfortably balanced at the table, bring your head more in line over the cue if you must. (Most of us are fine with the head a bit to one side and I would discourage you from adjusting the head in or near the final shooting position.)

The correct stance provides many benefits to the player, including the following:

▶ Allows the body to relax in place immobile, the shooting arm doing the work of the stroke

▶ Sets the player comfortably in place, avoiding neck and back strain

▶ Frees the shooting arm to move along a straight path without interference from the body

▶ Brings the cue stick to the same straight line for every shot, every time

Gripping for Distance

A S EXPLAINED IN Chapter 4 in detail, the long, skinny cue stick weighs just over a pound, and you will find its balance point, the spot near the middle where the cue sits levelly poised on a fingertip or two. Most players err with their grip by holding the cue too far back from the balance point.

Experiment if you wish, but several inches behind the balance point yields the best results for *most* players. The novice must persevere, however, to become accustomed to the unnatural feelings of guiding the cue from this spot, fighting the desire to hold farther back.

Grip your cue three to nine inches behind the balance point. Most sticks give maximum "feel" from this area. Exactly where you'll grip depends on shot requirements and your physical attributes.

Average Hold

In Figure 5.12, I have placed a white cue ball beside the cue stick at the spot where I typically clasp the cue with my shooting hand. The balance point on the stick in Figure 5.12 is near the base of those pretty red points on the cue. My right hand is set about six inches to the rear of this spot, and your hand may be a bit closer or farther back, depending on your height, cue length, and wingspan.

Figure 5.12
Ready to roll.

Gripping slightly behind the balance point allows the right forearm and wrist to do their work. During the stroke, the cue sways back and forth, the right forearm moving *like* a pendulum from the elbow down. Holding the cue to the rear yields more *leverage* but forces the player to pump their entire arm up and down, striking up or down at the cue ball instead of straight back and forward.

PLEASE BEWARE

Greater leverage with the arm, though it feels more powerful at first, ruins play and does not yield more control over the shot. You want a freely flowing motion, creating a powerful stroke. Squeezing and tensing muscles for leverage compromises power and accuracy.

For Gentle Strokes

Figure 5.13 demonstrates the best way to adjust for added feel on especially delicate strokes. Many *Straight Pool* experts (see more on Straight Pool in Chapter 15) hold their cue this far forward for most shots, allowing for the ultra-precise cue ball control for the game and shortening the stroke for convenience.

Figure 5.13
Choking up.

For now, be prepared to grip forward for a shorter, slower cue ball movement when you need one.

Adding Power

Figure 5.14 shows my hand as far back along the cue ball as the yellow ball, for more speed. The expert pool shooter gets a bit more of the weight of the cue stick behind the shot with this technique, rather than squeezing the cue stick harder or forcing an awkward stroke movement.

Simply grip the cue more toward its rear for added speed and power as needed. Going to the extreme rear of the cue doesn't work well for most players in most situations. As we will see shortly, the bridge hand will also come back to help keep a proper stance alignment.

Figure 5.14
Back for power.

Bridging for Distance

I N FIGURE 5.15, the bridge hand, my left hand, is set a few inches back from the 8-ball I am aiming to hit.

Figure 5.15
Bridging for distance.

This represents an average bridge distance for an intermediate player of about seven inches from the center of the ball near the cue tip to the loop of the closed bridge formed by thumb and forefinger. I am set for an average shot.

Make your bridge hand immobile. Novices move their bridge hand during the stroke, ruining their shots.

PLEASE BEWARE

For your pool stance, the bridge hand is to always sit as a dead weight during the shot. Relaxed muscles allow the cue stick to glide through the fingers of the bridge hand easily. You'll tighten slightly for more control only on those shots requiring extra spin or power.

Added Accuracy

Figure 5.16 has the bridge hand held much closer to the 8-ball, alongside the maroon 7-ball. With a bridge distance of just an inch or two, I am ready to shoot gently and with heightened accuracy.

Figure 5.16
Ready for a delicate stroke.

Many beginning players would do well with a closed bridge length of two inches for some time until they develop as pool players. Beginners tend to miscue (slip the tip entirely off the ball at impact) using a lengthy bridge.

A Power Stance

My hand has moved as far back as the yellow 1-ball this time for a powerful stroke, perhaps a break stroke.

It will require more than beginner skill to use this long of a bridge accurately. Build up to such a long bridge through practice to learn how far away you can rest your hand from the ball before you begin to miscue shots. Playing weekly, it might take a year before you are comfortable with a lengthy bridge distance.

TAKE A TIP

Did you note that the balls and distances did not change at all between Figures 5.12 – 5.14 and Figures 5.15 – 5.17? Remember to always adjust *both* hands back about the same distance for power shots or forward for deliberate, gentle strokes.

Figure 5.17
Bridged for power.

A Bridge Not Too Far

Once you have your approximate stance including both hands, you get set into a final position before beginning a few practice strokes and then a final stroke. Get set first with your stance so that the cue tip is as close as you can make it to the cue ball (without touching the cue ball in advance of your last stroke, which will move it and cause a penalty foul).

As in Figure 5.18, the cue tip is to line up as closely as possible to the impact spot of choice on the cue ball for the final stroke.

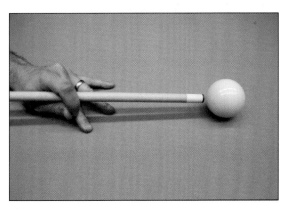

Figure 5.18
Right up to the ball.

The next photo shows where many players ruin the work to build a good stance so far.

Off Base

In Figure 5.19, although I exaggerate a bit for effect, I am demonstrating how the amateur addresses the cue ball in their stance. The cue tip is far from the actual point of contact on the ball.

> **TAKE A TIP**
>
> A good time to set the tip close to the ball is just after the bridge hand is set on the table but before the stance position is completed. It's easier to see the cue tip's position close to the cue ball from a point somewhere between fully upright and in the final, lowered stance.

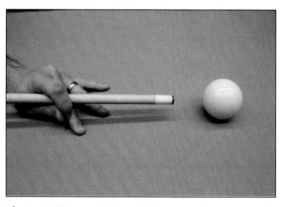

Figure 5.19
This bridge too far could cause a disastrous miscue.

Most players cannot see this error from their stance behind the ball. Have a pool playing friend stand alongside you to explain whether your cue tip is in the position of Figure 5.18 or 5.19. If you play with the stick far from the ball, you must adjust your comfort level for a new stance, holding your entire body and cue much closer to the ball or you will not improve as a player.

Three-Legged Stance

Let's check on bridge hand pressure, as there should be little weight on that hand and arm. When you are in the set position and feel comfortable, lift your bridge hand (and arm) from the table, not moving other parts of your body.

Were you forced to shuffle or adjust to maintain balance or could you lift the arm freely? You do not want a tripod stance leaning on both feet and your bridge hand.

If your bridge hand is part of your stance, your stance is weak. You are unknowingly putting tension into your bridge hand and arm. Tension in the bridge hand plays a role in the performance of the stroking hand. Less tension in the bridge hand relates to a comfortable grooved stroke.

Three Last Stances

W E'VE EXAMINED TWO WRONG stances and a good one, and average bridge and grip length plus two variations for more power or more delicacy.

Let's take a look at a final set of three positions, three stances as seen from the side. Only two will work out well for the player.

Well Cued

In Figure 5.20 I am captured in full stance from the shooting side. My hand is set comfortably back along the length of the cue, behind the balance point but not extremely far back. My bridge hand is set back from the cue ball, but the cue's tip is quite close to the center of the cue ball where I plan to strike.

Figure 5.20
Ready for action.

We want a comfortably level cue, as level as possible without undue strain. My cue angles down a bit from butt end to tip, but I can make a good stroke from this position.

The forearm of my shooting hand is near perpendicular to the cue stick. It could also be held forward as in the next photo.

My upper arm from the shoulder is near parallel to the table. It is not held there rigidly, it is simply the outcome of placing my arm and stick on line and then lowering my body weight while leaving the cue where it lies, as explained above.

Different Yet Adequate

Figure 5.21 shows the cue ball in the same position, but my stance is somewhat different. For added accuracy, I have hunkered down over the cue stick a bit. My head is lower than in the previous position.

Figure 5.21
Still fine.

My shooting arm has drawn forward also, and rather than hanging down from the elbow, my forearm is bent along and above the shot line.

This other stance is for a player to develop heightened accuracy and shoot gentle, quiet shots not requiring much speed. Although unorthodox and rarely seen today, this reigning in of the hand for delicate shooting works fine.

Figure 5.22 is the one that sets my teeth on edge when I see a beginner do it. Worse still, more experienced shooters stand like this, and other players consider them models to imitate.

Why Beginners Miss

I HAVE LOOKED BACK in shock to catch my shooting arm high in the air in Figure 5.22. I no longer have a near level cue.

Figure 5.22
Don't!

I exaggerate what I see beginners do. In some cases, however, this is no exaggeration! Students come to me complaining of missed shots and shots badly miscued. Here is the culprit.

We will discuss raising the shooting arm *slightly* in the next chapter, but this extreme cue elevation in Figure 5.22 is done (wrongly) for one purpose, to hit the cue ball hard and with leverage.

I can't tell you how many beginners and intermediates I have stood behind literally, holding down their shooting arm with mine so they can feel and see the difference between a near level cue and an arm playing pool from outer space high above the table.

Can You See It?

The elevated arm is a tough fault to catch on your own as players usually raise the cue high *after* assuming a decent stance, angling it too much to shoot properly. Greater leverage with the right arm, though it *feels* like a solid hold on the cue, does not mean added control over the shot.

In contrast, Figure 5.21 is better, and Figure 5.20 a rare sight in most pool halls. You must maintain a correct stance by leaving your shooting arm in place from beginning of stance to end, or your pool career will leave much to be desired.

In other words, basic shooting technique lies in a low, relaxed "gun hand." Lifting the hand by jacking it high wastes energy moving down rather than forward and is certain to cause a disastrous miscue eventually. On a draw shot, the cue ball will leap right off the table in an embarrassing, sometimes window-shattering fashion.

TAKE A TIP

The best way to check against this bad habit is to have a friend critique you while shooting. Most players lift the hand unconsciously, often just before the final stroke is taken. Keep your shooting hand close to the felt instead.

Note that the cue stick cannot be level when shooting over an obstacle such as a rail or an interfering ball. Most players position the cue at a slight angle and shoot "down" a bit at the ball. The key word here is slight.

Where You Now Stand

L ET'S ENJOY THAT lovely stance we now find ourselves in:

▶ You've walked behind the shot as naturally as strolling down the block.

▶ Stepping forward and lowering your trunk, your field of vision focuses on the shot and not distractions in the room.

▶ You are comfortably balanced, facing about 45 degrees to the shot line.

▶ Your shooting hand is a free agent that comes back and through without interference.

▶ Your head is comfortably over the stick or slightly to one side, your preference for accurate aiming.

▶ Your body weight is lowered with ease as though you are sitting in a chair next to the table.

The steps outlined above take only a few seconds to perform. Braced and aligned properly, you are now ready to shoot twice as well as the untutored amateur, using half their effort at the table, too.

After learning the basic stance, the intermediate should check on exact body position only at the start of play (or when one's game slumps). Being overly conscious of your precise distance from the table or obsessing over the position of a foot or a shoulder wrecks feel, touch, and the pleasurable relaxation of pool. Save the stance work for practice time, not tournament play.

Good Job, Reader

YOU'VE BEEN PATIENT with me through many tips on equipment, stance, and grip. This is a great way to get ahead of the competition. Most of your opponents will never take time to learn to play better and go by trial and error only. Your hard work pays off as we explore the correct stroke next.

A Final Tip

The pro pool player sometimes gets into her stance but feels misaligned or uncomfortable. At this point, an average player would twist his arm or wrist into final position or wiggle his cue about to get ready. This is a great error.

TAKE A TIP

The professional instead gets upright again from a poor stance, and he starts a new stance until he is satisfied, his mind freed of anxiety. Doing the same by reacquiring a correct stance for any shot if needed will help you make a half-dozen shots you would otherwise miss.

Try the right and wrong stances in front of a mirror and at the pool hall. When you are ready, let's move ahead to stroking the cue, in the next chapter.

Simple and Straight: Stroking
Your Cue

Why can't the English learn to stroke?

*W*HY CAN'T THE ENGLISH *teach their children how to stroke? This foolish pool distraction by now should be a joke. If you stroke as he does, ma'am, instead of the way you do, Why, you might be selling flowers, too.*

It's not just a British or American problem anymore, but an international one. Most pool players have never taken a lesson, knowing the tip end of the cue strikes the ball and that's about all.

Building upon our platform of selecting quality equipment (Chapter 3) and gripping the cue wisely and standing at the table in good position (Chapters 4 and 5), we are ready to get to the secrets of a great stroke. As a bonus, I am going to show you three different methods you can use to build a lovely stroking motion.

Want to Know a Secret?

PLAYERS HAVE BEEN SEEKING the Holy Grail of stroke for a long time. It's a tempting thought—could there be one unique way to stroke a cue stick to make the balls obey your every whim on the table? Reviewing most pool literature, it sure seems like pros have been withholding secrets.

Most pool instruction books contain a short paragraph or two on stroke. A recent few have sought to give more detail; however, some of these books have entire chapters on stroke theory without information on how to start or end a stroke, how to grip the cue, whether to push or pull the stick, etc.

I honestly do not worry about trouble with industry pros for spilling the beans. My philosophy? If you learn many pool secrets from this book and DVD, and can play as well as me soon, I'll at least have a good challenge when we shoot pool together!

Have 10,000 Spare Hours?

There *is* more than one way to stroke a cue and win. Willie Hoppe learned his chicken wing stance at the age of five, reaching far along dad's giant billiard table to make shots. He knew his stance was unorthodox to maintain as an adult, but held fast that anyone could overcome his obstacle if he simply devoted enough practice time. Hoppe not only played constantly, he refused lifelong to drive any car (in the days before power steering) so that he wouldn't strain the delicate muscles of his wrists!

Keith "Earthquake" McCready, one of pool's most entertaining personalities (he played hustling pro "Grady Seasons" in 1986's *The Color of Money*), also holds his cue sidesaddle to stroke, yet he could demolish most players in the world for cash now. The sidesaddle hold was adopted as a child, when he also cashed in heavily against his adult opponents!

You might also succeed with an unorthodox stance or stroke if you have thousands of hours to devote to practice. Let me save you the effort and demonstrate the basics of a great stroke that works for my pool students.

First Thing First

TO DETERMINE WHERE the big money games are in a pool hall, watch how the players chalk their cues. Before taking any stroke, the expert always chalks carefully to prepare for the shot.

It's so vital it bears repeating—rub the cube on the tip gently and evenly, like a woman applying lipstick precisely over the entire surface of her lips. Grinding stick into chalk absentmindedly causes straying from the tip, and can scratch the ferrule.

Examine the cue tip after a miscue, and telltale black spots will show you where chalk wasn't applied properly. The most important area is the tip's outside edge where it contacts the cue ball on shots other than dead center. The pros are sure to chalk extra thoroughly before using extreme spin, adding extra chalk so the tip adheres to the ball an additional moment.

Establish the habit of chalking faithfully. As mentioned in Chapter 3, showoffs shoot the last few balls without it. As likely as not, they wind up with egg on their face.

PLEASE BEWARE

Figure 6.1 is punishment for the student who refuses to chalk. Carry chalk in your hand for half an hour at the table, never putting it to rest, and you'll realize how little you chalk now and how vital chalking is.

Figure 6.1
Chalk on.

A Lighter Cue

"This cue feels good" is not enough for the winning player. Much of pool is setting the shooting arm on line (see Chapter 5) and moving the cue stick straight back and through again. A lightweight cue is easier to manipulate with the hands backward and forward without needing to be manhandled into position.

The cue should feel substantial enough in your hands to hit a ball without twisting or shattering, yet light enough to allow great freedom of movement.

Obey the Laws

A quick review of Newton's Three Laws of Motion affirms a light pool cue and helps us to understand how a good stroke *feels*. Sir Isaac Newton played a mean game of billiards in his day and knew his physics well, too.

Newton's First Law

"Every body at rest tends to remain at rest, while every body in motion tends to remain in motion, unless it is acted upon by unbalanced external force."

This physical law describes the concept of *inertia*, with which we are all familiar. If you have ridden in a car that stopped abruptly, following which you personally flew forward, you understand inertia. You do wear a seatbelt in a car or truck, right?

We are going to strike the white cue ball with a forward-moving cue stick. Following the shock of contact with the white ball, the cue stroke will have momentum to go forward. We want the cue stick to naturally *follow through* the stroke as it takes force (effort of force twisting away from the straight line path) to stop or slow this momentum.

An unforced, graceful follow-through is the hallmark of a job well done in many stick-and-ball sports, including pool.

Newton's Second Law

To paraphrase Newton's Second Law, the acceleration of any body is directly proportional to the force acting upon it and inversely proportional to the mass of the body.

This energy of a moving object is *kinetic energy* (sometimes called "energy of motion"). The kinetic energy of a crash should be absorbed by a car or plane to protect its occupants. Modern cars and planes have fronts of soft metal that crumple upon impact and absorb otherwise deadly kinetic energy.

Kinetic energy increases dramatically as weight and speed increase. If your cue speed triples, it would need nine times the distance to stop (unless it strikes a ball or is impeded by the bridge hand as happens).

For a powerful break shot, you want as much speed as you can muster. It's easier to accelerate a lighter cue stick than a heavier one. Many pros reach for a light stick for this important stroke.

Heavy for a Novice

The beginning player should use a heavyweight cue stick instead. The added mass means the cue will stay on line longer, moving forward with kinetic energy, on any halfhearted or off stroke.

The intermediate or advanced player will use a lighter cue when they feel ready. The light stick is more easily and subtly controlled as you develop feel or "muscle memory," as discussed in Chapter 2.

Newton's Third Law

Newton's Third Law describes a relationship between acting and reacting (opposing) forces: "For every force exerted on a body by another, there is equal but opposite force reacting on the first body by the second."

Figure 6.2
What would Newton think?

For every action in the physical world, there is an equal but opposite reaction. A 6-ounce cue ball resting on a pool table pushes down on the table with a force of six ounces. Similarly, the table pushes up on the weight with a force of six ounces. A dynamic example is a water-operated mill. The water on the millwheel exerts a force on the arms of the millwheel, which makes the wheel rotate.

Consider the powerful break stroke again, used to scatter the balls across the table. A cue stick's shaft has some degree of flexibility, and in the first moment of impact before the cue ball moves, the cue shaft bends away from its spine, creating a wave of motion running through the stick as the cue is foreshortened and compressed, imparting energy to the ball.

The action of the cue bending looks just like pole vaulting turned to one side. The stick and ball collide and react to one another, but the moving cue's energy wins and the ball moves forward.

The pros tend to reach for a 17-ounce or 18-ounce break cue (flex level based on personal preference) so they can quickly accelerate the stick into the back of the ball and bend it into the shot also.

Smooth and Clean

Friction is not considered one of the laws of motion but is important to understand as it relates to pocket billiards. Pool players could love or hate friction. If you are hitting a basic shot, you want a well-chalked tip that will adhere to the cue ball longer, providing spin and speed with ease. Chalk dirtying the balls, however, provides friction at the wrong time (see Chapter 8 for more on friction induced *throw*).

Newton's Laws and the response of friction tell us a few things to help you stroke a cue stick:

▶ Use the lightest stick you can guide comfortably.

▶ Make a clean hit on the cue ball with the stick moving straight back and forward (for most shots).

▶ For powerful strokes, emphasize smooth momentum rather than clenched muscle and dispersed energy.

▶ Stroke through the cue ball and after, look for a smooth follow-through motion.

▶ Chalk the cue adequately between each and every shot, promoting friction at impact.

Forget Leverage

I'VE SAID IT SEVERAL TIMES and several ways throughout this book, but you want reduced movement in your stroke, straight back and through, and not leverage and exertion of strength. Precision and flowing follow-through guarantee good results with balls that weigh just a few ounces rolling along the extremely smooth table surface.

The average player is astonished at how much spin, speed, and accuracy the pool pro achieves with delicate cue movement. Experts seem to get more momentum out of the same cue weight and specifications amateurs use, even with the same stroke speed and length, as the amateur. Words to describe a pro stroke might include "silky," "smooth," "oily," and "gliding."

Clasp the cue gently and stroke it easily to get pro action. University tenure or elementary school dropout, most still hit the ball way too hard.

The irony is the more conscious muscle you put into pool, usually the less snap, speed, and momentum you get from the stroke.

How Long Is the Stroke?

THE NEXT ILLUSTRATIONS give a good basis for an average stroke.

In Figure 6.3, I've drawn the stick back from just behind the cue ball to within the loop of my finger bridge. Much further back and the tip would slip from the finger loop entirely.

Figure 6.3
Length of backswing.

I do not force, pull, or in any way try aggressively to bring the cue this far back as shown. It's an extension of smooth, gentle hand and arm movement.

Back to Point One

Here's an actual stroke taken with high-speed photography alongside a cue ball in Figure 6.4. I simply return the cue stick tip to where I had aimed it, in this instance where the center of the cue ball would rest.

Figure 6.4
Coming through.

You don't need to consciously imitate all aspects of my motion as illustrated but let your right, visual brain understand the general flow of motion.

At Rest

Figure 6.5 illustrates the length of follow-through. Not a hard and fast rule, in this instance the cue tip has come to rest along the felt.

Figure 6.5
Follow-through.

The cue stick was held nearly level throughout the stroke, but as it was angled a bit above parallel with the table, the tip traveled vertically from the center of the ball into my bridge hand, back to ball center, and down to the cloth—back and through straight-line travel at an angle.

It's been said to hold the cue "as level to the table as possible," but on most strokes with a perfectly level cue stick, your hand would painfully graze the felt or strike a rail or pocket. A few degrees elevated above level is fine and the common practice.

I hold the cue stick higher than other players, but I am compensating for my 6' 2" frame and long arm and leg length. I know pool tables were designed centuries ago in Europe, for shorter people on the average. Drink milk!

Practice Strokes

MOST PLAYERS EMPLOY three to five practice strokes before making the final stroke, subtle rehearsals of the movement they are about to perform.

A good use of the practice stroke is to feel the *approximate* speed and line of the stick for the final shot, taking firm, controlled practice strokes to prepare for a firm, controlled shot or gentle strokes before an especially gentle shot, etc. Concentrate on the force you plan to use to hit the ball. It is not necessary, though, and may be even harmful, to imitate the final stroke's *exact* speed with practice strokes.

Besides speed, you may practice direction. On a shot requiring a sharp downward angle into the cue ball, set your bridge hand as needed and practice the downward glancing blow with the practice strokes and so on.

The pro makes fine adjustments of the bridge hand and feet as he settles down in preparation for the shot, too. Aim might be adjusted in small increments.

Smart players, if hesitant before the final stroke, stand up, take a quick break, and then reset, like a baseball player who steps out of the batter's box to mentally prepare for the next pitch.

In contrast, the novice lunges at the last moment with the cue stick in an effort to compensate for practice stroke shortcomings. This adds quickly to general frustration with the game.

Take What You Need

Some players use one practice stroke only or, quite rarely, none at all. Some use 10 to 20 practice strokes (and incur the wrath of their playing partners and extensive table rental fees), but the main point of practice strokes is to loosen and relax the body and mind before performing the final stroke. The athlete is ready to use procedural memory to perform (see Chapter 2) by keying in muscles and movement rather than starting from an immobile, static position.

You might pause after your final practice stroke before beginning your final stroke, or you might blend the last practice stroke into your final *backstroke* before returning to the ball. Do whatever feels comfortable. The ball responds only to the final stroke.

Butterflies Okay

On the practice strokes or final stroke, I often butterfly my shooting hand open as in Figure 6.6. The fourth and pinky fingers come off the cue entirely for many pros, opening their hand even further. This unique perspective shows the palm of my right hand making only incidental contact with the cue stick. The meat of the palm is off the cue entirely.

Figure 6.6
Open on the backstroke.

The stick weighs about a pound, the ball a few ounces—I only need a few fingers to get power and spin on shots, and so will you following the precepts in this book.

Let's Get to It

NOW COMES SOME of the action we've waited for, how exactly to stroke the cue stick. These revealed secrets will take most players' games to new, soaring heights!

Deviating the Wrist

Let's take another look at the shooting hand from this angle, this time as a final stroke has ended. The set of my wrist (note the creases in Figure 6.7) indicate that my wrist has moved from a hanging-down-natural position to use *ulnar deviation* (see Chapter 4) on the follow-through.

Figure 6.7
Forward stroke perspective.

A true pendulum stroke would loft the stick high into the air abruptly and force my hands, arms, and shoulders to do strange things to hold the stick on line. My wrist has bent using ulnar deviation instead to complete a near pendulum stroke.

You can just make out a gap of blue felt glimpsed between the palm and the cue, emphasizing the finger grip. There is no forcible hand movement on this follow-through.

Radial Deviation

In Figure 6.8, you can see a similar stroke, but this time I have chosen to demonstrate *radial deviation* of the wrist. This movement brings the fingers and hand in and up a bit through the stroke.

Figure 6.8
Another look.

Either ulnar or radial deviation blends nicely with arm and hand movement and won't interfere with a straight stroke. You might prefer to break your wrist toward your thumb or away from it with radial or ulnar motion, and on gentle strokes, you will not need the cue moved enough to bend the wrist at all.

To feel a radial deviation stroke, stroke through the cue ball, finishing the stroke with a caressing movement of the ring and pinky fingers of the shooting hand. Allow the shooting hand to sink alongside the cue stick's side as the top of the stick rises up and through the loose thumb and forefinger. This radial movement requires a conscious intention on the forward stroke; ulnar deviation or a neutral wrist position going forward with the stroke is the passive, unconscious norm.

Why It Works

Why do these two wrist movements work fine and why does a light finger grip help? Bending the hand with ulnar or radial deviation or its close cousin, closing and opening the fingers during the stroke, does not interfere with a straight movement.

Wrist deviation and opening and closing fingers may interfere with the stick on its vertical plane only. The hit on the cue ball could wind up higher or lower than where you aimed, providing unwanted topspin or reverse spin, called *draw*. While preventing fine position with the cue ball, it will still hit the target where you aimed.

Wrist twisting or any movement that changes the horizontal plane of the cue means a hit to one side of the cue ball or the other; and besides unwanted english (see Chapter 9), having jerked the cue stick off line, your cue ball may miss the target ball or rail entirely!

I recognize that some great players (who also have enough discipline to play with nearly locked wrists) have their wrists bent out from the plane of their stroking arm. Most shooters keep the wrist flat so the back of the hand is near parallel to the forearm, and use ulnar or radial movement only as needed.

PLEASE BEWARE

Nervous players who start with a cue cradled in their fingers may tighten a bit and not get the roll they want. But nervous players who palm the cue (or clench their wrist or arm) get unexpected sideways action on the cue ball. A finger grip on the cue stick is usually a winner.

Wrist movement of ulnar or radial deviation is a choice; experiment and see which one fits your basic stroke and temperament (and the stroke requirements at hand). See Chapter 4 for more on the six wrist movements you can make, and why four of them twist the cue off line.

Licensed to Stroke

W E'RE READY TO STROKE a cue together, and to ask the questions you want answered—how do I start the final stroke and what do I look at? How does a good pool stroke feel?

In the Pocket

Figure 6.9 was taken when I felt ready to send the cue ball straight ahead into a side pocket. My checklist is complete in this photo:

Figure 6.9
Ready to roll.

► I chose a straight-line path for the cue ball, set my shooting arm along that line, and balanced so only my shooting arm need move (see Chapter 5).

► My cue stick is held lightly in the fingers; I won't need to twist or flop hand or arm to maintain a straight movement (see Chapter 4).

► My head is comfortably resting to see the shot (not directly atop the line) and my cue tip is close on the cue ball, helping ensure I can get back to this spot for the hit (see Chapter 5).

► I've taken a few gentle warm-up strokes in preparation to send the cue into the pocket.

You can take a few practice strokes or many and pause before the final stroke or not. It's a matter of personal preference. I'm going to bring the cue back next for the final stroke, though a word about arm position is needed first.

Relaxed Forearm

The lower portion of my shooting arm is roughly perpendicular to the cue stick. It's hanging straight down or nearly so. Here is when many beginners pull back with the hand or raise it in the air before the final stroke is taken in an effort to gain strength and leverage on the cue. Let the forearm hang down by itself instead.

PLEASE BEWARE

Forming an angle between upper arm and forearm of 90 degrees (or less) is helpful. That right-angle might be high in the air but still 90 degrees to itself and the stick. But once it becomes an obtuse angle, once the hand and arm are lifted toward a straight line from the shoulder, all bets are off and anything unwanted can happen in the stroke.

Quiet Upper Arm

Allow the upper arm to be somewhat relaxed also. Flexing the biceps would tend to cause a wrist twist, the corkscrew motion we want to avoid in the stroke. All is relaxed with the exception of the shoulder, locked firmly enough to align the arm. Consciously feeling the shoulder resting in place is enough to hold it in space without undue clenching or squeezing.

The upper arm is somewhat parallel to the table and floor. I stood on the line with the arm along the shot line, and lowered the trunk of my body, as discussed in Chapter 5. The arm came into position with little conscious thought. If you prefer your chin close to the stick, your elbow and upper arm will be above the parallel plane.

Some players raise their upper arm into this position (or higher) intentionally. You may need to lift your arm a bit based on your body dimensions or preference. Do not raise your head and eyes to achieve this lifting action.

I find it tiring to hoist my upper arm into the air for every stance at the table, adding to muscle fatigue. There are good players who complain of a sore arm after play, but the sole thing that slows my game is mental fatigue from extended intense concentration. By relaxing my shooting arm and hand, I can play for hours on end before tiring.

TAKE A TIP

If you prefer to lift your upper arm for play, as many successful players do, be sure to settle into your stance and after, lift the upper arm gently by pulling back and lifting from your elbow (the elbow has no muscle but the sensation will aid you). This technique leaves your lower arm hanging down and sets your upper arm in place without undue tension, which causes fatigue and off line strokes.

A Full Backswing

I have taken a final backswing with the cue stick in Figure 6.10, bringing the cue tip stick back inside the loop of my bridge hand where it sits along the line.

Figure 6.10
Extent of backswing.

This shot line would extend in both directions between the side pockets. You can see the stick slightly angled above the pocket opposite the pocket where the cue ball will sink. The upper portion of my shooting arm and right shoulder are above the cue on line, the lower arm from the elbow down swings above the cue stick. My arm is along a straight line, as almost all pool strokes are straight strokes.

The cue tip is withdrawn all the way into my bridge hand. To go any farther back, the cue would slip from my left hand and fall to the table. I did not force this position; I simply slid the cue back and am ready to change direction and go forward again.

The hand has butterflied open, not a requirement, but I wanted such a free, unrestricted motion that even my pinky finger has lifted from the cue entirely. Again, let me encourage you to divert little awareness to such movement. Let your hand remain closed if that's within your comfort level.

The Hit

At high-speed stopped motion we see the cue returned to the cue ball at impact in Figure 6.11. My shooting arm is roughly in the position where it began. Nothing is in motion except the cue stick and my shooting arm, and that mostly from the elbow down.

Figure 6.12
Follow-through.

Figure 6.11
At impact.

My shooting hand's fingers have closed around the cue again, but not forcefully and almost without conscious thought. My hand is blurred in motion in this photo but is not rigidly held or tightened in any way. I'm gliding the cue forward, and what I am *feeling* we will discuss soon, too, so you know how to picture yourself with a great pool stroke.

Mission Accomplished

The payoff is shown in Figure 6.12. My shooting arm's fingers are loosely gripping the cue, so much so that the cue has slid along them and through them, and my wrist is fairly straight without much radial deviation.

The stroke is completed and the cue ball is headed toward the target. The cue stick angle, a few degrees above horizontal, is nearly the same as at address and on the backswing—but above the angle shown in Figure 6.11, at impact. Study each of the four photo angles carefully. At impact, my cue stick was more nearly parallel to the table.

This purposed change of angle illustrates an important point. Many fine players have a looping action to their swing, a large pendulum arc in their movement or some type of hitch or abrupt change of direction between backswing and final swing—but in a vertical fashion only. The tip still returns to the point of aim or nearby. Horizontal movement would destroy aim upon impact or wrench the stick from the bridge hand during the stroke.

You will see all types of bizarre-looking pool strokes changing direction through the air, even on tour, but unwanted *horizontal* movement of the stick can produce disastrous results.

The Nitty Gritty

L ET'S DISCUSS HOW a good stroke feels and how to make one, before we dive into the details on pocketing balls at will in the next chapter. You have choices and a bit of experimentation ahead to see what's best for your game.

Pull, Toss, or Cast

Three descriptive words could describe a good pool player's practice strokes and final strokes—"pull," "toss," or "cast," while bad strokes are "yanked," "jerked," or "twisted" off the shot line. There is more than one way to stroke a pool stick with ease, and I'll share all three with you, dear reader.

PLEASE BEWARE

The sliding motion of the cue stick (for most strokes) is without undue muscle tension. As you read the following three descriptions, plan to keep the motion of your stroke fluid and rhythmic, whichever method you choose.

Pull the Cue

The word *pull* is a helpful keyword for many players. Some teaching professionals use this term to describe how the cue stick may be guided straight back and forth along the shot line.

Pulling a cue stick must be distinguished from most pulling movements we make on a daily basis, however. I squeeze a rope or door handle just before I pull it. I grip firmly onto a handle before

pulling luggage, a milk bottle, or tugging a dead weight behind me. You will not want any excessive squeezing, yanking, or muscular exertion at any time during most pool strokes.

Another issue involves the unusual direction of the pull in pool. Ulnar and radial deviation of the wrist in pool or simply pendulum-ing the cue without bending the wrist at all is not a typical direction of motion we make to pull an item.

Place one palm flat upon your chest as if you are about to pat your breast or recite a pledge. Now brush the palm of your hand along your chest slowly. This is the same motion we use to wipe windows clean or to move a cue along the shot line (with thumbnail facing parallel to the shot line and the arm turned over).

Place your hand on your chest again and close it into a fist. Rub the fist along your chest by pulling it from near the elbow up and down, without moving the upper arm much, and you feel what a pool player feels who pulls their cue as their stroke thought.

If you choose to be a "pool puller," think of the cue more like a sheet of paper that is wet and happens to cling to your fingers or hand along its bottom or side here and there. The pulling motion may feel as though it comes from hand, forearm, even the upper arm a bit, as long it is gentle and does not disturb the angles for a good stroke.

TAKE A TIP

In Figure 6.13, we again regard the end of the backswing. I can at this point use my choice of pulling, tossing, or casting the cue forward—and so can you. All three methods will work fine going forward, whatever style you used to draw the cue back.

Figure 6.13
Any option open.

Toss the Cue

If you are in the school of players who cannot find best results pulling the cue gently, try tossing it along the line instead. Dean of Master Instructors Jerry Brieseth uses this concept as his core approach.

There is more than one way to win at pool, and I love the concept of tossing the cue softly into the shot. The sports terms *backswing* and *forward swing* or *forward stroke* unfortunately prompt thoughts of powerful, sweeping movement, when a gentle toss of the cue is all that's needed to move the stick perfectly straight.

I've seen hundreds of pool players make all varieties of exotic, deliberate movements to try to send the cue perfectly along a straight line. Trying for a perfectly straight stroke kills touch and feel. These shooters hunting for the ultimate straight stroke would be comical to watch if they weren't saddening. Painstakingly, they pull their cue back and forth, searching to carve a path straight as a laser beam! The rhythm and feel needed for pool quickly break down.

Most of their muscle flexing, hesitation, and super-straight attempts break the rhythmic free glide of the smoothly moving stick. If I asked the same player to toss a ball straight to me underhand, they would do so without hesitation or numerous practice strokes, and free of care!

Feel the Toss

Hold a pool ball in your hand at your side, palm up, and heft it back and forth a few times. Moving mostly from the elbow down, bring it back and forth as if you were going to toss it a few feet to a waiting friend. Do you need to make a conscious, muscled effort to bring your lower arm straight back and through the motion? Of course not, indeed, any muscle tension or conscious effort slows the motion. Squeeze the ball with all your might and make the same tossing motion. Tough to perform now, isn't it? You can see how muscle tension might ruin a tossing pool stroke.

Hold the ball again at your side in the same starting position. Now rotate your hand from the elbow, 90 degrees inward, so your thumb is now near the top of the ball and the pinky finger near the bottom. The loop of your forefinger faces up and forward along with your thumb. Bring the ball up and down several times in the same plane of movement as before, as if you are going to toss the ball straight ahead of you again. That's basically the pool toss stroke when you are bent over a table!

Too many players stroke by tightening their grip just before impact, anticipating the hit, and decelerating the tip. It's natural to want to tighten to add power, but that tension diverts energy to the hand and not the stick and ball. The pool pro does the opposite, often finishing the stroke by *loosening* the hand as the tip is about to strike the cue ball, releasing energy into the throw and accelerating the cue tip into impact. Boom!

Toss It Straight

It so happens, fortunately, that the tossing underhand motion will send the entire cue stick from butt to tip straight back and forward with ease. *The more your momentum is a toss forward with the stroke, the more straight the cue will shoot,* as that inertia will overshadow any sideways movement.

To demonstrate in clinics I will literally throw the cue, launching it out of my hand with both cue ball and cue stick tip finding the pocket!

If tossing the cue rather than pulling it is your key thought, you want to focus on your shooting hand, feeling as though you are cradling the weight of the cue at that part of your hand closest to the floor.

You will focus on tossing forward the weight of the cue as it sits in that hand, not the butt of the cue and not the tip, and feel as though you are gently throwing that section of the cue through the cue ball and toward your target.

The tip will behave itself very well, especially if you allow freedom of movement in your arm. Feedback movement from your arm will educate you quickly, and you will soon learn to get the desired cue ball movement from the lower arm without much input from the upper arm, as shown in Figure 6.12.

TAKE A TIP

When you toss the cue stick, it may brush the palm or pads of the fingers, as in Figure 4.4 in Chapter 4. The concept that the cue stick may move through the hand at times, not glued to any one spot, is hidden from most casual observers because it is subtle in nature. Again, a loose hold on the stick enables this movement as needed. I have even seen top players run rack after rack with a teacup grip and the stick held (and sliding across) only a thumb *tip* and two *fingertips*.

No matter your practice stroke or backstroke movement or thought, all you need do on the last stroke is gently toss or throw the stick from the hand forward on the final stroke. You can easily gauge the force you need to throw a ball five feet, ten feet, or fifty feet. In the same way, you can easily judge the force of tossing motion needed to send the cue ball various instances. Enjoy!

These stroke images of *pulling* the cue or (gently!) tossing the cue stick work well for many. I will show you a third way also, next.

Cast the Cue

I use the word cast to describe a third way of stroking the cue stick successfully, a gentle thrust from the elbow down using the forearm and without conscious hand movement.

Figure 6.14
A wild toss?

No matter how you get from point A to point B with the backstroke, you can make a beautiful, accurate stroking motion forward using your fore-arm only and without manipulating your shooting hand in any way.

Take a drumstick or similar shaped object in hand—even a light pen, pencil, or drinking straw. Sit down at a table with your hand at your side, your elbow resting on your hip, and the stick or straw poking up through the loop of your fist into the air, as if you are about to play the drums.

Go ahead and drum the table with the object while consciously moving your forearm vigorously, your hand much more passively, to move the stick. Your wrist will naturally get in a bit of ulnar or radial deviation as it needs, and you can "play" the drums at many varied speeds and strengths with

the forearm alone. Turn the arm so the forearm hangs down in a pool stance and you can shoot great pool.

If shooting pool with the forearm below the elbow, I clasp the cue as lightly as I possibly can in the fin-gers, just barely closing my hand around the cue if I feel I need to do so. I judge the distance I need to send the cue ball with a straight cast from my fore-arm. The hand and cue simply come along for the ride, and it is a smooth ride indeed.

The arm from the elbow will of its own accord thrust straight and then up into the upper arm, folding in a bit as in Figures 6.11 and 6.12 on many shots, and the hand will do all it needs to shoot pool without conscious thought added.

If your key thought is to cast the cue stick with the forearm, you'll want to use the shooting fore-arm to thrust a passive hand forward, and think of that hand as then taking the cue stick with it for the ride.

TAKE A TIP

As you develop feel for the stroke at dif-ferent speeds, you will want to settle into a relaxed frame of mind where you don't focus particularly on pulling, tossing, or casting the cue. When you simply *play* pool and achieve the results you visualize before the stroke, you are in dead stroke.

Glide Now, Jab Later

THERE *WILL* BE TIMES when you will jab or poke at the cue ball rather than glide through the stroke in one of three ways. We will review those in Chapter 9. For now, realize that the classic billiards stroke involves flowing, silky movement.

You can choose in advance of any stroke to pull the cue back, and through the stroke, gently *toss* the cue through the shot or *cast* the cue with the lower arm only. Watch great players and you may see them using any of these three families of stroke.

I demonstrate all three methods of stroke plus what not to do on the companion DVD that accompanies this *Picture Yourself* book.

More Stroke Thoughts

I HAVE MORE INSIGHTS for you to better develop your pool stroke. Regard the following pointers with care.

Don't Anticipate a Hit

Another concrete fact of great pool shooting the pros know—unless they want to jab or tap the cue ball purposefully, they avoid feeling the actual ball impact during their stroke.

As Newton's Third Law describes, upon impact the cue ball resists the cue stick's motion, so vibration travels through the stick to the player's body and provides feedback to the shooter. Excessive vibration is unwanted but a smooth stroke, as if the ball was not there, is.

If the movement of the stick is forward and straight through, most of the shock of impact reverts to launching the ball straight ahead. Too much vibration and the cue might be deflecting off line, ruining the shot. The sideways movement of vibration is slight, but the concept of stroking smoothly through, not at, the cue ball, is vital.

The butt end of the cue with its rubber bumper absorbs vibration as does your body if you are in a balanced stance, and in recent years, manufacturers have gone so far as to market *cue stabilizers* and *cue dampeners*, shock absorbing cue extensions to soften the hit. You may have a preference for a hard or soft hitting cue.

Ignore the cue ball impact on the final stroke forward, looking at your target as you stroke and not the ball. Anticipating the hit on the cue ball, and worrying about returning the cue stick to the precise point where you aimed, creates unwanted muscle tension in the stroke.

The cue ball is highly resilient; if you drop one from a height of three feet onto a concrete floor it will bounce up nearly three feet high again. The cue ball is elastic (springy) and you cannot feel the hit too much to begin with, so ignore the hit sensation; it's a potential distraction in your game.

My swing thought in Figure 6.15 is to pull (or toss or cast) the stick through the place where the ball rests, as if the ball was made of air and not plastic.

Figure 6.15
Not feeling it.

TAKE A TIP

For most shots, you are not trying to hit a spot on the cue ball; you are trying to stroke *through* a spot on the cue ball, which is different. Thinking about the actual hit may make you decelerate into impact, so ignore it.

Making Change

IF YOU HAVE BEEN keeping up with Mr. Newton's laws, you realize the inertia of the backstroke must be overcome before we can reverse direction to go forward again.

You have great leeway in how you will end your final backswing and begin the second part of the stroke. Some world-class players pause for a long moment at the end of the backswing, clearing their mind of distractions and recommitting to the stroke before coming forward. Some blend the two motions together so fast that is hard to tell just where the backswing ends and the forward stroke begins. You should consider this timing and rhythm as helpful to your stroke. Are you a smooth pause kind of player or a smooth blender instead?

How Fast Do I Stroke?

For now, keep timing and rhythm simple. Stroking speed and rhythm equals moving the cue as fast or slow as you need to send the cue ball a particular distance for the shot. It really is that simple! If your temperament is fast and loose, you will probably swing the cue faster overall than the more thoughtful, deliberate pool shooter. Both types of players still need to hit with speed X to send the cue ball X distance.

One step to outstanding play is good personal *tempo*, or rate of play overall. Tempo derives from the Italian "tiempe," meaning "time," and includes time used to plan and choose shots, in addition to shooting them.

A small percentage of players are too slow and cautious. Never moving fast enough to get hot at the game, they fall short of greatness. Most who stumble, though, move like the IRS is getting paid per stroke on the 16th of April.

Some of these speedsters, like top professional Lou "Machine Gun" Butera, who earned his nickname for rapid-fire shooting, do quite well. For most amateurs, an extra moment's concentration on aim or position would tremendously boost their play.

Your personal tempo, quick or methodical, should be dictated by your individual temperament. Only you can guess what speed of toss, pull, or cast will send the cue ball as far and as fast as you need. You will learn speeds fast if you commit to the fundamentals outlined in this book.

Without a second ball on the table, send the white ball half a table length, a table length, two table lengths, and other distances. How close did you finish to where you intended? Are you hitting the ball too hard or too soft? Let each shot be your learning or confirming experience. Watch the cue ball roll to a stop and start the process of adjusting cue speed for the shot at hand.

Controlling cue ball speed with the stroke is critical for great play, but a child can do it.

Trust the Hand

Take one last look at the end of the backstroke as in Figure 6.16. My shooting hand is behind my legs, along the shot line, behind my field of vision, separate from my body.

Figure 6.16
One more time.

The stick should move freely in a manner that is comfortable, even relaxing, to the player. I need to absolutely trust that my stroke will do what I need, especially since I am looking past the cue ball toward the side pocket throughout the stroke.

Most backswings require only a few inches of movement, with your shooting hand going back three to eight inches from the starting position; but until you learn to let your hand swing freely behind you and out of sight (almost out of feel and out of control "on its own"), your game will plateau in skill.

Nice and Easy

Hopefully, experience teaches a soft, smooth stroke. Pool great Willie Mosconi compared pool's basic stroke with the light, tapping touch he used for putting on the golf course. Pool balls roll several feet across a smooth, level surface—they're not pounded 300 yards down the fairway.

In golf, the gentle analogy is still apt. Muscular jocks without golf know-how often dribble off the tee a few feet, but you see a skinny pro or an overweight, out-of-shape pro smash a ball 300 yards via fluid, easy movement.

Pro golfers must add smooth movement to muscle action. Racecar drivers turn their wheel fluidly, not sharply out of control. Basketball pros, racquetball champions, tennis stars, and many more add flair and follow-through to their movements. Pool players strive to become silky with their strokes.

Most pool shooters hit the cue ball too hard. With gentle strokes, you gain sensitivity regarding cue movement and ball spin, too, and learn faster.

We'll thunderously smash a few *open break* shots together in Chapter 10. Even then, however, the smooth breaker is the most powerful at the tables.

Cue as Extension

A helpful image is to imagine the cue stick as simply being part of your body. Do you need to force or squeeze any muscle consciously to walk, to eat, to breathe?

When the cue stick is a part of you, a natural extension of hand, arm, and mind, it will do whatever your mind visualizes, rather than be a foreign, clunky object to you.

Stroke an Invisible Ball

When learning the correct stroking motion, it is helpful to simply send a cue ball into a corner pocket, as I have done in Figure 6.17, and forget the rest of the balls. You might even practice with no ball at all, checking on ease of movement, follow-through distance, and more.

Figure 6.17
On a roll.

Think "crawl, walk, run" for developing a pool stroke. Master the stroke a step each time and don't become discouraged because you can't shoot a five-rail shot or break the 9-ball into a pocket on the first try. Send a cue ball on its own or off a rail or two or into a pocket for a while as suggested. From then on, it's a matter of learning how to aim the cue ball itself (see Chapter 8) and making minor aim and speed adjustments.

Diamonds Are Forever

An old timer's stroke trick is to rest the cue atop one of the long rails of the table, then stroke the cue stick above one of the diamond markers along the rail to check for straightness.

Watch the cue tip throughout the stroke. Confirm whether it covers the diamond throughout the back and forward strokes or swerves to the side. Practicing this way for a minute is a real confidence builder before a big match.

I am grateful to Master Instructor Carl Oswald for pointing out the following helpful drill also—use the line created where cloth meets the rail along the table. The shooter or instructor can confirm whether the entire length of the cue is on line during the stroke.

Don't grow anxious if these drills reveal a slight flaw in your stroke. Most of us have such a flaw somewhere. Again, producing forward, unimpeded stroke inertia helps the cue fly straight, too. Loosen your grip on the cue and see if the stroke is now straighter above the diamond and alongside the rail. Check your stance alignment and ensure your shooting arm is along the shot line (see Chapter 5).

Snap, Crackle, Pop

Many good players give the shot extra *oomph* with a flick of the wrist. Added wrist action is controversial in our sport. Many experts state unequivocally the ball does not care whether your wrist is moving or bent at impact according to the laws of motion.

I agree that you can shoot without wrist flick or with wrist deviation. My observation, however, is that the pro often adds a bit of wrist action in the forward stroke but returns the hand and stick for impact to near where they started at address. In other words, they flick their wrist in the stroke based on need but at impact the cue is flying forward.

I demonstrate how and when to use your wrist for break and other strokes later in this book. For now, if you experiment with hand motion, study whether you are twisting the cue or accelerating it, and be sure the fancy stuff happens ahead of impact or after, during the follow-through, when the ball is well on its way.

Dropping the Arm

Upper arm movement (or its opposite, holding the arm immobile) is another theory battle fought between pool sages for ages.

To create a perfect pendulum movement, you might need to do much with wrist deviation, fingers, and the upper arm to perform a true, rounded arc. Most pool strokes go mostly straight instead, adding a bit of up and a bit of down somewhere. The typical pool pro strokes with an arc, but it has a long, flat bottom.

I want your cue stick to be going straight through the cue ball. Why add the trouble of timing the bottom of a perfect arc at the ball? You could not always be sure if you are hitting the ball at the bottom of the arc or on the upstroke or downstroke. The elbow pinned by a shoulder set immobile through impact creates a simple, repeatable motion you can easily train. It's near a pendulum with a straight line movement of one to several inches going forward during the stroke.

Allow your upper arm to drop an inch or two during the follow-through, and if it should drop after impact, well, that's not the worst thing in the world. I leave the upper arm mostly in place until my follow-through, but I neither hold it rigidly aloft nor consciously force it down through the stroke.

Head in the Game

The old saw, "Keep your head down!" has been laid to rest in golf, as it leads to back and neck problems among other troubles. Yet keeping the head down is still great advice for pool.

Figure 6.18
Pool is beauty.

Leave your head in position until the cue ball has come to a complete stop. That's a key stroke thought today of no less a luminary than Hall-of-Fame great Nick Varner, whose father trained him as a child to stay down until he saw the balls collide, and we could do worse than emulate him.

If you pop your head and neck up to watch the outcome of a shot, chances are you lifted your body through the final stroke and ruined the hit.

You will often see players leap into the air in the middle of the shot to watch the hit like their pants have caught fire. Quite often, the hit was a miss.

Stroke, Don't Broom

The rules of pool call for a continuous motion forward on the final stroke. The player may not touch the cue stick to the cue ball and then broom or push it along.

A perceptible backswing on every shot helps avoid taking this penalty foul.

Relax, Relax, Relax!

A maxim pool teachers like to use is to tell the student to relax, constantly, to avoid muscle tension. For my personality type, that is akin to telling me "Don't think about pink elephants" or "Jump out of a plane with no parachute but don't think about the ground." The admonition to relax actually tenses me.

Athletes in almost every sport seek neither total tension nor complete relaxation but something in between. I expect to feel keyed up and excited before a big game or a big match. I would be worried about making a speech if I had no thought for the audience, no rush of adrenalin, and I couldn't play my best pool without a bit of excited anticipation.

I seek for a heightened state of concentration at the table that includes clarity and simplicity of thought, including calm, clear insight on strategy and shots, and spinning and speeding the cue ball with ease. In that state of intense and also relaxed concentration, I merely think softly to myself, "hit this very fast and hard (I may even feel this speed need without conscious words)" and my body responds in the stroke without any conscious strain, with little effort. This elevated state of play is called "dead stroke" in pool.

Follow the stance, stroke, and equipment key thoughts I've outlined and let them be your focus in practice. During an important game, however, trust your fundamentals and think only about what you want the balls to do and where you want them to go. If you can be eager, animated, even a little wound up, but relaxed enough to rely on procedural memory (Chapter 2), you're ready to roll in dead stroke!

I trust the fundamentals and the aiming techniques I'll outline in Chapters 8, 9, and 10. I feel no more anxiety over a long, challenging shot than over an easy one most of the time. If not in dead stroke, I am usually in dead calm.

Still having trouble with *active relaxation* in the stroke? Imagine your elbow and wrist are machine parts, freshly oiled. Stroke back and forth and feel your cue in a straight line as if it and you are mounted on ball bearings, like the door sliding open on the finest car you've ever opened. This image should place you in a confident yet relaxed state of mind.

Summing a Great Stroke

L ET'S TAKE A QUICK refresher course on
stroking like a champion from this chapter.

▶ Use a fairly lightweight cue (intermediate
player) or slightly heavy cue (beginning
player) and chalk it well.

▶ Take a few practice strokes (or many) and
pause (or don't) before the final stroke.

▶ Draw back on the final backstroke and
pause for a moment (or don't) before going
forward.

▶ You might use some combination of
pulling, casting, or tossing for practice
strokes and the final stroke.

▶ Seek for a smooth stroke with a relaxed
body and mind—it is a pool axiom that less
is more with smoothness resulting from letting go of muscular effort.

Stroke Files

F ILE AWAY THESE TIPS in your stroke
knowledge, too:

▶ Build a personal sense of style and rhythm.

▶ Stroke forward when you are confident—
you hit the ball with the final forward
stroke only.

▶ Stay down until the balls collide. Where
possible, let the balls come to rest fully
before leaving the stance.

▶ Use the table diamonds or single balls and
pockets for stroke practice.

▶ Seek for the combination of intense excitement and relaxed effort that produce dead
stroke.

▶ Hit the ball softly, stroking through it, not
into it, and take note of your results.

▶ Consider the cue stick as part of your body,
a longer arm, a smoothly oiled, gliding
extension of your mind.

Ready, Aim...You Know the Rest

YOU HAVE A LOT OF TOOLS belted for a great stroke now. In Chapter 7, I will show you a lot of fun stroke variations the pros use to create fancy spin on the cue ball, jump it into the air, and much more. We'll even look at long-lost techniques from a century ago that you can enjoy today.

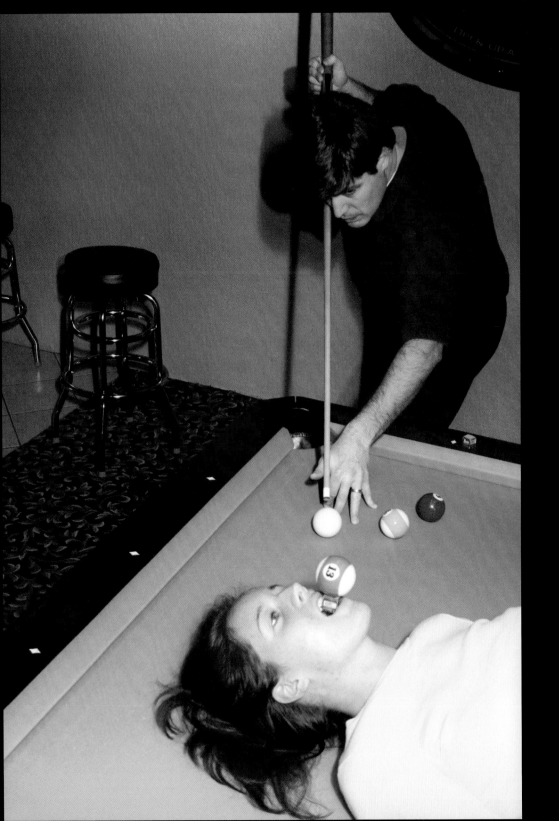

Adjust as Needed: Pro Stick

Moves

Many ways to skin the cue ball

T HE PURPOSE OF THIS CHAPTER is to teach different angles of attack on the cue ball, adding special effects to the cue ball's movement. Some of the techniques are quite old in invention but rarely seen today, even though they still work!

You are going to calculate aiming the white ball into the colored object balls in Chapter 8, but first we are going to make the cue ball dance. I will demonstrate how to make the cue stop on a dime (or less) and spin backward, forward, over, and sideways. You will even learn to send the cue ball high into the air, changing the flat pool table into a three-dimensional amusement park.

A New Route

W E'VE EXPLORED AT LENGTH taking a medium stroke into the *center* of the cue ball (center referring to stroking through the center of the sphere midway along its vertical axis as seen when facing the ball). Next, we are going to break some of the rules for the smooth, near-level stroke and learn how to make the cue ball do special spins and movement.

PLEASE BEWARE

Much of this chapter contradicts the advice given in Chapter 6! You will always develop a flowing, smooth cue movement with a near-level cue as in that chapter— that classic stroke will always serve you well. It's time now, however, to look at the many ways we can alter "normal" cue movement with a variety of exotic techniques for changing the cue ball's spin, speed, and path.

Old Friend

I N FIGURE 7.1 we regard our old friend, a basic center ball strike on the cue, as we used for learning general stance and stroke (Chapters 5 and 6).

A center ball shot is hit at the intersection of the center of the equator line and the center of the vertical axis on the sphere of the cue ball (as facing the player).

Figure 7.1
Center ball aim.

Figures 7.3 and 7.4 illustrate a medium center ball stroke, with its moderate angle of attack on the cue ball and a follow-through of several inches' length. Beginners should bring their bridge hand in closer to the target and make a shorter stroke as they learn the game.

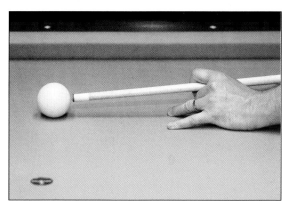

Figure 7.2
Center ball from the reverse angle.

Figure 7.3
Center ball final stroke.

Figure 7.4
Follow-through.

By "medium stroke," I mean that I am rolling the cue ball down the length of the table without any effort at intense speed.

In Figure 7.5, I have the same length bridge, and will adjust the motion of my shooting arm to come through the ball a bit harder. I am bringing the cue stick back farther than before, all the way into the loop of my hand to come forward again with a bit more dash.

Figure 7.5
Center ball backswing.

Figures 7.6 and 7.7 show the completion of this stroke. The follow-through is lengthier as a natural consequence of a faster stroke taken.

Figure 7.6
Forward stroke.

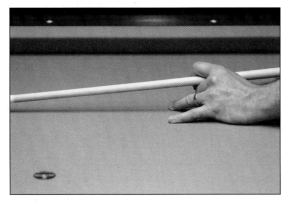

Figure 7.7
Longer follow-through.

TAKE A TIP

Why is only the bridge hand pictured in these illustrations? Direct your attention mostly to the bridge hand now, so you learn to adjust your angle of attack on the cue ball for different stick moves. (The shooting hand action is somewhat similar for all strokes with some slight and subtle adjustments.) For now, consider the way the cue tip is played into and through the cue ball to create different effects.

The center ball stroke will cause the cue ball initially to *skid* away from the cue tip rather than *roll*. The ball does not turn over its axis but slides or skids across the surface of the table for a time. The length of the skid is based on the force of the strike. A harder center ball hit will make the cue skid farther.

If I strike with medium force and the cue ball hits an object a few inches ahead of my cue tip, it will skid into that ball and stop dead in its tracks, an important position play for halting the cue's movement.

Aligning for Draw

FIGURES 7.8 AND 7.9 have me aligning the cue tip to *draw* the cue ball. Draw or backspin (a spinning ball that rotates toward the player on its vertical axis) makes the cue ball pause for a moment upon contact with an object ball, before it moves backward on the shot line again and toward the player's cue stick.

Figure 7.8
Drawing the cue ball.

Figure 7.9
Reverse angle.

PLEASE BEWARE

These varied stick moves are shown without an object ball for the cue to strike. Description of how the cue ball would respond off an object ball with these strokes is in general terms and based on a *full hit*, an impact when the sphere of the ball hits the sphere of the ball fully along the shot line. From the player's perspective along the shot line, a full hit looks like the moon covering the sun's disk in a full eclipse. Draw and other spin shots have subtle changes if there is less than full hit contact.

There is no object ball seen in either figure, which is fine, because fear of the drawn cue ball rebounding into the cue tip causes hesitation for new draw players.

Practice the stick moves in these illustrations as shown, without an object ball. Focus instead on the feelings of stick, stroke, and cue ball before using a second ball to hit against.

You may want to use a striped ball to acquire visual feedback on ball spin. Set the stripe facing you horizontally for each stroke. Be careful to remove all chalk from the striped ball before returning it to the set for play.

Figure 7.10
Ready to press forward.

Draw Stick Angle

Figure 7.11 shows the far extent of the backswing. Note the steeper angle from above the cue ball down to near its base. The cue stick is angled more above parallel to the table in Figure 7.11 than in 7.5, providing a hit lower than the center ball as seen, although still in the middle of the cue ball along its vertical axis.

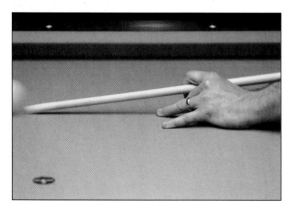

Figure 7.11
Up to down angle.

There are several keys to hitting the draw stroke with adequate spin. I share them all with my students, and one or two of them are usually enough for them to create draw with their cue.

▶ Chalk especially well before the draw stroke for added friction, applying a heavier coat than usual. Ensure the coating is uniform. Too much chalk can actually provide slippage to the cue tip.

▶ Check the loop of the closed bridge to ensure that it has been lowered (by spreading middle, ring, and pinky fingers to lower the loop)—if your loop is low, the stick will be as near level as you can make it and still aimed low (in Figure 7.10, the cue emanates from a bridge loop held as low as the ball itself).

▶ Stroke more authoritatively than usual, looking for an always accelerating cue stick, the cue traveling faster and faster through contact with the ball—think "five, six, seven miles per hour" through forward stroke and follow-through (or whatever mental image creates smooth acceleration).

▶ Strive for a lengthy follow-through on the stroke—it's almost as if you hit the draw point on a second cue ball several inches past the ball you actually contact.

▶ Some great draw players add a bit of wrist action to the stroke, looking to give the cue ball an extra caress with the cue tip—the longer the tip remains on the ball, the more draw spin is added.

▶ Do not raise the shooting hand more than an inch or so. Let the lowered bridge hand align the cue for you—a steeply raised shooting hand will mar the stroke or even jump the cue ball off the table.

▶ Know that most players actually strike the ball a bit higher than they aim in a draw shot. Even some pros aim lower than they strike. A deliberately relaxing grip hand is used by the pro to effect this motion. The beginner, however, must avoid dropping the elbow mid-stroke, which causes an undesirable high hit.

▶ Almost any contact below the equator of the ball creates some backspin.

I would not aim much lower than pictured in Figure 7.9. An extremely low hit on the ball causes the white ferrule of the cue to scoop the ball into the air, which is a foul stroke.

Draw Stroke Clench

It's not used enough in pool instruction, though I've emphasized it throughout this book—stroke smoothly and gently, and you will get the results you want. Having repeated that point again, I do need to tell you that the intermediate player applies a bit more muscle to the draw stroke, an added bit of tension, and clench until they get the hang of the draw stroke. Once the stroke is learned, resolve to use added force to draw but apply this force as smoothly as possible.

There should be a bit of punch or jab to the draw stroke. Since the ball will get underspin on any hit below center, I can make a smooth stroke (as in Chapter 6) and still get draw action on the ball for a short time.

Friction from the cloth on the table works against backspin and erodes it over time. To get plenty of draw spin on the ball so that backspin will last over longer distances, I need to really give it extra force. I will still release and launch the stick into the ball through impact, however.

It takes little force to roll the smooth ball with overspin along the smooth, level table, but extra force to provide a *backward* underspin motion to the ball while it is moving *forward* along the table surface. Think of a drawn ball as a roll of tape that is becoming a flat line of tape along the shot, spooling out across the felt. The tape is sticking to the cloth. Extra spin is needed for true draw motion after ball impact.

My cue stick is also writing on that line in Figure 7.12. You can see the white ferrule is going for a ride along the felt in this extended follow-through. Forward and through, forward and through, for added draw action.

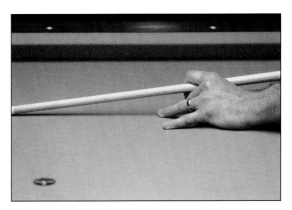

Figure 7.12
Brushing the cloth.

Some degree of below center ball hit, a draw or holding stroke, occurs more than half the time in play. Learn to enjoy and use this important stroke.

PLEASE BEWARE

Yes, the great draw player hits the ball a little harder, adds a little wrist flick or tightens the grip a little on the cue stick. But the key is, if you squeeze the life from the cue stick and pound into the cue ball with all your might, you will simply push the stick into the ball with deceleration and kill the draw action. Draw involves a hard, fast punch but not a smash.

Ye Olde Jab Draw

FIGURE 7.13 SHOWS the set position for a *jab draw* stroke. This lovely tool was promulgated in pool books a century or more ago, and it is just now coming into vogue again, as it breaks many of the rules we've outlined so far for a quality stroke.

I've brought my upper torso far closer to the ball than otherwise, with my head over the shaft toward the tip rather than the midpoint of the cue as in previous diagrams. My cue is lifted high and steeply angled, much more so than in the traditional draw shot (compare Figure 7.13 with Figure 7.8). My forearm is still above the cue and loose, but the cue stick is ready to jab into the ball quite steeply.

Figure 7.14 shows the angle of the jab draw, an angle so steep it seems that I might hit the cloth short of the cue ball itself. But I am going to not only jab or poke at the ball, I'm going to violate another rule of traditional cue stroking in spinning this ball.

Figure 7.13
Secret of the ancients.

Figure 7.14
Poking at the cue ball.

A close comparison of Figure 7.15 with 7.14 shows my bridge hand has actually slid along its base on the table toward the ball to enable this poking draw shot. This little-known draw technique is a lifesaver.

Figure 7.15
The bridge slides.

The jab draw may be used to bring exceptional amounts of draw spin when the balls are hemmed in and there is no room for a traditional draw stroke. It's also easily taught to students who cannot achieve traditional draw action. They use the jab in training to feel the backspin as applied to the cue ball. A real eye-opener!

TAKE A TIP

By sliding the bridge hand forward through the jab draw shot, we have opened the field of slip strokes. The habit some have of sliding the grip end of the cue through the shooting hand during practice strokes to acquire final hand positioning is called a *slip stroke*. Throwing the cue through the bridge or shooting hand and catching it again along the forward motion is a *reverse slip stroke*, as with this jabbing draw stroke through a moving bridge hand. Even Willie Mosconi liked to get his body moving forward a bit with the shot in a *body slip stroke*. Slip strokes are heady stuff and should be experimented with only after you are confident working with an immobile bridge and nothing in motion but the shooting arm through the classic stroke.

Top Stroke

APPLYING INSTANT TOPSPIN to the ball (sending the cue ball rotating over its axis forward as it leaves the stick with little or no skid like a center ball hit) is pictured in Figures 7.16 through 7.20.

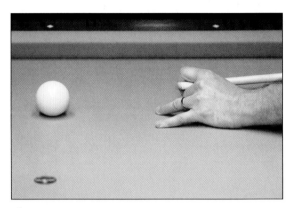

Figure 7.18
Extent of backswing.

Figure 7.16
Positioned for follow-through.

Figure 7.19
Impact.

Figure 7.17
Drawn back.

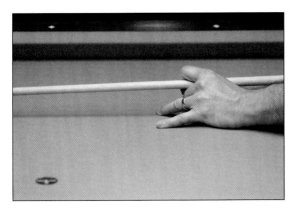

Figure 7.20
The end.

Figure 7.21
Tripod bridge.

Keys to a topspin stroke are setting a more level cue than in other strokes and raising the loop of the bridge (or channel of the open bridge, see Figure 4.27 in Chapter 4) by drawing the fingers into the hand, *not* by lowering the shooting hand. Simply aim a nearly level cue above center (north of the ball's equator) to get that lovely roll.

Striking the cue seven-tenths up its vertical axis yields immediate roll. We usually don't need to go any higher than 60% of the way from bottom to top, however, to get a little extra rolling distance on shots.

Figure 7.21 illustrates a tripod bridge (see Chapter 4) with the pads of three fingertips used to hoist the palm of the hand bridge completely off the felt. The cue is steeply angled downward but will strike the ball above center providing topspin, where a tripod bridge is required.

TAKE A TIP

You won't need topspin action on most strokes, because a center ball or even a draw hit eventually converts to overspin when the initial skid or backspin erodes on the shot line. Topspin is for decisively sending the cue ball forward through impact somewhere. We will learn more about using topspin to *shape* (position) the cue ball in Chapter 10.

Nip Stroke

THE PROS CAN BRING action to a cue ball in a tight space with a *nip stroke*, a sharply condensed stroking motion.

Figure 7.22 shows the full extent of a nip backstroke, this time with a raised open bridge. Up lightly a short distance, then perhaps a long pause, to ensure the forward stroke will be gentle but decisive.

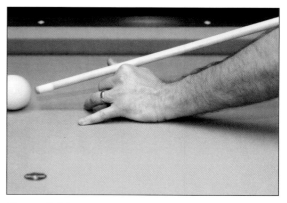

Figure 7.23
Cue ball is struck.

By Figure 7.24 the cue has ceased its follow-through and come to rest. This is literally a short, nippy stroke that takes a bite from the cue ball and sends it a tiny distance with follow-through. Apply more force with the nip stroke to send the cue ball a surprisingly great distance.

Figure 7.22
Tiny backswing.

In Figure 7.23 the cue ball has been struck. The key thought is to have the cue tip penetrate the cue ball but not to any great depth. We do not want to squeeze ball to cloth with force. Per Newton's laws of motion, the cue ball might take to the air as one result if we hit hard enough to press the tip to touch the table's cloth.

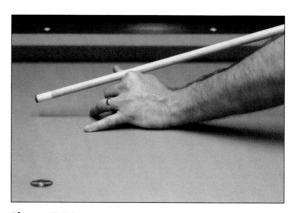

Figure 7.24
Stroke end.

Force Follow

By leveling the angle a tad and using a full wrist and lower arm release through the confined stroke distance, you can hit *at* the ball, not *through* the ball. The cue ball may then take to the air and impact a nearby object ball before rolling forward with topspin, a dozen feet or more! This *force follow* stroke is a firework that breaks all the rules.

Tight Center Stroke

THE *TIGHT CENTER STROKE* is rarely considered for play, even by advanced shooters. As one result they get too much action on the cue ball stroking in tight spaces.

Figures 7.25 through 7.28 reveal in high-speed photos this gem of a stroke. Again breaking a precept from Chapter 6, we seek to feel the cue ball impact; so instead of stroking through the shot, we come to an abrupt stop after lightly tapping the ball. Just touch the cue ball with your tip. As we bunt the cue ball a bit forward, the grip is like the hit, loose and light.

Figure 7.26
A short backstroke.

Figure 7.25
Tight center aim.

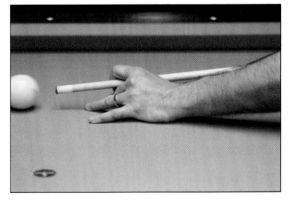

Figure 7.27
A light tap of a hit.

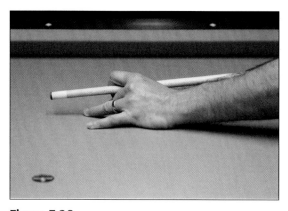

Figure 7.28
The finish.

The bridge hand is close on the cue ball, and the shooting hand has choked up on the stick (see Figure 5.13 in Chapter 5 for choking forward). Just nudging the cue ball with a tap or pop and not a full, flowing stroke, it serenely skids forward into place. A great shot for precision near a crowded corner or some other congested table zone.

As mentioned previously, taking at least a perceptible backswing on every shot helps avoid having a referee call a penalty foul for an illegal *push* of the cue ball.

Rap Top Stroke

THIS IS A STROKE that may come up ten times or more for you in a single playing session. It's easy to execute, once you've seen it and know what it can do.

In Figures 7.29 through 7.32, my cue ball was somewhat close to an object ball, and I wanted to rap on the cue ball and have it rap the object ball in turn to help ensure it would roll straight forward toward my target.

Figure 7.29
Aimed high on the ball.

Figure 7.30
Pulling straight back.

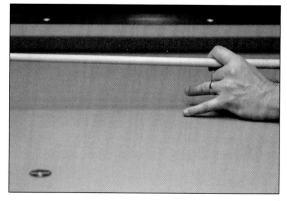

Figure 7.32
And away it goes.

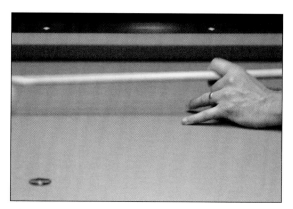

Figure 7.31
A high, thrusting hit.

Aim higher than you would for an ordinary top-spin stroke and give the ball a solid rap or tap. You may have noticed part of my bridge has come off the table with the stroke in Figures 7.31 and 7.32.

By Figure 7.32 I have gone so far as to hit a *British follow* stroke, named after shooters in Great Britain who employed this stroke for snooker and other games. By aiming quite high on the cue ball and rapping it forcefully forward into a nearby ball, the cue ball will jump a tiny bit before rolling forward a considerable distance. It's a pretty stroke when used for sending a cue ball after an object ball into the same pocket, for example.

Semi-Massé

THE LOVELY MASSÉ or *curve stroke* is seen next. It seems in Figure 7.33 that although I am standing more upright than usual at the table, my cue stick is poised to drive the white ball squarely into the maroon 7-ball at the foot of the table.

Figure 7.33
Ready for crazy action.

We have discussed avoiding making corkscrew cue movement, which produces an off-center hit in the stroke and unanticipated results. Horizontal motion can have any of several disastrous consequences.

In this case, a bit of twist is used to produce planned results. You can see in Figure 7.34 I have brought the cue down diagonally to my right, off the straight path with the follow through. The stroke is still straight but wends diagonal toward my right.

Figure 7.34
The corkscrew hit.

Figure 7.35 shows the cue ball just edging from the path to the 7-ball, and Figure 7.36 has the rotational spin veering the cue ball still farther to my right as forward momentum has worn down. The semi-massé can be learned with a few minutes' practice if you understand the concept of two momentums creating a gradually increasing curve as one momentum, directional speed, wears down, and yields to rotational speed.

Figure 7.35
What will happen?

Figure 7.36
Missed by a mile.

As with a sliced golf ball, the left-spinning ball carries the cue ball to my right, more as the forward energy of the ball begins to dissipate.

TAKE A TIP

The massé stroke family is featured in more detail on the companion DVD to *Picture Yourself Shooting Pool.*

Full Massé Stroke

A FULL MASSÉ IS A NOD to the greats of an earlier era. They astonished the large exhibition crowds gathered to watch their skills in pool and *Cushion Billiards* (game without pockets where balls must contact other balls to score points).

Note I am using a house cue (see Chapter 3) for this stroke. A good massé requires a vertical stroke taking the cue tip to the table bed or near it. One might lose a cue tip or warp a favorite cue shaft with this shot. This is no time to use a thousand-dollar cue stick—at least, until you learn to shoot these shots gently enough!

In Figure 7.37, I am lining up on the ball. A few firm practice strokes up and down one inch or two come next. In Figure 7.38, I have pulled the cue

back into my hand for the shot. In Figure 7.39, you can better see the reverse grip I have taken on the cue for this bizarre stroke.

Figure 7.37
This will be intense.

Figure 7.38
A straight backswing.

Figure 7.39
A bizarre curve.

The cue ball was aligned to strike the maroon 7-ball but has taken a sharp curve around it instead. You will better understand the massé and semi-massé strokes as we explore concepts of *english* (sidespin applied) in Chapter 9.

TAKE A TIP

The full massé stroke comes up rarely, so do not be intimidated by its apparent difficulty. It is more for trick shooting or showing off a wild curve than it is practical for everyday competition.

Jump Stroke

THE JUMP STROKE may be executed in several ways. In Figure 7.40, I have brought my bridge hand close to the cue ball for control. I have formed a tripod bridge with the cue gliding along the channel of my hand (a raised *open bridge*, see Chapter 4) so I can better see the shot and also *intentionally* allow my cue stick to leave my bridge hand on the forward stroke.

Again, I have violated a rule of the classic stroke by loosening the bridge hand guide for the cue stick, and hitting a blow sharp enough on the cue ball to send stick and ball into the air.

Figure 7.40
Reared back to strike.

Figure 7.41
Fly!

We will learn more about jump shots for position in Chapter 11.

PLEASE BEWARE

The jump stroke as illustrated in Figure 7.41 is not the fancy stunt stroke demonstrated at the front of this chapter. Do not try that one at home!

Adding to the Arsenal

WE'VE HAD QUITE A RUN in this chapter of pro stick moves. A good pool player will start learning properly with an elegant, graceful stroke as outlined in Chapters 5 and 6. The savvy player then adds some of the special moves outlined in this chapter:

▶ The draw stroke and jab draw stroke.

▶ Topspin strokes and British, rap, and force follow strokes.

▶ Nip strokes and tight center strokes for close work.

▶ Massé (curving cue ball) strokes.

▶ Jumping the cue ball.

Time for Pocketing

Next, we will explore aiming the cue ball to sinking an object ball. Anyone can hit the white cue ball into another ball. We will add precision and direction to targeting, too.

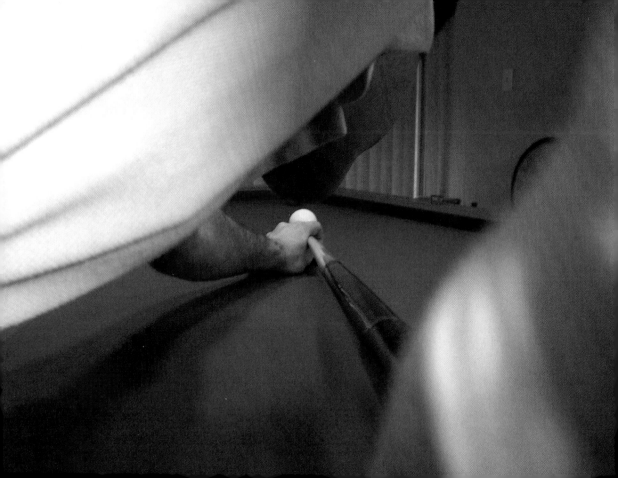

Aim True: Understanding Ball Impacts and Paths

Aiming to sink more shots, quickly

IMAGINE TELLING FRIENDS, "At the poolroom for three hours, I shot hundreds of balls in the pockets—without missing even once!"

Pool's greatest—including Willie Mosconi, John Schmidt, and Nick Varner, among others—have shared that statement with the world. They managed to run 300 to 500 or more shots even under the constraints of Straight Pool, a game we will explore in Chapter 14.

To run balls, of course, you must know how to aim them to hit the pockets. This chapter is the salt to your stroke's pepper. You have a decent pool stroke from Chapters 4, 5, and 6 and will now learn to aim the cue ball to hit targets with accuracy.

Aim is for many the single toughest pool subject to comprehend. Many pros aim by instinct and are unwilling or unable to teach aim methods. Pool literature, even instructional material, has had little to date in the way of helpful advice.

In step-by-step fashion, this chapter reveals aim tricks that top players use to sink many more balls than they miss, visualizing lines of travel and adjusting for ball spin and table condition. You can learn to aim superbly and win as a result!

Music of the Spheres

EVERY INTERMEDIATE *SHOULD* be able
to run 10 or 20 shots in a row without a
miss. In practice, aiming spheres to collide
together accurately gives most amateurs fits!

I will provide many tips in this chapter to aid your
aiming. You need not struggle as I did to decode
these essential secrets of pool.

PLEASE BEWARE

We will shoot at ball targets now instead
of pockets as by now you have some skill
at sinking a ball in a pocket as in "Stroke
an Invisible Ball" in Chapter 6. If not,
review your stance and stroke and re-read
Chapters 5 and 6 before progressing
through this chapter.

A Full Hit

FIGURE 8.1 WAS STAGED with the white
cue ball touching the blue-striped 10-ball
along a rail. Imagine I rolled the cue along
the rail with my fingertips.

We see a full hit here. In a full hit, most of the cue
ball's momentum transfers to the object ball.

PLEASE BEWARE

Picture Yourself Shooting Pool relates inex-
act physics and geometry. We are not concerned with exact drag coefficient,
perimeter velocity of a colliding ball, tan-
gential frictional force, etc. General terms
like "stop," "stun," or "most of momentum"
are simplified explanations so the player
learns to make the balls move as desired.

Figure 8.1
A full hit.

Think "Sun and Moon"

In our sky, the circles of the moon and sun are equivalent. Wondrously, the moon's diameter is about 1/400th the sun's diameter, and the moon is also 1/400th the distance from Earth as the sun, making the circles equal from our Earthbound perspective.

In a total solar eclipse, therefore, the moon's disk covers every part of the sun. As the Earth, sun, and moon travel through space, a tiny misalignment of the two circles, even a sliver crescent of sun, glares bright light everywhere and ends the total darkness of the eclipse.

In the same way, covering or incompletely covering the object ball with your cue ball provides different effects than the full hit. The full hit (full eclipse) tends to stun the motion of the cue ball, momentum released to the object ball, which then rolls straight forward.

Figure 8.2 shows a full hit from a perspective beneath the "shot." Because the photo was taken below the ball, you can just see the striped 10-ball rather than not seeing it at all.

If the 10-ball were on a table ahead of the cue ball along the shot line, impact makes a full hit on the 10-ball. The cue ball is your moon, sent to cover the sun of the 10-ball, making a full hit.

Figure 8.2
A full cue ball eclipse.

Pocketing Balls

L ET'S POCKET A BALL using a full hit as most pool strokes involve the intention to pocket one or more balls, clearing the table toward victory.

Full Hit Sinks It

Consider the shot shown in Figure 8.3 How would you aim the cue ball labeled "C" to strike the orange five into the side pocket? Stroking the cue ball directly into the 5-ball knocks it straight into the pocket.

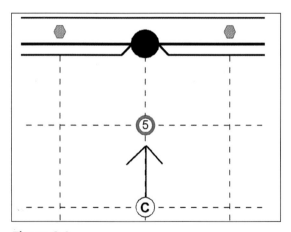

Figure 8.3
Full hit into side.

PLEASE BEWARE

Table diagrams including ball sizes in *Picture Yourself Shooting Pool* are not to scale. Enlarged balls, rails, and pocket openings help illustrate the principles of good pool.

Playing this shot on the table, your cue stick would rest behind the cue ball, aimed directly through the center of the cue ball, the 5-ball, and the side pocket. Your head may be directly over the shot line or watching from one side based on your preference and comfort (see "Head and Eye Alignment" in Chapter 5).

As your cue stick comes straight back and through, the white ball goes squarely into the 5-ball, which releases after impact and moves straight into the center of the side pocket. A perfectly straight follow-through would leave the cue stick atop the dotted line, too.

The full hit is important to know, because it is both simple to aim (a "full eclipse" viewed from the shooter's perspective along the shot line) and tends to *stun* or halt the cue ball. Leaving the cue ball where the 5-ball sat might prove important for the next shot taken.

Make This Shot

Prepare and stroke this shot several times at your table. What happens when you make a gentle stroke on the cue ball, striking it in the middle at its equator? What happens when you stroke through the cue ball harder or softer? Try shooting at different speeds and at different spots along the vertical axis of the cue ball (you might review Chapter 7 for cue stick positioning for specialty shots).

On this shot, stun action will cause the cue ball to stop dead upon impact, leaving it where it struck the 5-ball. If you can duplicate Figure 8.4, the cue ball skidded to the hit with no over- or under-spin, no rotation. Forward roll makes the cue ball drift after impact to replace the 5-ball's spot, rather than sticking behind it.

There will be few directions on cue ball speed throughout the book as you are to experiment and set a personalized gauge for speed, but a medium speed stroke, striking dead center as facing you, should stun the cue ball on this shot.

Figure 8.4 shows the impact moment of the stroke of Figure 8.3 and the pre-visualized contact point for the balls.

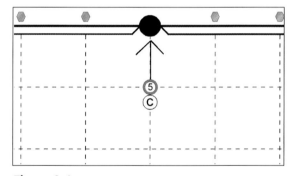

Figure 8.4
Cue ball at impact.

Diamonds Are Still Forever

If the 5-ball misses the pocket entirely, it's time to have a friend check your cue alignment to the shot from all sides. Alone, you can use the diamonds of the table to check on your straight stroke (see Figure 8.5 and the section "Diamonds Are Forever" in Chapter 6).

As shown, you may check the tip's movement or else align the cue along three table diamonds or a rail to check the straight motion of the length of the cue stick.

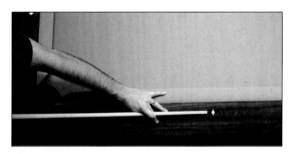

Figure 8.5
Aligning with a diamond.

The Aim Line

THE FULL HIT IS UNIQUE in that the *shot line*, the path the cue ball takes from cue tip to impact, is a continuation of the *aim line*, the path the object ball follows to the target. Other shots send the balls in divergent directions.

Stunning the cue ball with skid will become an important tool in your game. Let's consider a few shots where the cue ball will escape, going to one side as the object ball goes the other direction.

Expert's Aim Line

On any shot where cue ball and object are aligned with the dead center of a pocket, a full hit will sink the ball. More than 99% of pool shots require aim adjustment, however, some angle made between the straight shot line and the straight aim line.

How does the pro aim any ball into the pocket? He begins with determining the advantageous path the ball will take *inside* the pocket.

The amateur plans for the *back* of the ball to strike the back of the pocket. The expert aims the *base* of the ball to cross the middle of the pocket *opening*.

I can't see where the base of the 8-ball touches the cloth but it is directly opposite the top of the ball. In Figure 8.6, I hold a cue stick above the ball's top to aid my visualization of the aim line. I'm using an open bridge to prop the stick above the ball. If the stick touches the ball, a foul is incurred and my turn is forfeited.

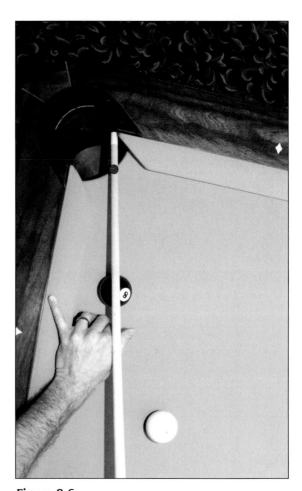

Figure 8.6
Aiming true.

My stick is extended to cross the middle of the pocket opening (marked by a red dot in Figure 8.6).

The Pocket Is a Mouth

From my perspective behind the aim line, the 8-ball will enter the pocket from its left side, cross the middle of the pocket opening at its *lip* where the ball falls into space to land somewhere in the right side of the pocket.

Think of the pocket as a mouth to swallow shots. The 8-ball will contact the pocket at its *jaw*, the straight diagonal edge of felt meeting the black pocket itself.

Balls tend to rebound from the rails reflectively at angles equal to the angles they enter, including the rail jaw. By playing the pro side of the pocket, the jaw, which frustrates the beginner by blocking shots from falling, helps the expert bounce balls off the jaw to within the pocket.

The 8-ball need not go far and strike the right jaw near my cue stick's tip. A gentle shot would simply tumble off the felt at the pocket's middle.

PLEASE BEWARE

The *aim line* is the plotted line of travel for the object ball. The *shot line* is where the player will place their cue stick and shooting hand to send the cue ball to impact. Don't confuse the two. The skilled player works backward, figuring the aim line first, then the shot line that brings the cue ball to impact.

"Pro Side" Explained

THERE IS ANOTHER ADVANTAGE to shooting balls into the pro side. I am considering the same line of play in Figure 8.7 as Figure 8.6. The two olive-colored circles are the same size as the 8-ball and represent how far to either side of the shot line I can miss but still sink the 8-ball.

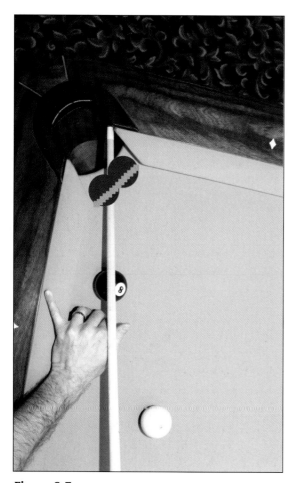

Figure 8.7
Room to wiggle.

The pink line in the illustration runs between the *jaw points* of the corner pocket, where the rails meet the pocket jaws. Past the olive circles, some edge of the 8-ball strikes a rail or jaw point and misses.

In other words, the pro side of this pocket is the aim line giving the 8-ball an equal chance of drifting left or right and still sinking. If the *base* of a ball travels past the pink line, it will sink if it has momentum.

Viewed from the player's perspective over the aim line, the pro side is the right side of the pocket. Any ball to the left of a pocket has a pro side on the right and vice versa.

Tournament pro, trick shot artist, or gambling hustler, the expert takes the best chance to sink the ball even if they miss the aim line. The corner pockets become effectively the same size, with the same width of opportunity, from anywhere on the table!

The pro side of any corner or side pocket:

▶ *is derived from an aim line that may be missed by an equal distance left or right and still work*

▶ *turns the pocket jaw opposite the shot from adversary to friend*

▶ *makes a fast-moving shot coming from the left strike the right side of the pocket or vice versa*

▶ *is easily calculated using a straight line from ball center to the lip of the pocket at its middle*

Half Ball Hit

There are pool terms in common use to describe select degrees of impact angle. One common shot is known as a *half ball* hit.

I'm aligning the equator of the cue ball marked by the red dot to the right edge of the 10-ball in Figure 8.8. If my eyes are above my right hand I am seeing a half ball impact.

Figure 8.8
A half ball look.

The half ball hit is frequent in pool, providing reliable, predictable ball paths, and may be aimed to sink a great many shots. The reference is handy, too—use the rightmost or leftmost edge of the object ball as the target.

On Edge

Figure 8.9 is a cue ball's half ball impact on a yellow ball, seen from the shooter's perspective behind the shot line.

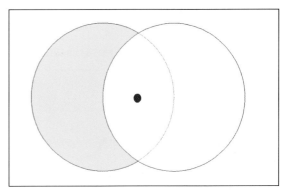

Figure 8.9
Shooter's view.

Cue ball center is aimed straight to the right edge of the yellow ball, making a "half eclipse." Note the center of the yellow ball also meets the edge of the white ball in this symmetrical shot.

Do the balls impact at their middle and right edge as used for aim? Unfortunately not, which is one reason why beginners have trouble with concepts of aim.

The impact is hidden from view at a point opposite the brown dot in Figure 8.7. The half ball shooter chooses to align as if half of one ball will actually touch half the other ball.

Five in the Side

Let's knock the five in the side again, this time from the right side of the pocket as taken from the shooter's perspective.

In Figure 8.10 the aim line, the shortest line between the 5-ball's center and the center of the side pocket lip is shown, with the pro side being the left side of the pocket.

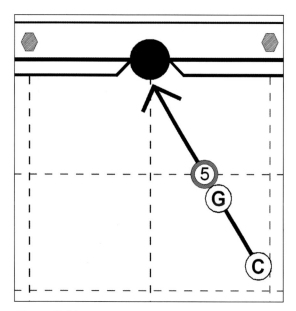

Figure 8.10
Full hit on the five.

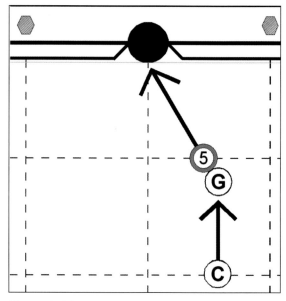

Figure 8.11
Half ball play.

The cue ball "C" makes a full hit on the 5-ball sending it into the side pocket. The ball marked "G" is the *ghost ball*, an imaginary ball players use to visualize the collision or "eclipse" between balls at impact. The player may send the cue ball to replace the ghost ball to sink the 5-ball.

The shot is similar to that of Figure 8.3 with an aim line the same as the shot line. What if the cue ball's starting position was not along the aim line?

Half Ball Shot

With the cue ball at the starting position of Figure 8.11, it still needs to contact the 5-ball in the same spot as in Figure 8.10. The *bottom of the cue ball must still be along the aim line at impact.* From the shooter's vantage point, however, this particular shot is a half eclipse, not full eclipse—a half ball hit.

The ghost ball remains the same in both illustrations. The shot line remains the shortest line to get the cue ball centered on the aim line at impact. At impact, we align the two balls' centers with the middle of the pocket opening.

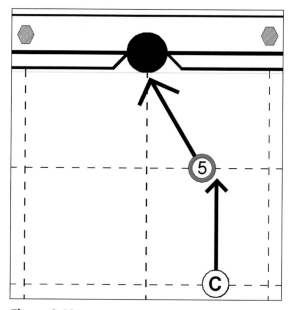

Figure 8.12
Aimed at the edge.

Figure 8.12 is the same shot as the previous diagram. Without the ghost ball, we can see that the shot line aims the center of the cue ball at the right edge of the 5-ball. The cue ball will *never hit that edge*, but the half ball concept makes a convenient aim guide.

TAKE A TIP

Recall that most every shot line is a straight shot, cue ball releasing from impact with your cue tip along a straight line. We can simplify object ball travel in the same way. In general, objects take straight paths following impact.

Measuring Challenging Cuts

I N FIGURE 8.13, I face the double challenge of a cue ball far from the object ball and an object ball far from the intended pocket in the upper-left corner. The shot is not a full hit, but is it a half ball aim or subtly different?

Figure 8.13
Judging 5-ball impact.

I am estimating the *cut angle*, the degree of eclipse or cover the cue ball will make on the 5-ball. Pool players talk in terms of cutting an object ball with a half ball or full hit or perhaps *thickly*, eclipsing more of the ball, or *thinly*, for less of an "eclipse."

As you mark the spot of impact in this manner, picture the ball rolling into the pocket down the aim line. Over time, you will rarely need to use the cue stick to aid your aim line visualization as I am doing.

Experts check the line with a stick when competition pressure runs high or their distance eyesight fatigues.

Figure 8.14 is the same shot as Figure 8.13. For an especially challenging play, take time to walk behind the intended pocket and rest the cue above the aim line. From facing the pocket as in the previous photo, however, I can better focus on the spot from the time I mark it to assuming my stance.

Figure 8.14
Visualizing the aim line.

Yes, the 5-ball as illustrated will require close to a half ball hit. Practice shots like this one with the cue ball closer to the object ball and return to long-range shots after you feel capable with the cut angle.

Quarter Ball Impact

The *quarter ball* hit is another cut term describing a common aim and providing players with a frame of reference.

Figure 8.15 illustrates a quarter impact on the striped 10-ball. When gazing down the shot line behind the cue ball, one-fourth of the cue seems to strike or eclipse (cover) one-fourth of the object ball.

Figure 8.15
Quarter hit.

Figure 8.16 is another look at a quarter hit. The cue ball is in the center of the illustration and probably would be centered in your vision at impact.

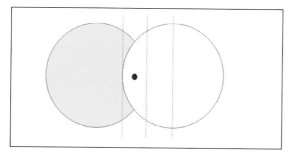

Figure 8.16
Quarter impact.

Besides the resemblance to the logo of a popular credit card, this hit brings an imaginary line on the cue ball's vertical axis, halfway between cue center and left edge, to meet the right edge of the yellow ball.

The three lines suggest imaginary quarters of the cue ball, and one-fourth of the cue ball eclipses one-fourth of the yellow ball. You were correct if you guessed that as with the half ball hit, actual impact on the spheres takes place at the brown midpoint where the circles intersect.

I consider quarter ball and half ball hits rarely in actual play (I shoot them but do not aim by ball sections). Sections are a frame of reference for us, however, because pool literature frequently labels shot diagrams with this terminology.

Many fine players divide the balls into these general sections and take the pressure off aiming to ultra-specific points of impact.

Where Does the Cue Go?

L ET'S USE A QUARTER BALL HIT to see what happens to the cue ball if it is *stunned*, skidding at time of impact.

Figure 8.17 shows cue ball "C" along a shot line parallel to the side rail. The 6-ball aim line is a dotted path between the base of the six and the pocket's middle.

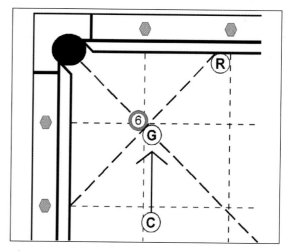

Figure 8.17
Quarter ball with skid.

The ghost ball impact on this quarter ball hit is represented with cue ball "G." "R" is the cue ball reaching the long rail. The 6-ball will sink in the corner, but how do we know in advance that the cue ball will travel to "R"?

Stun Principle

The 6-ball will be cut to the shooter's left as viewed from behind the shot line CG. The *stun principle* or "90-degree rule" states that a cue ball skidding at impact will travel along a tangent line GR perpendicular to the aim line.

On any cut shot like Figure 8.17 to the left of the shot line, the cue ball must rebound to the right of the same line (every action has an opposite physical reaction, see Chapter 6). If the cue ball has no spin at impact and is stunned, it travels a 90° tangent perpendicular to the aim line. Note the tangent line runs between the edges of the balls where they impact.

The stun principle works no matter the cut angle. If the cue ball impacts with stun, without rotating or revolving, it moves along the tangent line. The tangent and aim line are always easy to imagine as forming a right angle or corner.

Cut Speeds

Here's something as lovely and helpful as the stun principle. Recall that the full ball hit played with cue ball skid stuns or kills the cue ball in place, momentum transferring to the object ball. What about the half ball hit transfer of energy?

The *speed principle* states that ball speed following impact is in direct proportion to cut angle. A half

ball hit means the cue ball will retain half the speed after impact it had before, a quarter ball hit as in Figure 8.17 will retain 3/4 or 75% of cue ball speed following impact on line GR. A cue ball traveling 10 miles per hour that cuts about nine-tenths of an object ball leaves impact moving about 1 m.p.h., and so on for all percentages of cut.

Object ball speed is also estimated easily. Due to conservation of energy, the object ball gets the rest the cue ball didn't keep, half speed on a half cut, approximately 25% of cue speed on a quarter cut, etc.

PLEASE BEWARE

Don't be concerned if you do not fully grasp the stun and speed principles. You will see them clearly illustrated for the remainder of this book. For now, recognize the opportunity to predict the cue ball's path and speed based on the cut angle at hand. Predicting cue ball path and speed equals near limitless pool success.

Thin Hit

A *thin hit* takes some thin sliver or slice of the object ball with a cut, making a minor crescent of an eclipse at impact.

Figure 8.18 shows a glancing blow of the cue ball on the edge of the 10-ball. Since we know the 10-ball would move away from impact, compressing into the rail in this instance, we are approaching a 90-degree play. Much beyond this angle and the shot will become impossible to execute.

Figure 8.18
A thin slice.

This is a thin hit indeed. Beyond 90 degrees of impact, we would not impact the ball at all. There must be at least a partial eclipse to move the object ball.

As per the speed principle listed above, the thinly cut object ball will move much slower than the cue ball following impact. The cue ball, therefore, must move quickly to send a thinly cut object ball even a short distance.

Cut as Context

Before going forward, consider that Figure 8.19 is only half ball impact when the cue ball has traveled along the brown line marked "Half Ball." The *same impact* is instead a full hit if the cue had rolled along the green "Full" line. Aiming any cut is contextual, based on the path the shooter uses to impact.

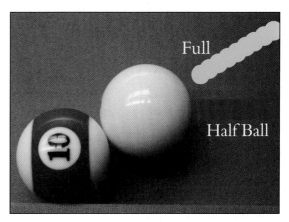

Figure 8.19
Half or full, depending.

Ghost Ball Adjustment

NEXT WE MUST CONSIDER when and how the ghost ball system will aid us for aiming. If you can grasp the next few concepts presented, you will be well on the way to pool excellence.

How Most Shooters Aim

Most beginners use a method of aim I am illustrating in Figure 8.20 using a real ball. I want to cut the orange 5-ball into a pocket, so I take aim at the ghost ball location, which is here represented by the striped 15-ball.

So far I've undergone the method I've recommended to you. Let's recap:

1. Select the ball and intended pocket.

2. Determine the aim line between ball base and the middle of the pocket lip.

3. Determine the shot line, the shortest line to get the cue ball centered on the aim line at impact.

4. Imagine the ghost ball at the end of the shot line and shoot the cue ball to become the ghost ball.

The imaginary ghost ball is a real 15-ball now. If a friend lifts it from the table without disturbing the 5-ball, I simply send the cue ball forward and make the shot, right?

Figure 8.20
Ghost ball becomes visible.

Here's the saddest issue with the ghost ball method—sometimes it works and sometimes it doesn't. Two main factors make ghost balls unreliable:

▶ at times, the ghost ball hit requires effort of will as it feels like the ball will be missed entirely

▶ the phenomenon of *throw* pushes balls off line

Let's address these issues in order and fix our aim accordingly.

Aim Point Miss

Figure 8.21 displays a classic case of not being able to reach the contact point directly.

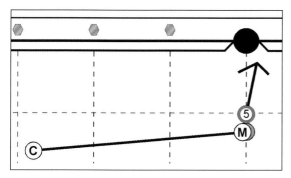

Figure 8.21
Swing and a miss.

You know the aim line from our first shots in this chapter. We want the 5-ball to go straight into the side. The typical shot line straight from cue ball to contact point, however, will bring the cue to strike the 5-ball at "M," for miss, before it ever reaches the blue ghost ball. See how the ball position at "M" almost fully eclipses the blue ghost ball? The little

sliver of distance between equals missing the 5-ball to one side of the pocket if aim is taken at the contact point along the shortest possible shot line.

In the photo sequence of Figures 8.22 through 8.24, I am sending the cue ball to impact the sighted contact point with all the skill and care I possess. Can you see how I will just fall short of the aim line in Figure 8.24?

Figure 8.22
Correct impact upon object ball.

Figure 8.23
Aimed at contact point.

Figure 8.24
Tragic mistake.

In Figure 8.25, you can see the actual position of the balls at time of impact. Compare this illustration with the ghost ball as depicted in Figure 8.22.

Figure 8.25
Actual contact.

Side Cut Solution

I've got to *overcut* the ball beyond the aim contact point by striving to replace the ghost ball instead. In pool, to overcut is to hit the ball more thinly, stretching a wider than typical angle between the aim line and shot line.

The beginner when overcutting this aim point feels as though they will miss the 5-ball entirely and indeed they usually do several times before clicking in a success. It's a thin cut for certain, and according to the speed principle, the 5-ball will trickle toward the pocket despite a fast-moving cue ball.

You need to pick the contact point for the 5-ball, then school yourself to shoot to its side a little to replace the ghost ball instead, cutting the 5-ball more than you've dreamt possible, or it won't sink in the side pocket.

At times, shots require instead an *undercut* adjustment, which is of course, to hit a cut shot more thickly or fuller than the contact point suggests. We will see an example of *driving* the ball in Chapter 9.

PLEASE BEWARE

The shot diagrammed in Figure 8.21 should become part of your practice routine immediately if you want to improve at pool (and sink side pocket balls to impress your opponents). This particular play or a similar angle becomes an opportunity several times in a single session of pool. Until you train your procedural memory to feel what is hard to see, you will miss the cuts you need to become proficient at pool.

Throw

ONE OF THE FRUSTRATIONS pool players share in common is the phenomenon known as *throw*, when balls cling together for an extra duration following impact, due to dirt, chalk, or humidity on balls or cloth. I say the balls "cling together," as that is the simplest way to predict resultant object ball path. In physical reality the balls are not impacting together for a longer time.

In Figure 8.26, we send the cue ball to ghost ball location "G" to sink the 5-ball in the corner. The next diagram, illustrating throw, will be a greatly exaggerated one.

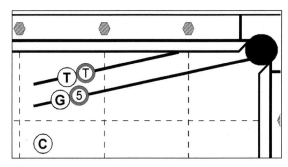

Figure 8.27
Exaggerated throw.

The cue and 5-balls have clung together and are marked with "T" for throw in their final positions before release. After clinging or throwing, the 5-ball will still travel a path parallel to its aim line. It has now been *thrown* off line. A shot aimed accurately and executed correctly was missed, the 5-ball hitting the rail and rebounding away instead of sinking.

Again, this illustration has been greatly exaggerated to show huge amounts of throw not present on the table. Even a few degrees of throw can ruin a shot, however, and throw can be as much as 5° off line.

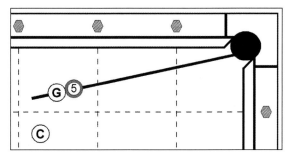

Figure 8.26
Understanding throw.

Imagine the dirtiest table and balls ever played for the exaggerated throw diagram of Figure 8.27. At impact, the balls have "clung together," stuck with dirt, chalk, and humidity (and my imagination) before releasing again.

Throw Adjustment

If a table or balls are dirty enough to cause noticeable throw, I simply roll the object balls a little slower, and watch impact closely. If the initial movement of the object ball following impact is on the aim line, the shot should succeed down the line.

Cutting the ball thinner on a cut like that in Figure 8.26 can help. The ball throws releasing with a shallower angle into the pocket.

With Little Throw

If the table's felt is clean and the balls just polished or washed, I am in for fun. I can cut most any ball without throw anxiety, slicing balls thinly and quickly into the pockets.

Pool experts also use *english* (sidespin) to all but eliminate throw error, spinning revolving balls into the pockets. I will demonstrate how the pros use english to counter throw in the next chapter.

Expert Aim

THERE ARE SEVERAL WAYS to stroke a cue and succeed, and it seems, a wide variety of aiming methods pool experts use to calculate ghost ball adjustments. Most pros fall into general categories, however, in how they sight the shot and compensate for the ghost ball and throw.

Most say they first learned the ghost ball method and then through practice and dedication, how to adjust the ghost ball method for shots that need a change. For example, when a top cash hustler or tournament pro misses a crucial shot in a match, they will revisit the shot in practice—200 times.

While there is no substitute for practice, let me make several recommendations so you see what they see at aim time.

Practice Missed Shots

You might not redo a shot 200 times, but you can take any missed shot in practice again one to five times, however long you need to sink the shot and record the successful aim in your procedural memory.

Repeating a challenging shot soon makes it a reliable shot, reducing anxiety at the table, which can only aid your fluid pool stroke.

Head Lowered

Some pros use the bottoms of the balls only in aiming while others urge players to "keep their head down at all times." Some stroke low with all practice strokes, regardless of how high on the cue ball they plan to make the final stroke. Some lean their head far lower to the cue than I do. Why are pros aiming and thinking "low" always?

I believe there are several possible reasons for this behavior.

► Head down forces concentration on the table, not on distractions outside the playing area.

► With head down at impact, the body was also lowered and did not jerk the shooting arm from the shot line.

▶ The base of the cue ball at address will become the ghost ball center, for those pros who aim by adjusting ghost balls.

▶ The actual contact point on the object ball is lower than it appears from standing above the table before bending to the stance.

▶ Eyes raised to see from a lowered head release the brain's function to make alpha waves, known to stimulate a relaxed but clear state creative visualization—some pros set head and eyes to get in "the zone" of enhanced performance.

Regarding the fourth bullet above, note that as you choose a place or edge for object ball contact from the standing position, the actual contact point needs to be slightly lowered at stroke time. Accordingly, shooters may find it helpful after head, body, and cue are in position to glance away from the object ball before focusing upon it again for the practice and final strokes.

Edge-to-Edge

Many of the best players start by learning the ghost ball method and then progress to some type of *edge-to-edge* aim system. They consider what edge or section (half, quarter, or an imagined slice) of the cue ball needs to hit what section of the object ball at impact.

I usually play edge-to-edge, aiming at a real ball instead of an imaginary ball. Those who play using a ghost ball have better visualization ability.

TAKE A TIP

One of the issues raised by the ghost ball system is its reliance on visualizing the cue ball's center at impact. You may use the top of the ball, its base, or its true center at the core. No matter how you aim, your ghost center is an invisible marking more than an inch distant from impact. When your focus changes to hit an edge, you aim at the actual object ball rather than an imagined ball in empty space.

Off the Runway

A challenging cut is presented in Figure 8.28, the 9-ball into the lower left-hand corner pocket. Think of the cue ball's path as an airline runway, with the cue ball an airplane increasing speed before takeoff.

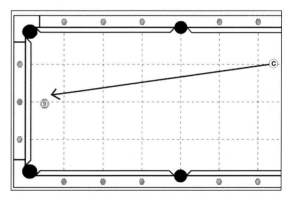

Figure 8.28
A long cut shot.

It's looking up and down the runway length that sabotages many beginners at aiming. The pro regards the cue ball and the object ball only. Distracting felt becomes ignored space.

As the beginner looks at all points up and down the runway, their eyes attempt to focus and refocus along the indistinct blue or green blur that is the felt. The shooting hand and arm may wander with the eyes as the brain tries to prepare the stroke.

In contrast, the expert looks only at the two balls, one at a time, shifting as needed. On the final stroke, only the 9-ball will be used for aim.

Object Concentration

Pool experts mentally mark a spot on the object ball (or edge or section or ghost ball) and then aim at it continually until they settle into their stance. The object ball becomes their whole world of vision.

You have peripheral vision. Use it with confidence. You can unconsciously see the cue ball and a distant intended pocket, bring both into play as needed.

I hardly look at my cue ball or cue tip other than a brief glance ensuring the tip is close to the ball before the final stroke. I regard the object ball and the first inches of the aim line, not needing to look at the pocket.

I concentrate so wholly on the object ball that it sometimes seems all object balls are the same size whether inches or many feet away. I have felt at times of peak performance that my stance was balanced at the object ball and not on my two feet, all of me striving to meet the balls together correctly at impact. Object ball concentration has an added benefit, the tendency to stroke through, not at, the cue ball with smooth motion.

Figure 8.29
Object ball focus.

Not the Drop

By all means, strive for precise impact with the object ball. Most pros look at the object ball last before the final stroke and until a moment after impact.

If you see an impact, you can learn from the result to become better at pocketing balls. But the moment impact is complete, or soon after, I change my focus to the cue ball—avoid watching the object ball drop in the pocket on cut shots.

Recall how when cutting an object ball to my right, the cue ball must diverge to my left and vice versa. So worrying over the aim line means I can never watch the all-important position of the cue ball for the next shot.

If you can sink each ball in its intended pocket and place the cue ball well for the next shot, you will never miss!

Plot the Cue Ball

In Figure 8.30, I use multiple balls as ghost balls to illustrate the intended path of the cue ball. I plan to shoot the cue ball to where the 8-ball rests now and sink the orange 5-ball on my left. The cue will travel along the perpendicular stun line to the rail where the green 6-ball lies, and out again on a near equal angle toward the 12-ball.

While I don't envision 14 ghost balls when I play, I do picture lines of travel for the cue ball on every shot and a landing spot for the cue ball.

This aim technique releases anxiety over sinking the object ball. I usually ignore the pocket during the stroke, and the corner pocket is hidden from view accordingly in this photo. I am thinking "send the cue ball to hit the edge of the five here (replace the 8-ball), and the cue ball will proceed to follow this line to the rail and out."

Not looking at the pocket and trusting my shooting arm, I increase confidence and can hear the object ball pocket or not to learn whether the impact was correctly aimed.

Figure 8.30
Visualizing cue ball path.

As a bonus, shooting object balls but not caring to watch them fall deflates my opponents. I enjoy banking or bouncing balls off the rails into pockets behind me, striding to the next shot before they sink from the table.

A Bit of Blur

Great pool shooters often reach career peaks later in life in their 30s and 40s, when table knowledge has grown, age has quieted a restless spirit, and some astigmatism has taken away the opportunity to stare down the object balls too much. I hit shots as well with weaker vision than before, and further trust edge-to-edge aim.

I've personally found the green 6- and 14-balls and the purple 4- and 12-balls tough to sight on precisely, and you may have difficulty with certain colors also. We can still make shots sending the cue ball to a general area.

You can eliminate color errors further through practice. Carl Oswald uses a set of 16 black cue balls to practice shooting dark object balls.

You might even want to aim some easy shots and then shoot them with both eyes closed to restore your confidence in your aiming.

Aim with Heart

The final word on pro aim technique may be the most important tip for you. The pool expert knows pool is more a matter for eyes and mind than a shooting arm.

In other words, subtle adjustments for throw and ghost ball error are best made letting the hand and arm bring the cue stick's tip to the aim of need, with a heartfelt but near unconscious level of concentration. Let it roll!

Think of the cue stick as an extension of your body. Do you need to tell your hand with a conscious verbal instruction how to toss a ball to a waiting friend, or do you toss it without thought?

Not Magic

Let me emphasize that I am not referring to a pro's wondrous hand-eye coordination (many are not enormously coordinated). I am referring to *your* ability over time with practice to make last-moment adjustments that sink shots.

Players get mired in worry over aim and throw (and deflection and english as in Chapter 9), so they grow unable to relax and perform their best. Meanwhile, a cue need not even be straight for pool! I've played intentionally with crooked cues and still made many shots. Think "I can bend this cue into impact if I need" and watch your pocketing skill increase.

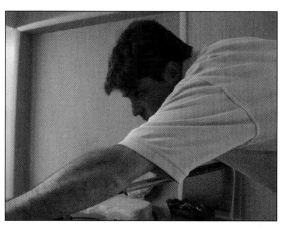

Figure 8.31
Head downward, eyes rolled up.

Aim Is Picturing Yourself

The left, logical side of the brain sends a cue ball instruction "a bit to the left," which the right brain sees reversed as "tfel eht ot tib A" along with some visual picture of choice. If you think, "A bit to the left or I miss!" the right brain tends to send the cue ball for that miss as pictured. Remember saying, "I *knew* I was going to miss...."?

I recall Hall of Fame shooter Nick Varner saying, "I pause long enough with my backswing so my fingers and arm make the shot without my thinking about it," a way of conceptualizing the need to aim then feel rather than obsess over trivia.

Take the aim techniques I've demonstrated in this chapter to the table, but on occasion sink a few shots by feel only without much conscious aim thought. Watch your confidence level improve.

Other Aim Techniques

SOME EXPERTS USE other aim methods you might find helpful.

On the Spot

A few top players use one specific spot on the object ball, sending the cue ball to that spot. I find my concentration wavers after a short duration of this method, but there are some who can do this for hours without tiring, even in intense competition. Most players reposition the ghost ball or aim edge-to-edge instead.

Measuring Lines

A few use their cue stick to guide aim, such as "I'll aim the right edge of my cue stick through the cue ball to the center of the object ball" and so on.

When aiming on the object ball, I find the cue stick can blur in my vision and does not make a reliable aim aid, but you might succeed with this method.

Measuring Tips

Some players use their cue tip as an aim aid, as in "I will aim at the center of the object ball, and then adjust my cue stick two tip widths to the left." Whether using the cue tip or cue stick to aim, it helps to have a personal pool cue (see Chapter 16) so the width of the cue does not change and alter your measuring system.

What if you change tables but not your cue stick, and the balls themselves are different sized than before? A tip or stick aim method could become unmanageable on different equipment.

Make This Cut

I STRONGLY RECOMMEND the following practice drill, which includes enough variety in stroke and speed to keep you amused. This exercise will benefit your game greatly.

Place any ball of your choice about one diamond's distance from both the short and long rails along one of the corner pockets. Place a cue ball at "C" or anywhere in the shaded box area in Figure 8.32. Keep to the inside of the dotted line so you can cut the ball in the pocket rather than hit it full.

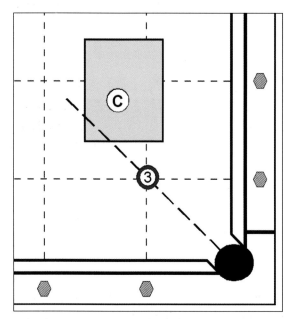

Figure 8.32
Basic practice shot.

Shoot this shot 10 to 20 times at different cue ball speeds. For the first tries, strike the cue ball center ball with your cue tip.

The 3-ball is aligned directly opposite the pocket's center, so there is no pro side to the pocket. You are looking to see how precisely you can make the ball in the pocket's middle.

Are you able to cut the 3-ball into the pocket easily? If you can pocket the ball with some regularity, are you able to *split the pocket,* making it in the true pocket middle each time, or do shots wobble in, off one jaw or the other? Pocketing this ball cleanly should become simple for you.

Observe how the balls cling together at impact for fractions of a moment before releasing again. There is always some degree of cling or throw, however minor.

What is the slowest speed you can put on the stroke and still sink the 3-ball? What is the fastest stroke you can make on the shot successfully?

TAKE A TIP

Stay encouraged even if you miss simple cut shots like this one. Impacting a simple shot at varying cue ball speeds and distances is far more important to study than difficult cut angles or even sinking balls. The more easily you can guide the cue ball and understand cue ball impact, the better your pocketing skills will become.

Above all, begin to plan your own aiming methodology with this drill. Are you comfortable with a ghost ball for this shot or not? Do you prefer some type of edge-to-edge or sectional aim instead?

Hard to Miss

Note there is some margin of error with the stroke of Figure 8.32. In Figure 8.7, we observed the safety margin of error at the pocket. Now consider the margin of error tolerable at time of impact.

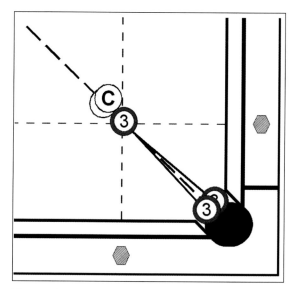

Figure 8.33
Margin of error.

The two cue balls, two lines of travel, and two 3-balls pocketed show the greatest possible misses to either side that still work.

The more precise your stroke and aim, the closer the 3-ball will come to dead center across the middle of the pocket lip.

Play the Cue

When pocketing the 3-ball becomes simple, do the same drill but see how accurately you can predict the landing spot for the cue ball, as shown in Figure 8.34.

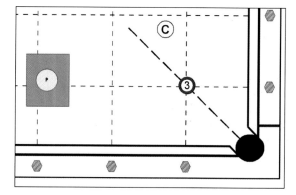

Figure 8.34
Landing targets.

The beginner hopes to land the cue ball on any given shot within some vague area. The intermediate should be able to send certain shots to land on a sheet of paper (the blue box in this diagram).

TAKE A TIP

Take an actual sheet of paper and move it to all parts of the table as a cue ball target for this shot.

The strong player looks to play cue ball position within the space of a six-inch circle (the yellow circle), the pro a spot the size of a quarter (the letter "P" inside the yellow circle)".

If you tire of using this shot to sense impact with the 3-ball or position the cue ball, use this angle to warm up cue ball speed, sidespin, rail play, etc.

Incorrect Mechanics

IF YOU STILL HAVE TROUBLE pocketing simple shots like that of Figure 8.34, review basic stroke and stance as outlined in Chapters 5 and 6 and watch the same chapters on the companion DVD.

Let's be honest, pool players miss due to nerves, the dreaded choking that athletes refer to when tense, even panicked, lacking calm focus. Forget the pocket for now and visualize the cue ball path instead.

I find I remain as calm over a long, challenging shot as a simple cut. I can only get tired mentally at the table from thinking about strategy, not physically from nervous tension and muscle clenching.

Aiming Like a Champ

Did you know that nine of ten pool players do not know basic pool aim principles? In this chapter of *Picture Yourself Shooting Pool*, we've fully begun to explore pocketing balls—the heart and soul of the game.

Let's review briefly the main keys that experts use to aim. The best pool shooters:

▶ build aim backward from pocket to cue ball, starting with the aim line reaching to the pro side of the pocket before tacking on the cue ball's shot line

▶ use ghost ball imaging as a starting point before moving the ghost ball or sectioning balls or aiming edge-to-edge

▶ settle into stance and take practice strokes and final stroke aiming at the object ball

▶ adjust for throw and other factors by trusting hand-eye coordination to bring the balls on line

▶ focus on impact to evaluate every shot before turning to watch the cue ball

▶ may keep their head low and eyes tilted up to lock out distractions and calm the mind

Moving On

I T'S TIME TO CONGRATULATE you on having learned much about pool. I am confident that your game has increased significantly since we began.

Chapter 9 includes dazzling shots as we discover how to bend, bank, and spin the cue and object balls. Opportunities to sink tough shots and awe fellow pool shooters await you.

Master Moves: Guiding Your
Cue Ball

Spin, english, and choice

"*LOOK AT THAT GUY—can't run six balls and he's President of the United States.*"

—Top hustler John "Johnny Irish" Lineen on Richard M. Nixon

You might not become president of your country, but I can show you how to run six or more balls. In the game of Straight Pool (see Chapter 14), experts often play "ten or no count" and do not score any balls pocketed unless the shooter has made at least ten in a row without a miss. Dick Lane, a professional shooter from Dallas, Texas (not to be confused with Hall of Fame footballer Dick "Night Train" Lane), has been known to play 100-point no count!

To pocket more than a ball per turn, you can be lucky or learn to position the cue ball, directing it to move into place. Experiencing play as if a magnet is beneath the table, dragging the cue ball to the precise spot you want it for the next shot, is one of the greatest thrills that pool offers.

Without exception, pool winners have pocketing skill, but champions also have superior cue ball position skill, as taught in this chapter.

Stop the Cue

TAKE A TIP

Now that you understand basic aim principles (see Chapter 8), this chapter will
serve as a companion to Chapter 7,
"Adjust as Needed: Pro Stick Moves." This
chapter plots the path of the cue ball,
while Chapter 7 can aid you in executing
the strokes as diagrammed.

M UCH OF GUIDING the cue ball
involves planning ahead, consistently
choosing wise sequences to remove the
balls from the table.

A simple way to run multiple shots is to seek *stop
shots*, where the shot line and aim line are one.
You get the greatest power of choice when receiving *ball in hand*, the ability to place the cue ball
where you like at the beginning of your turn. How
might you place the cue ball for Figure 9.1, as you
must shoot the object balls as they lie?

I've illustrated a simple way to run the 4-, 5- and 2-
balls, all with stop shots. You could place the cue
ball as indicated and shoot it on three successive
full hit strokes to positions A, B, and C, sinking the
four, five, and two in that order. As mentioned in
Chapter 8, the full hits made are easy to aim and
require no ghost ball adjustment.

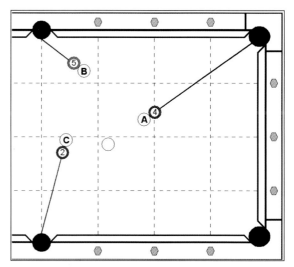

Figure 9.1
Three stop shots.

TAKE A TIP

I'm not implying that my sequences are
the way to run a table. In fact, a good
practice drill is to create three methods of
accomplishing any sequence before com-
mitting to one for play. How can you
improve this sequence?

Playing Stop

S TOP STROKES, IN GENERAL, take place at the cue ball's equator or below. Figure 9.2 diagrams a center ball stroke. The cue tip strikes the edge of the ball facing the shooter at the intersection of its vertical and horizontal axes.

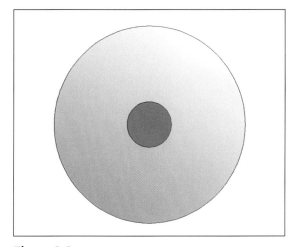

Figure 9.2
Center ball hit.

A level strike through the middle of the cue ball sends it skidding along the surface of the table—at least for several inches until friction against the felt causes the ball to roll instead of slide.

A skidding (sliding) cue ball is stunned upon impact with the object ball. A center ball stroke will provide this stun action over a short distance. What about stopping the cue ball over a longer distance?

Stop from a Distance

In Figure 9.3, you plan to stop the cue ball dead in its tracks after it impacts the purple 12-ball. A gentle center ball hit wears off, and the cue ball will be rolling when it strikes the twelve. Fortunately, there are three techniques for halting a cue ball over a long-distance shot:

▶ aim lower on the cue ball than its center

▶ hit the cue ball harder

▶ aim through the "magic spot"

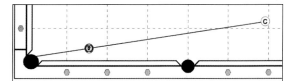

Figure 9.3
Long stop.

Lowering Contact

By aiming to stroke somewhere through the cue ball below center, you play a draw stroke, providing underspin to the cue ball. Tip contact anywhere below the horizontal axis of the cue ball provides draw spin.

A forcible enough stroke will create just enough backspin to erode over the felt so that at impact time, the cue ball is skidding again.

I recommend setting the shot as illustrated and trying to sink the 12-ball with the cue ball as pictured and over varying distances, as well. You will know if you did not get enough draw action on the shot when friction erodes past skid to create overspin (a rolling ball). The cue ball will finish beyond the 12-ball's position.

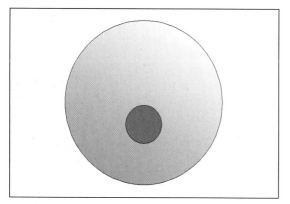

Figure 9.4
Some draw.

Hit It Hard

You can simply hit the center ball shot more forcibly to create extra skid distance. Experiment to learn how hard and how far you can stop straight-in shots. Skid will last for several inches along the shot path. Therefore, there is some speed flexibility with this stop stroke.

You will discover that for better results, you both lower the tip aim on the cue ball and hit the ball faster and perhaps harder. I use the term "hit the cue ball" rather than "stroke through the cue ball," because with this drill you are learning to alter the ever-fluid stroke to create a bit more punch with the stroking motion, a bit of a hit or pop on the cue ball.

Keep your aim focus on the object ball, however, during the actual final stroke.

Magic Spot

I was privileged to have world champion Nick "Kentucky Colonel" Varner share with me his tip for stopping a straight-line shot over any distance. Aim the cue tip to strike roughly between the center of the cue ball and its absolute bottom (see Figure 9.5). It's just one of those marvels of pool physics that it works. Thanks, Nick.

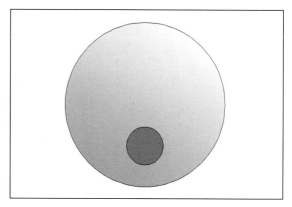

Figure 9.5
Magic!

Your shooting hand may be lifted, if slightly, to provide the cue ball somewhat of a glancing blow from the cue tip. Taking a cue far above level can cause all sorts of problems over a long-distance shot.

Think "Precision"

For any full-hit stop shot, visualize the result before you stroke. Will the cue ball stop dead in its tracks or rebound off the cue ball, coming back half an inch? Will it roll into the object ball instead before sliding further forward?

Considering subtleties of cue ball position vastly improves your concentration and results. You will need to be as accurate as an inch or two many times to win.

Stun Principle Revisited

BEFORE WE MAKE the cue ball dance, let's review the critical principle of stunning the cue ball. It is the key factor unlocking myriad cue ball possibilities.

In Figure 9.6, I am confronted with a difficult cluster of three balls I want separated. I am playing a center ball stroke into the red 3-ball.

By Figure 9.7, I have completed my stroke and the 3-ball is disappearing into the confines of the bottom left-corner pocket. The cue ball will gently bust the cluster, separating the balls for upcoming shots.

Figure 9.7
Trouble repaired.

Figure 9.6
Trouble.

It's 90 Degrees

It's always 90 degrees in pool land. I'm not thinking of temperature but the 90-degree tangent the cue ball follows if stunned at impact.

Figure 9.8 is the same stroke as Figures 9.6 and 9.7 in diagram form. Starting with a cue ball at "C" and sending it to ghost ball position "G," the stunned ball travels to position "B" to break the cluster. *The stroke I used to sink the 3-ball was the same center ball hit I'd use to stop a full hit from the same distance.*

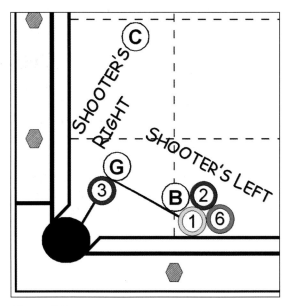

Figure 9.8
See the box.

Don't think I used calculator, slide rule, and PC to plot this stroke. I simply noticed the aim line for the 3-ball implies a tangent line to send the cue ball into the cluster if and only if it was stunned.

If you can see the aim line and cluster break line together forming a "box corner" like the edges of a cardboard rectangle, you are on your way to mastering cue ball play. Tangent line, 90-degree rule, or stun principle, whatever you wish to call it, it's the most vital concept in positioning the cue ball.

I knew the 3-ball and cue ball must take divergent paths. The 3-ball was cutting to my right (viewed from behind the shot line), so the box corner line, the tangent line, must point to my left. If an object ball goes one way, the cue ball must take the other per Newton's law of opposite reaction, or energy following the path of least resistance.

When a cue ball's obvious tangent helps the shot succeed for position, it is said to be a *natural play* or *natural angle.* Choose the natural play where you can—it is often the easiest.

TAKE A TIP

When discussing one's right or left side in pool, these terms are always absolute. Whether you shoot pool right- or left-handed, direction is always taken from the perspective looking down the shot line behind the cue ball. Hold up the diagram in Figure 9.8 and turn it about until you can picture yourself behind the cue ball, making the same shot and sending the 3-ball right and the cue ball to your left into the cluster of balls.

Cheat the Pocket

A FUN WAY TO MANIPULATE the cue ball is to intentionally use the tolerable margin of error by design. Risking a smaller margin of error play to change the cue ball path is known as *cheating the pocket.*

The 11-ball and cue ball should seem familiar in their positions in Figure 9.9. In other circumstances, we would play a full hit and probably stop the cue ball. Here, we wish to send the ball to our right so we choose to cut the 11-ball to the left (remember right and left are relative to our position behind the cue ball).

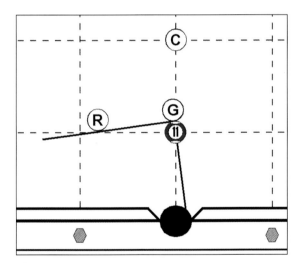

Figure 9.9
Cheating the side.

The 11-ball has enough room to go in the left side of the pocket. Sending the cue ball a bit to our right to "G," the cue ball is then destined to travel the tangent line toward "R" *if it is stroked the same way as a full-hit stop shot from the same distance.*

Do you see the box corner formed by the 11-ball's path and the line the cue ball will travel? Every adjustment to the cue ball path involves progressing from the tangent line as our frame of reference.

With just the cue ball and eleven as pictured, did you know you can send the cue ball anywhere on the table, simply by cheating the pocket and stroking follow, stop, or draw at varying speeds?

Cheating is handy at a side or corner pocket alike. How far from the pocket can you cheat the object ball? If a ball is much more than a foot from the pocket, even the expert treads with care.

Cut or Drive?

ADDING TO THE STUN principle is our impact speed principle (see Chapter 8) that has ball speed after impact in direct or inverse proportion (depending on whether you are considering the object ball or cue ball) to the degree of cut angle. A cue ball traveling 20 m.p.h. sends the object ball it quarter hits at 5 m.p.h. while retaining about 15 m.p.h. of speed. The $1/4$ of speed goes to the ball cut one quarter, while the remaining 75% stays with the cue ball.

You can often *drive* an object ball by cutting it thick and thus alter ball speed and direction.

Figure 9.10 presents unobvious cut angles on the 6-ball. From the cue ball position, you can consider ghost ball "G," which will hit the 6-ball thick, *driving* it in the side pocket or another shot line to the purplish ball behind G, cutting the 6-ball thinner, across the middle of the pocket. Can you see both box corners formed by the four lines in this diagram?

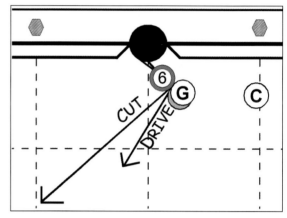

Figure 9.10
Speed choice.

The opportunity to choose some degree of angle between thick drive and thin cut comes especially with balls close to the pockets. The beginner who is locked into the typical aim line misses an easy way to manipulate the cue ball.

What a variety of shots to please pool shooters! First, we learned to aim for the pro side of the pocket consistently, but now we've chosen to avoid the pro side to work the cue ball. Both choices were straight strokes but with different shot lines.

Draw the Cue

W E CAN USE STUN to visit many parts of the table, but draw shots make pool plain fun. Draw in pool is bowling's strike, golf's 300-yard drive, and baseball's home run; draw gets players excited about its mystery backward action and deep table curves. On a drawn full hit, the cue ball hesitates for a dramatic moment as impact reduces momentum before rolling back toward the cue stick again like magic.

As a refresher on draw, let's watch the cue ball action in Figures 9.11 and 9.12. Review the slightly up-to-down draw angle of attack as outlined in Chapter 7 if you need.

Figure 9.12
Draw delivered.

Figure 9.11 is the set for the draw stroke. The tip all but touches the cue ball to heighten accuracy of strike as I will play a full hit on the yellow 1-ball into the side pocket.

I plan to hit the cue ball near the spot illustrated in Figure 9.5. Much lower and I risk a miscue, the white ferrule hitting the cue ball and scooping it into the air.

Recall that my bridge hand will stretch, lowering the cue so that I need not lift my forearm much from the elbow, which can ruin the stroke.

Figure 9.11
Draw ready.

In Figure 9.12 the yellow ball is hitting the rear of the side pocket, as I have completed my follow-through. My cue stick shaft is flexible and slightly curves as the white ferrule slides along the felt. The cue ball spins away from impact and will hit my cue tip unless I lift my stick from the table soon.

A Bit More "Oomph"

If an object ball is six feet away or more, go slightly lower on the cue ball and hit it a little harder. Beware as clenching muscles on a forcible draw stroke can ruin the shot. The harder you strike at the cue ball, the more difficult it is for reverse spin to take effect because of forward momentum. My key mental image, therefore, is "smooth through the cue ball" on any strong draw stroke.

The draw stroke is also a chance to experiment with wrist snap. The cue stick's tip has no care for whether your wrist is rigid or flexing at impact, but a wrist move of less than an inch can help accelerate the cue stick with impunity. An ever-accelerating tip helps draw action immensely.

A good way to gauge your ability to draw a cue ball is presented in Figure 9.13. Shoot full hits into the 7-ball at varying speeds and different aim points along the cue ball's vertical axis. Your goal is to sink the 7- and 8-balls with a single draw stroke.

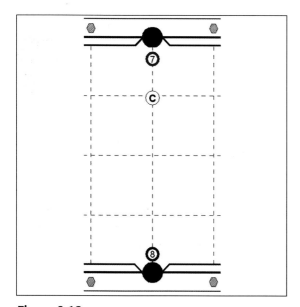

Figure 9.13
Draw test.

You can adjust the distance of the cue ball from the 7-ball based on preference and the need to lift the stick before the ball rebounds. If you can cross the table width about half the time you take this stroke, you are doing quite well with draw. The expert can draw a ball the *length* of the table or more anytime when needed.

Try the jab draw stroke, too, as outlined in Chapter 7, especially for strokes where the cue ball is relatively close to the object ball.

If you do not reach the 8-ball, take notice of whether the cue ball remained on the shot line. Drift to either side indicates some flaw in your alignment to the shot line or your straight stroke.

TAKE A TIP

Beginners tend to clench and add muscle when first learning draw, indeed a little added effort may help to learn the skill, but later clenching can dampen a silken stroke. In contrast, the expert may loosen his grip to begin his final backstroke and loosen still more just as the cue tip is about to hit the cue ball. This is one way that experts generate more power with less muscle effort than the novice.

Follow the Cue

HITTING A CUE BALL with follow (top-spin or overspin) can provide pretty, if sometimes humorous, results on the table.

In Figure 9.14, I am stroking through the cue ball higher than center. Hits anywhere above the horizontal axis of the cue ball impart forward roll or *topspin* to the cue ball with little or no skid.

Figure 9.15
Follow-through of stroke.

Figure 9.14
Follow stroke.

In Figures 9.15 and 9.16, the follow-through of this stroke is displayed. Again, my cue tip has come down a bit from the aim position as the cue stick was nearly level but slightly tilted in space high-to-low.

Figure 9.16
Toward disaster.

The humorous consequence of this lovely stroke is that the white ball will follow the full hit on the 3-ball to sink in the same pocket.

Play this same stroke on your table, again with various points of aim and speed.

Figure 9.17 shows a cue tip aim point about 70% to the top of the ball along its vertical axis. From this point, the ball has topspin immediately after contact. In actual play, a tad above center, perhaps 60% to the top of the ball, gives plenty of spin.

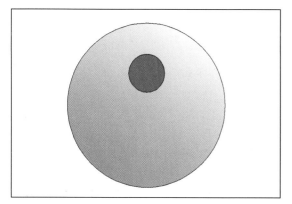

Figure 9.17
Immediate roll.

We are revisiting Figure 9.3 as Figure 9.18, a long, full hit on the twelve. You know that hitting a cue ball in the center or even below center, it eventually acquires topspin from friction. In this shot, it can even follow into the same pocket as the 12-ball.

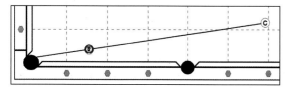

Figure 9.18
Natural topspin.

Natural topspin, follow via table friction, accrues quickly, so that many players make shots more complex by aiming for topspin when center ball would achieve the same effect.

PLEASE BEWARE

Beginners and even some experts believe wrongly that hitting as high as possible on the cue ball provides added topspin. Many shots provide natural topspin from friction. Top players hit about half their strokes with some degree of draw or "hold" to slow the cue ball, and most of the other strokes near center ball. Topspin aim is rarely needed.

Top Taps

Chapter 7 describes topspin variant strokes, including *British follow* and *rap top*, when the cue ball is hit much higher than usual to achieve special effects. Other than these atypical cases, the expert tends to stick to the blue tip area shown in Figure 9.19 for topspin, center ball, and draw.

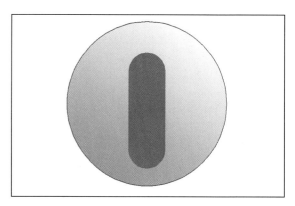

Figure 9.19
Vertical play area.

Dozens of conceivable tip positions are possible along this axis, but after trial and error, you will acquire some favorite specific aim points on the cue ball.

Draw and Follow Positioning

MUCH OF POOL takes the tangent line and shapes it to move the cue ball into position. You should, therefore, visualize up to three lines for a shot, including the:

1. *aim* line from ball to pocket

2. *shot* line sending the cue ball to impact

3. *tangent* line, which a stunned cue ball follows after impact

These imaginary lines follow repeating geometric patterns around the table. Soon you will recognize them in a second or less for any given shot.

Curves Ahead

Pictured in Figure 9.20 are sample effects of topspin or draw on less than full hits. The fern-like shape of the drawing is not to scale but a mere rendering of the visual image I bear in mind when spinning the cue ball.

The cue ball is hit into impact "I" to sink the 10-ball in the corner. The black tangent line if the cue skids into impact takes it toward the side pocket—unless spin is added to the stroke.

The red lines represent the effects of draw and the green lines, topspin. The shot curves a bit before finding a straight path again. On a half ball hit (not pictured), maximum draw sends the cue ball sideways, straight left or right of the shot line.

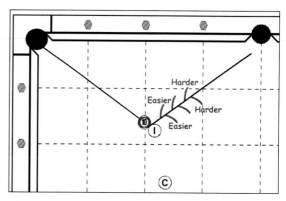

Figure 9.20
Bending the tangent line.

All paths are toward the shooter's right side since the 10-ball was cut to the left. The curves are somewhat symmetrical in nature. Two essentials should be remembered about draw and topspin at an angle:

▶ the cue ball travels along the tangent line, curves, and then rolls straight again

▶ the harder the cue ball is struck, the longer it travels the tangent line before the curve begins, and the shallower the curve will be

These are not the extreme curve massé shots in Chapter 7. The gentle curve appears as the cue ball transitions between the tangent line and the new line as spin grabs cloth. Like a pitcher's breaking ball or a bowler's hook, forward momentum erodes until sidespin begins to "take" and curve the ball.

Again, with time and a little practice you can calculate the specific cue ball path before any shot is taken. These curves will come in handy to amaze your opponents as you shoot the cue ball *around* an interfering ball.

This type of shot is invaluable, so don't practice only maximum topspin and draw!

TAKE A TIP

Remember: a drawn cue ball, hit full or not, tends to return toward the shooter, but a topspin shot tends to travel away.

Rails and Speed

THE RAILS OF THE POOL TABLE are cushioned with springy rubber bumpers to send balls bouncing off them back into play. Below are a few rules of thumb to understand the interplay of cue ball and rail.

Mirror Image

Reflection is a basic rail principle stating that a ball striking a rail at any angle tends to rebound at an equal angle. An approximation, this rule works for most practical purposes.

Table condition is important, too. Broken and worn rails make calculating angles tough, as they tend to be uneven in quality along their length with good and bad spots here and there.

Figure 9.21 shows a fun illustration of the reflection angle concept. The shooter pockets the 2-ball with a full hit draw stroke, bouncing the cue ball off the long rail then back across the width of the

table to pocket the 1-ball. Set the balls inside the middle of the pockets yielding easier angles for the full hits. Beginners who can reach the rail at all are doing well.

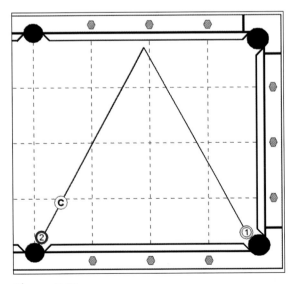

Figure 9.21
Bouncing back.

Note that the angled lines do not touch a rail at any point. Diagram lines display the base of the cue ball while the leading edge touches the rail. Another reason to think *edge-to-edge* when aiming.

Balls also come closest to exact rebound angles like this V-shaped path when they are skidding at impact. The ball must roll as it hits the rail in this illustration.

Drive or Cut the Rail?

Just as certain object balls may be cut or driven with thin or thick hits, the cue ball can be aimed on different angles into the rail.

The drive angle is marked in Figure 9.22 with a thick line. The cue ball "S" would be hit almost full into the rail. The cut line involves a more glancing hit against the rail by the left edge of the cue ball.

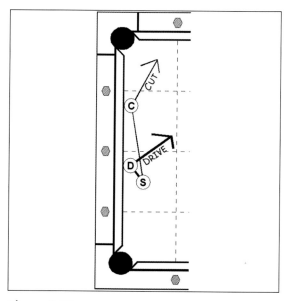

Figure 9.22
Cue ball choices.

For either shot, aim would be improved by plotting the course of the *edge* of the cue ball where it touches the rail, as cue ball *center* must be aimed beyond the actual rail contact point.

As with object ball impact, the cue retains more speed with the glancing hit than the thick drive into the rail.

Rails and Speed

Like Goldilocks' search for porridge, we are looking for something just right in Figure 9.23. In this example from the game of Eight-Ball, the opponent's 3- and 4-balls are blocking some of the shooter's paths to the 15-ball.

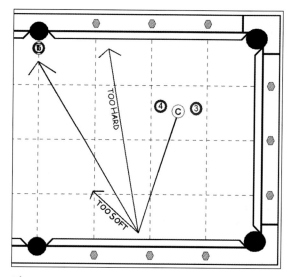

Figure 9.23
Speed control.

Too hard a stroke and the rail quickly and deeply compresses, springing the ball back on a tighter angle than the mirror angle bounce that makes the fifteen. Too soft and the ball turns a bit along the rail for a long moment before bouncing wide of the mark.

The best way to play the rail is to not anticipate the hit. Aim using the rail but ignore it on the final stroke so the follow-through is not halted in anticipation of impact.

Pick the rail impact point by aiming toward the bottom of the rail near the table felt. The rail top can create an illusion that the target is farther away than it is. Walk around the table if you need to calculate the mirror angle.

For any rail play, a fast, hard shot tightens the rebound but a soft shot widens the return angle.

Rails and Spin

Draw, like a harder stroke, tightens the rebound angle. Topspin (follow spin) widens the angle, as in Figure 9.24 (an approximation as these lines may have a bit of curve to them). If you have trouble remembering the rebound rules before shooting, visualize the action of the ball at the rail. Think of draw grinds or gears deep into the cloth, bouncing back straighter into the middle of the table.

Like draw or a hard stroke, humidity in the room also tightens the angles on a table. Let's sum up what we've learned about vertical spin before progressing to sidespin:

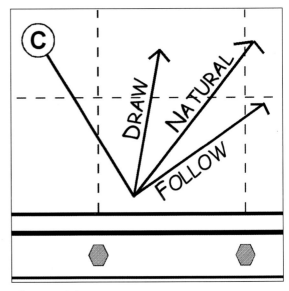

Figure 9.24
Spinning to a rail.

► cue ball path is calculated based on the tangent line created by a skidding ball traveling 90 degrees opposite the path of the object ball

► draw returns the cue ball toward the player; follow sends the cue ball beyond the tangent line

► thick impacts with an object ball or rail reduces cue ball speed, while thin cuts preserve more speed

Comprehending English

S IDESPIN OR *ENGLISH,* (the term is not capitalized in pool) whether intended or incidental to friction on the table, is a source of wonder to most people. Its effect is most noticeable on the cue ball, which can be made to curve dramatically, speed up or slow down after impact, and take wild turns.

Figure 9.25 shows our aim points using the circular cue tip against the cue ball for the vertical axis (blue, no english) and points adjacent where the tip can safely create english (in red).

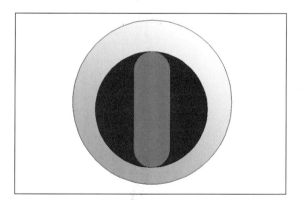

Figure 9.25
Points of english.

Any shot where the tip or a section of the tip strikes off the vertical axis provides sidespin. Shots beyond this red circle may be taken, but I recommend that beginners stay within its confines. The farther from the vertical a stroke is taken, the less mass there is to cushion the blow, and the more likely the player will *miscue,* slipping the tip off the cue ball.

Clock System

There are dozens of possible tip aims on the cue ball within our red circle, but pool instructors often refer to english using clock points of reference. The purple aim points in Figure 9.26 are with right english at 3 o'clock on the cue ball and left english at 9 o'clock.

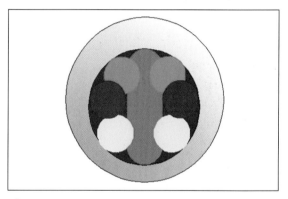

Figure 9.26
Around the clock.

The green points approximate 1:30 and 10:30; the yellow points are english taken at 4:30 and 7:30. You can go a bit lower with draw, as indicated, but there's no reason to stroke english high on the cue ball since it cannot add further topspin.

The purple circles represent english only, a pure revolving ball motion. The green and yellow points show sample places to combine either follow or draw (respectively) with english.

Pool shooters also refer to *tips of english*, such as "one [cue] tip of bottom right," which is the same as a suggestion to hit the cue ball at 4:30, with some draw spin and also some right english.

English Off Rails

Although english affects the paths of the object balls, the expert plays english primarily to manipulate the cue ball. On any one shot, one side of english is *outside* the stroke, also called *running english* or *natural english*, and the other is *inside* or *reverse english*. Outside English tends to speed the cue ball faster and widen rail rebound angles, but inside spin tightens angles and slows the cue ball.

In Figure 9.27 a cue ball will be shot toward the rail. When hitting a rail with a ball, take a line in your mind's eye to the side of the table you face. Right english will be outside english for shots played toward the right-hand side of the line and vice versa. The next diagram helps clarify this concept.

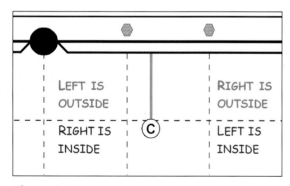

Figure 9.27
Off the rail.

Playing the Rail

Figure 9.28 shows that when pointing your cue tip toward the right at a rail, right english is running english, and left side english is inside english, pulling the cue ball more toward the original shot line or vice versa.

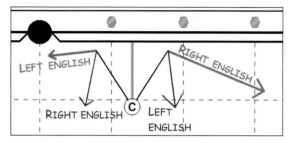

Figure 9.28
Off the rail.

Off an Object Ball

A common use of english is to enhance the cue ball's path off the rails of the table after it has already contacted a ball. There the rule is simple. *When cutting a ball left, right english is outside or vice versa.*

The pool shooter is cutting the 8-ball to his left and wanting to get across the table for somewhat of a full hit on the 9-ball in Figure 9.29. Topspin and right english on one stroke makes the shot easily. Bottom or draw spin and left english will ruin the position.

Try this stroke with and without topspin. Can you move the cue ball to the left so that draw will help flatten the angle to the 9-ball?

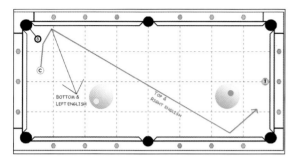

Figure 9.29
Opening the angle.

TAKE A TIP

Note that in Figure 9.29, the paths are one and the same until after the cue ball has struck a rail. For practical purposes in most cases, consider english as affecting the cue ball only after rail contact has been made. Follow and draw will take effect before rail contact, but in Figure 9.29 are presumed to be equal in measure.

Let's review cue ball action before we see how to stroke english. In general:

▶ use the choices of draw, inside english, and harder strokes to tighten cue ball angles off the rail

▶ follow, outside english, and softer strokes widen the rebounds off the rail

▶ draw and follow bend a cue ball away from the stun or tangent line, but english has little effect until after a rail comes into play

Three English Strokes

FINALLY, WE'LL CONSIDER three methods you can use to add sidespin to a cue ball before moving to key shots taken around the table. Three ways that players generate english include:

▶ parallel english

▶ pivot english

▶ carabao english

Parallel English

Applying english becomes simple using the parallel system. Address the cue ball along the shot line as normal and add any desired topspin or draw aim along the vertical axis. Then move the bridge and shooting hands both to create a line parallel to the shot line.

In Figure 9.30 I begin the stance for parallel eng-lish. I set the cue for the desired vertical spin first, in this instance, a center ball stroke.

I have moved the whole apparatus just about one inch to my right in Figure 9.31. Both the shooting hand and bridge hand have moved, keeping paral-lel to the original shot line. The bridge arm moves as one unit from the shoulder, like a gunbarrel on a swivel base. I could have moved more or less dis-tance depending on what degree of right-hand english I choose.

Figure 9.30
Center ball aim.

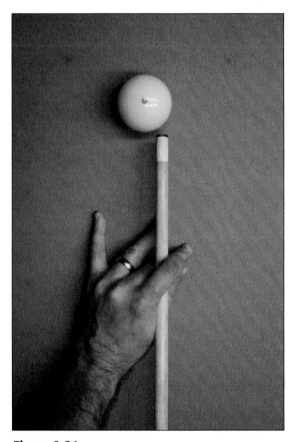

Figure 9.31
Right-hand english.

Through the Cylinder

It is important to finish the parallel english stroke along the same line where you aim. Figure 9.32 shows the cue ball as if it has been hollowed through.

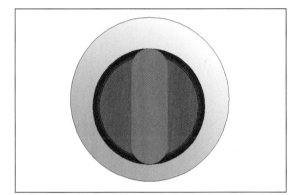

Figure 9.32
Through the cue ball.

When you play parallel english, think of the cue ball as a cylinder extending into space. Keep your cue stick along the cylinder until the end of your follow-through.

I have chosen left parallel english in Figure 9.33. The loop of my bridge hand with the hand moved a small distance from center ball to play this shot. By moving my shooting hand also, I've kept a straight stroke for this play.

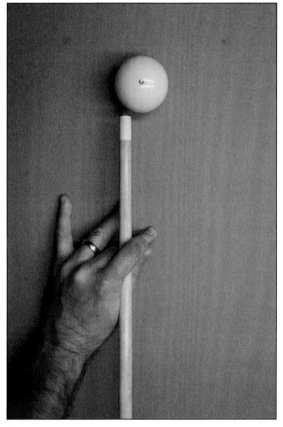

Figure 9.33
Left-hand english.

Deflection, a.k.a. "Squirt"

You are probably asking whether the cue ball will still travel the shot line being hit to one side or the other with a parallel cue. Pool players sometimes knock the ball off line due to *squirt*, the natural tendency of the cue ball to move opposite the force applied upon it. English applied with a cue tip edge causes the cue ball to deflect or squirt away from the shot.

With a parallel left english stroke as in Figure 9.33, the right edge of my cue tip, not its center, will strike the cue ball. Since the rounded edge of the cue tip faces to my right, the cue ball has the tendency to be pushed to the right, off line and missing the shot.

Pool players go to considerable lengths to avoid deflection, including purchasing shafts and cues tested to reduce squirt. We need not worry too much about the phenomenon of *sideways* cue ball travel if we maintain a near level cue, as squirt minimally affects most straight strokes.

If your cue is hoisted high in the air as warned against in Chapter 7, the ball will curve quite a bit along the table as seen in "Semi-Massé" and "Full Massé Stroke" in that chapter. If the cue is close to level, deflection is minimal, as most of the momentum is forward, and sidespin momentum is parallel to the table, effectively not pulling the cue ball sideways.

We'll discuss further, in Chapter 10, why the pros rarely worry about deflection and why you don't need to either.

Pivot English

A second way to generate english is to leave the bridge hand in place and pivot the cue stick through the bridge hand at an angle.

Beginners are able to produce lots of spin using this method, and it feels easier to stroke than parallel english. As shown in Figure 9.34 with pivot left english, however, since the shooting arm moves, the cue is off the shot line to the left ahead of the bridge and to the right behind it. The cue is pivoted fully off the shot line.

Figure 9.34
Left english by pivot.

I do not advocate the use of pivot english because with all but the simplest shots, it makes the shot line challenging to calculate. There is a third way, however, providing benefits of both parallel and pivot english with one stroke.

Carabao English

The term *carabao english* is derived from the Pidgin English spoken by the Filipino pool experts who have brought this stroke into recent prominence, though some Americans were known to employ the technique as long ago as the 1930s. The word *carabao*, also spelled as "karabaw" but pronounced "ka-ra-bao," refers to water buffalo—laminated water buffalo hide being a substance often used for cue stick tips.

Simply performed, carabao english is an eye-opener for most players. Address the cue with center ball aim along the shot line and on the final stroke forward, then swerve the shooting hand and stick so the cue tip strikes the intended spot for english.

As seen in Figure 9.35, despite the extreme left english with which I will strike the cue ball, near my shooting hand the cue is closer to the shot line than with pivot english.

My understanding is that in applying carabao, forward momentum dominates the stroke above the small swivel of english. The sum effect is carabao may be considered as a diagonally held cue stick with tip thrown mostly forward along the shot line. Pivot english, in contrast, is an entire stick plus tip pointed diagonally to one side.

Carabao players stake great claim on their method's ability to all but eliminate english deflection. While this technique remains controversial among pool's top players, it works well for my students. I am comfortable with it and with parallel english also, so feel free to try both methods.

Yes, there are players who aim center ball for all shots, using carabao last-second motion to apply draw and topspin, too. Try it and see if you like it.

Figure 9.35
Carabao left English.

Time for High Fun

You are well on your way to mastering ball movement, including cue ball tricks even some pool *hustlers* don't know.

Next we will have fun playing key shots to get out of trouble and plain show off, including pool kicks, combinations, and banks like you've seen made on TV and in the movies.

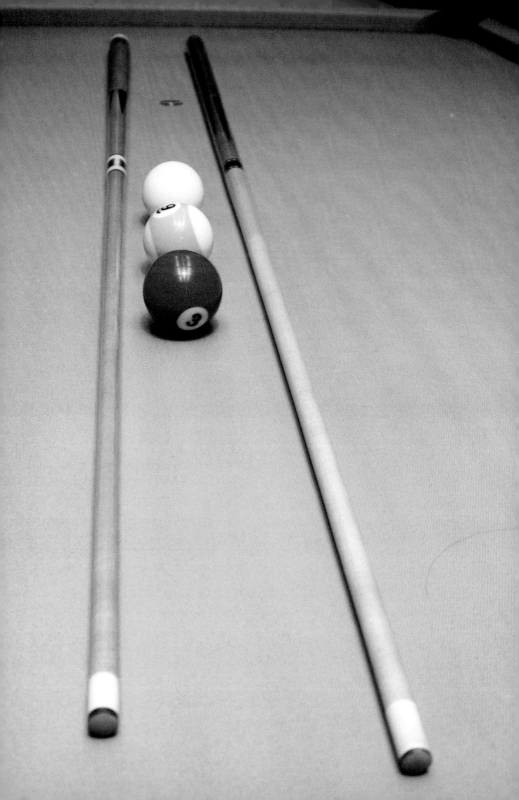

Tools of the Trade:
Key Shots

From rescue missions to grand explosions

10

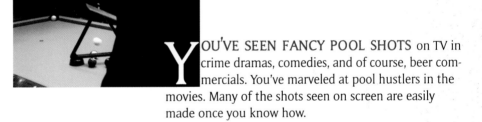

YOU'VE SEEN FANCY POOL SHOTS on TV in crime dramas, comedies, and of course, beer commercials. You've marveled at pool hustlers in the movies. Many of the shots seen on screen are easily made once you know how.

A small child could make many of the caroms, banks, and combinations in this chapter once you help them aim as illustrated. Take this book to your table and shoot the shots in this chapter—they are as fun to watch as perform!

These are also practical shots I resort to over and again when the cue ball or object balls find trouble and I lack clear paths to the pockets.

Combination Shots

WHAT POOL PLAYER hasn't dreamt of knocking a ball into another ball—into a ball—into a pocket? Two or more object balls may be shot as *combinations*, driving balls to one another with the final ball as the prime target. "Combos" plain look and sound cool when stroked. "Click-click-click," then the last ball drops.

Stand up taller on combination shots to better see the interplay between balls. You must calculate more than one impact for one shot. The experts aim combos backwards, as with all shots, starting with the intended pocket. A two-ball combo (as illustrated in Figures 10.1 through 10.5) is aimed in three steps:

1. Find the aim line bringing the final object ball to the pro side of the intended pocket.

2. Find a shot line for the first object ball as if it were a cue ball.

3. Use the first ball's shot line as your aim line to find the cue ball shot line.

Figure 10.1
Ready, aim.

Figure 10.2
Firing.

Figure 10.3
Two hits the three.

Figure 10.4
Follow-through complete.

Figure 10.5
3-ball sinks.

This three-step method is illustrated in Figure 10.6. Send the cue ball to ghost position "G" and it will drive the 1-ball to its ghost position at "N" to sink the 2-ball. You began by aiming the 2-ball to the pocket, then the 1-ball to strike as if it were a cue ball, then the cue ball into the one.

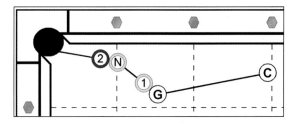

Figure 10.6
Two ball combo.

Remember that all works best if the 1-ball is close to skid when it collides with the two. Take extra time for precise aim on this challenging stroke.

PLEASE BEWARE

Margin of error increases exponentially as more balls are used in the combination. Separated balls have to be resting in fine position indeed to pull off the rare three or more ball combination shot.

Wild Stuff

Change your mind from standard ways of thinking about pool possibilities and enhance your game. In Figure 10.7, we use a cue ball as an object ball during a shot.

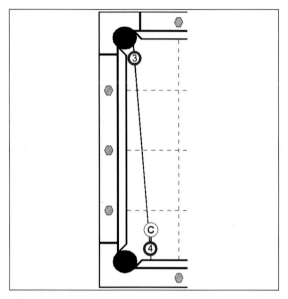

Figure 10.7
Backwards combination.

We may shoot the cue ball to make a full hit on the 3-ball into the corner pocket, but how about stroking the 4-ball to the rail to have it come back, hitting the cue ball as if it were in the middle of a combination on the three? Experiment and learn, but for this play, you probably want a soft stroke with draw spin.

Try this shot as diagrammed, since it may not appear often but the underlying principle will. *Cushion Billiards* players, who use tables with rails but no pockets, constantly use cue balls as targets and combination balls. Many of pool's greatest champions were billiards players at some point in their career, which greatly enhanced their pool problem-solving skills.

English Combos

ENGLISH OR SIDESPIN affects the object ball and cue ball both and can become vital to our combination plans.

We reviewed the effects of english on the cue ball in Chapter 9, learning sidespin cannot substantially alter the path of the ball until it contacts a rail. English noticeably alters the path of an object ball immediately, however.

Think of any ball collision as two balls gearing against one another, and you will be able to visualize results to anticipate from impact. A cue ball with *right english imparts left english to an object ball* from the gear effect and vice versa.

In Figure 10.6, hitting the cue ball with left english would send the 1-ball with right english into the 2-ball, which would have left english following impact. Sidespin cannot be transferred down long chains of object balls, so transfer need only be calculated for the first ball in most instances. We will see about applying english again with our next key stroke, a *frozen cluster* shot.

Cluster Shots

WHEN BALLS CLUSTER together, the many collisions can make it frustrating to determine lines of travel. We are always looking for *dead clusters*, balls aligned at rest in convenient positions.

A Dead Cluster

Remember working to sink balls in the side for much of the last two chapters? In Figure 10.8, the 15-ball that in ordinary circumstances would require judgment of a thin angle, is now easy, so easy that the expert calls it a *dead* ball.

In this *dead combination shot*, most any angle and speed of hit on the 5-ball will send the 15-ball into the side pocket. The 5-ball becomes the cue ball in this combination and, happily, is *already positioned on the 15-ball impact aim line*. The 15-ball would need to be thrown a tremendous distance to miss.

In contrast, some clusters require english to be thrown into sinking position.

Figure 10.8
A dead combination.

Dead Set Advice

Coming in from an angle to one side, as in Figure 10.8, the fuller you hit any *frozen cluster*, where the balls rest touching like the 5- and 15-balls, the greater the tendency to throw the shot off line. Shoot a glancing blow on a dead combo when it is far from the pocket.

Cluster with English Shot

Figure 10.9 shows the 11- and 12-balls *frozen* or touching one another. Frozen balls travel along the lines of centers, as we've seen a cue ball and an object ball do. The 11-ball as pictured will head along the aim line created by the 12-ball as if the twelve were a cue ball. The 11-ball will ultimately miss the corner pocket on its right.

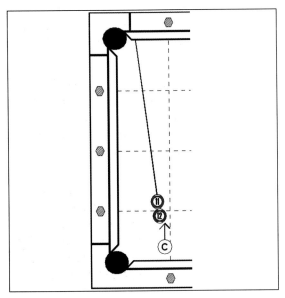

Figure 10.9
Frozen throw with english.

Once we understand that *balls with english throw an object ball in the direction opposite the english,* we can work backward to repair this line of aim.

We want the 11-ball to dance over to the left. Stroke the cue ball softly and with *left* english. The 12-ball receives *right* english, which throws the 11-ball to the *left* and into the pocket! The second object ball receives little english, but at times, every bit helps.

We stroke slowly as the less forward momentum, the more the sidespin can dominate the shot and enhance this english throw effect. We further enhance throw hitting the combo on the right-hand side of the cluster. This aim sends the end of the cluster, the 11-ball, so far to my left that spin will take little effect, and even a center ball hit will "throw" the object over far enough to sink.

Let's review what we've learned about english and cluster throw:

▶ A ball with english throws a ball it strikes in the direction opposite the english.

▶ English transfers from ball to ball, reversing direction each time, like gears turning one another.

▶ A small cluster of balls may be thrown to one side by striking it on the opposite side.

All three of these throw rules suggest opposites as every force experiences an opposing force (see the physical laws listed in Chapter 6). Left english becomes right english on the object ball; left english throws an object ball to the right, while a cluster of balls struck on its right side slides to its left. Another illustration may help fix these principles in mind.

Throw Stop Shot

The cue ball is aligned with the 2-ball in Figure 10.10 such that you can make a full hit and halt the motion of the cue ball. Add some left english and the 2-ball is thrown to the right, sinking in the corner pocket. Experiment with speed and you'll soon learn that the slower the stroke, the more the english throw is enhanced.

You may elevate the cue stick to further enhance the throw effect. I raise my shooting hand *slightly* for this stroke.

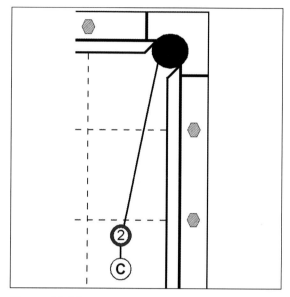

Figure 10.10
The thrown ball.

Again, these illustrations are not to scale but are illustrative of sound pool principles.

Thrown Cut Shots

This next concept shot may prove the most important of the chapter for you, since it affects every shot. Now that we've explored throw and english, it's time to tackle one of pool's thorniest problems, throw's affect on every pool stroke taken.

The Battle Rages

All pool balls, like all objects in our physical world, are subject to immutable physical laws including those discussed in Chapter 6. Vehicles in collision compress against one another and cling together before yielding and crushing. Resilient pool balls cling, throw, slide, and transfer spin at impact, but being resilient, go on their merry way rather than crushing. (At least most of the time. I've shot hard at cheap clay balls before and had them break in half, with only one piece entering a pocket. I was unsure whether I scored half a point or not!)

Some pool experts are certain that *throw*, the tendency of balls to leave the aim and shot lines at collision, occurs on every shot. Others say throw itself is myth. Who is correct, and why are there arguments even among pool's best?

You can see balls cling together on any stroke taken slowly enough. I *want* to see the balls throw together for a moment if I am seeing the object ball traveling the aim line on its way to the pocket. The balls do not physically cling together, but this is the simplest way to visualize and predict throw-altered paths.

A fine experiment to test the reality of throw was conducted by pool teacher Bob Jewett, who suggested placing three balls in a fashion similar to what I've arranged in the next two photos. Jewett confirms what pool shooters with physics education know—throw is real.

Figures 10.11 and 10.12 illustrate a three-ball cluster perfectly aligned to sink the red 11-ball in the distant corner pocket. The table is level, the felt is clean of debris, the balls are clean, and the cue tip adequately chalked.

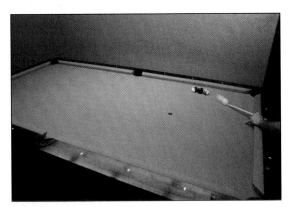

Figure 10.11
Three frozen balls.

Figure 10.12
11-ball throw is partly factored by speed.

With both the 13- and 8-balls along the aim line into the center of the corner pocket, the 11-ball should find the pocket every time. It does not, especially as speed of the cue ball is altered to a harder stroke, based on the reality of throw. Throw appears on a soft stroke, but in small enough degree to insubstantially alter the path of the 11-ball to the pocket. The 11-ball can be made to throw backwards toward the cue ball and strike the short rail to the left of the pocket in Figure 10.12.

The reason why certain experts do not believe throw exists is they subconsciously adjust for throw with their strokes (see "Aim with Heart" in Chapter 8 for more).

Anti-Throw Choices

I F IT WEREN'T FOR COLLISION throw and english-induced throw, an intermediate pool player might be able to run 100 balls or more without a miss. How can the shooter adjust for throw on every cut shot?

Shooting Harder

I am an advocate of shooting softly as much as possible to give balls every chance to find the pockets. Faster cue ball speeds create less throw on a single object ball, but it's impractical to shoot everything hard and fast, besides being destructive to a silky stroke motion.

Stay Level

Like harder strokes, a nearly level cue removes throw to some degree. While most strokes cannot include a perfectly level cue due to the table rails, keeping the butt end of the cue from lofting high in the air is easily accomplished with a freely hanging lower shooting arm (see Chapter 5).

Outside English

Pool experts know they must adjust the ghost ball for throw or shoot cuts with outside english (or both methods at once).

Figure 10.13 is an exaggerated diagram showing the effect of outside english. The cue ball cuts the blue ball to the shooter's right, along the green line. Outside english on a cut to the right is left english. Rather than clinging to the blue ball and pushing it off line, outside english makes the cue ball revolve and gear around the blue ball with minimal throw.

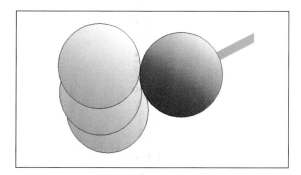

Figure 10.13
Outside english gears a ball.

Outside english tends to speed the cue ball, sending it longer distances with ease. Not only does the pro spin a ball to avoid throw, they get extra distance with the cue ball, too!

Anti-Throw Throw!

Before you rush to cut every ball with outside english, recognize that sometimes inside english or no english is demanded from a shot. Besides, english is a harder stroke to master than a vertical axis stroke. A third consideration is this—outside english throws the object ball, too, doesn't it?

Since outside english throws the ball inside the shot, the pro cutting a ball to his left applies right english *and* hits the ball more thickly than the center ball player, driving the object ball right to counteract the left throw of english!

Your head may be spinning more than a pro's cut ball from the last sentence, so let me sum up throw and anti-throw cut shots:

- ▶ Skilled shooters who play center ball learn to consciously or unconsciously cut balls more thinly than the ghost ball suggests.
- ▶ Skilled shooters who play outside english learn to consciously or unconsciously cut balls more thickly than the ghost ball suggests.

How Thick or Thin?

You may be asking to what degree the center ball or outside english player adjusts the ghost ball for any given shot. There is no rule to share because there are different english strokes, as shown in Chapter 9, each of which implies aim adjustment and deflection; and different cue ball speeds affect throw and subtleties of cut angle, etc.

The best advice I can give for cut shots is to practice at different angles and speeds. Certainly, get lots of vertical play accomplished before you tackle the addition of english. Most teaching pros recommend several months of pool with no english first.

What about the experts who say there is no throw ever? I humbly suggest that these players subconsciously overcut balls or add carabao english (see Chapter 9) to their stroke, a bit of swerve adding outside english at the last possible moment.

Your choice on cut shots remains—avoid english and its complications and get plenty of cut practice, or use english and still practice.

The Cluster Buster Shot

HERE ARE TIPS for separating a cluster at will, like the mess found in Figure 10.14. Before you stroke into a cluster, you'll want to predetermine the paths of the cue ball and each of the cluster balls.

Figure 10.14
Cluster to bust.

Consider Topspin

Topspin helps a cue ball burrow through trouble. Follow should not be played on a full break shot to begin most pool games (more on break shots in Chapters 14 and 15) but can help the cue to travel through a clustered pack. Perhaps some topspin applied could help the shooter in Figure 10.14.

Ralph Greenleaf, who dominated the sport through the 1920s and 1930s, could play so much topspin with his stroke that he could double drive clusters, sending the same cue ball spinning into the pack and away before it spun into the clusters a second time!

Contrary to widespread belief, sidespin does not better split clusters and only serves to confuse plans for clustered balls.

Consider a Jump

A bit of aerial maneuvering can help, as sometimes the player needs a jump shot to clear the edge of an interference ball and pocket a ball on the far side. A jumped cue ball can add a little power into a breakup play from above, too.

Luther "Wimpy" Lassiter, perhaps the greatest Nine-Ball player ever, was famous for jumping balls into the middle of troubling stacks to bust them apart.

Play the Tangents

In general, hit any two balls clustered together and one will go straight down their combined aim line, and the other will travel perpendicular to that line.

In Figure 10.14, striking the 6-ball directly with the cue ball should send it fractions of an inch down the tangent line to strike the 12-ball with the 15-ball sent straight away from the 6-ball into the rail.

Leave One

To fully separate a pack, you need only move two balls from a cluster of three, three from a cluster of four, and so on. You might stroke the cue into the 3-ball in Figure 10.14, clearing the 14- and 12-balls,

following which the three continues to hit the six and fifteen pack. The 6-ball might not move at all, and the other four balls will separate.

Seek Dead Combos

Examine any cluster carefully and once again if it is even slightly disturbed out of place by a passing shot. Check all six pockets for dead on combos as in "A Dead Cluster" earlier in this chapter.

Study String Theory

Set clusters on the table and then bust them apart. Before stroking, however, pick one ball from among the pack and estimate its path. Most players don't practice cluster shots, but besides looking dramatic when played for pockets, they often have easy possibilities waiting inside.

Carom Shots

A BALL DIRECTLY BLOCKED by another may often be pocketed using a *carom* shot, where the cue ball bounces off a ball as if it were a rail. Again, we may accurately predict the cue ball's path. We will go even a step further in the next photos and shoot an object ball to a carom with a second ball.

You can shoot the 9-ball in the pocket easily, as shown in Figures 10.15 through 10.17, if you know your tangent lines. The 9-ball is sent to meet the 6-ball where the two form a tangent line for the pocket. Let's take a look from above to clarify.

Figure 10.15
Aiming the 9-ball.

Figure 10.16
The 9-ball caroms off the 6-ball.

Figure 10.17
Almost home.

The cue ball and 9-ball are aligned so that a full hit sends the 9-ball to "G." At impact, the 9-ball and 6-ball have a tangent line to the pocket. If the 9-ball hits the 6-ball with stun or close to stun, it will sink.

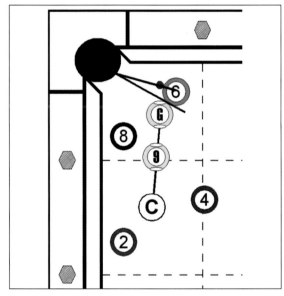

Figure 10.18
Two aim choices.

As advised earlier, most pool calculations are derived from stun tangent lines. Make sure your carom ball slides into the target ball.

You might be an old hand now at seeing prospective tangent lines; if not, I suggest an alternate carom aiming method. Aim the 9-ball straight into the purple spot representing the edge of the 6-ball closest to the pocket!

Kick Shots

KICKING THE CUE BALL refers to sending the cue off a rail before it touches any intended ball. You already know much about kick from your cue ball rail study in Chapter 9, but a practical application is presented in Figure 10.19.

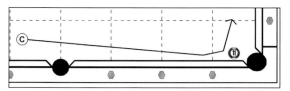

Figure 10.19
Short kick.

The cue ball is near straight onto the 11-ball, limiting cue ball possibilities, but a short hop off the rail knocks the 11-ball in the corner and allows less than a full hit, preserving cue ball speed.

A bit of outside english can help on this stroke. Indeed, if the object ball is within about a foot of the rail as the 11-ball is, measure the distance with fingers or cue stick from the edge of the ball to the edge of the cushion. Continuing along this line, count off the same distance from the cushion past the edge of the table.

Aim the center of the cue ball to that spot in space adjacent to the 11-ball, using medium speed and a tad of outside english. Experiment to learn how degrees of english will alter cue ball path and also the precise spot on the rail you will need to contact to sink the 11-ball.

TAKE A TIP

Kick shots like this one can be difficult to estimate from the shooter's position behind the shot line. But standing behind the pocket and facing the 11-ball to look back toward the cue ball, the kick line should become clear almost instantly.

Deep Kick Shots

KICK SHOTS ARE CHALLENGING when playing to a ball far from the rail. I find the parallel kick method the simplest for calculating the point on the rail for impact.

Figure 10.20 outlines this easy system. You'll want to memorize this system. Most would miss the 7-ball by a foot or more without it.

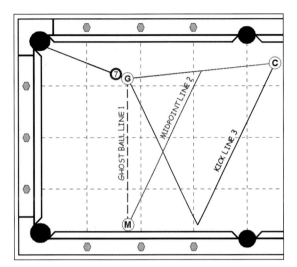

Figure 10.20
Long kick calculation.

1. Draw "Ghost Ball Line 1," an imaginary line from the ghost ball impact on the 7-ball in the corner pocket to an imagined ball, "M," perpendicular to the kick rail.

2. Draw "Midpoint Line 2" as a direct line between the center of ball "M" and the midpoint of the shot line from cue ball to ghost ball.

3. Use "Kick Line 3," a line parallel to Midpoint Line 2, for the cue ball. The reflection angle will bring the cue ball to sink the seven!

Use your cue stick above the felt to measure and visualize the last two parallel lines.

Certainly, you may want to use a bit of draw and speed to come as close as you can to skid action when the ball kicks the rail. Reflection angles for banks and kicks are based on skidding, not spinning balls.

Bank Shots

S OME PLAYERS LOVE *bank shots*, bouncing object balls off the rails into the pockets. Others famously loathe banks, not wishing to add any element of surprise (like a broken, inaccurate rail) to play. Single-rail bank shots may be calculated as shown.

Let's learn how to calculate the starting angle for a bank shot. In Figure 10.21, you wish to send the 5-ball into the rail and bounce it into the bottom side pocket.

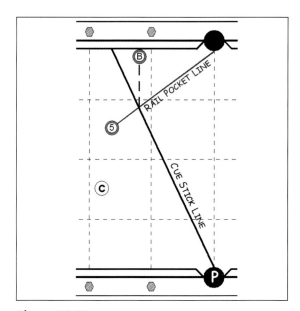

Figure 10.21
Bank assessment.

1. Hold your cue stick on a line from the target pocket "P" to a point on the opposite rail perpendicular to the 5-ball's center.

2. Imagine the "Rail Pocket Line" between the object ball center and the middle of the pocket opposite P.

3. Drop a line from the X shape you formed between cue line and pocket line straight to the rail. The 5-ball must strike at that point, "B," to bank one rail into the side.

In takes less time to perform this task than to read about it, especially since you will always be aiming the rail pocket line for side pocket shots that aren't banks. In short order you will be able to plot the bank angle without a cue stick in mere moments. A touch of outside english (left for this stroke) helps achieve the bank angle, too.

Aim by viewing the base of the rails and mouths of the pockets in your calculations. The tops of the rails create an illusion that can affect your estimate of distance.

Hard Inside Bank

Why do good players who shoot gently change to bang certain banks to the pockets?

The answer lies in manipulating balls off the cushions as discussed in Chapter 9. Harder strokes take tighter angles off the rails than the typical reflective angles. So do balls banked using inside english.

Stroking any bank hard and with inside english, the rebound angle comes closer to vertical, providing a straighter shot into the side pocket. You can also, therefore, bank balls resting rather close to the side pockets and on tight angles.

Which english is inside for a bank? English transfers between balls at impact, so when banking to the right, as with the 5-ball in the diagram, inside english will actually be right english.

Spin Bank Shot

I heartily recommend opening any bank practice session with *spin banks*, shots using maximal english and slow strokes to open the angles. Don't use follow; hit left or right english only for this drill.

When you can spin a ball near a corner pocket to the side pocket on the same rail with a one-rail spin bank, your confidence and comprehension for bank technique will soar.

Shoot a few spin banks wide and then a few hard inside banks on narrow angles to warm your banking skills at the start of a new pool session.

Easier Banking

Work to incorporate as much feel as you can with banks. Try shooting them without advance measurement to begin to develop your table sense. You are always shooting to points not in your field of vision with banks, so get used to shooting and trusting without watching the results.

TAKE A TIP

A great way to handle most any rail or bank shot is to pretend the rail is not there at all. When you stroke toward the rail without an abrupt hitch in anticipation of impact, your banking percentage increases.

Frozen Banks

What play could be made from the starting position of Figure 10.22? To bank the 14-ball one rail, shoot center ball with a firm half ball stroke (from the shooter's perspective, aim the cue ball's center to the left edge of the 14-ball).

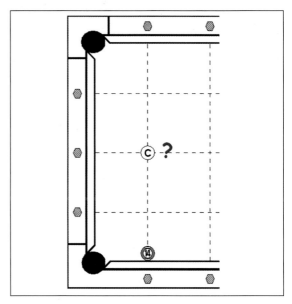

Figure 10.22
What to do?

The half ball stroke avoids the 14-ball hitting the cue ball a second time, called a *double kiss.* The speed tightens the angle enough to pocket the ball and plows the 14-ball deeper into the rail, giving the cue ball time to escape.

This same stroke could be played from the short rail for the length of the table, from the middle of the rail, as it must travel a longer distance along the same angled line. Have fun showing this shot to a friend and daring them to make it before you accomplish it as they watch!

Systems and Theories

SOME POOL TEACHERS could fill an entire book with only banks, kicks, and caroms (and indeed, have done so). We haven't looked at multi-rail banks and kicks, or even *cross corner banks*, the lovely little banks that hit a side rail and then travel across the table to pocket in a faraway corner.

What has been presented in this chapter is a basic introduction to key shots making the game fun and also a creative endeavor. Whoever can see more possible shots on the table is the likely winner.

Side Pocket Shots

The side pockets present added challenge. We shoot at their middles as with the corner pockets, but they present less opportunity than the corners. From many table points, they simply may not be reached with a straight aim line, the object ball colliding with the rail instead.

Requiring extra accuracy (though they are larger than the corner pockets as partial compensation), side pockets give many players a fright!

The easiest way to improve your side pocket accuracy is to aim to bank balls off the pocket facing on the pro side, rather than limply tumbling balls off the lip. Stop worrying and fly a ball inside.

Figure 10.23 represents the approximate area of the table from which balls may be pocketed in the nearest side pocket without needing to resort to a delicate stroke.

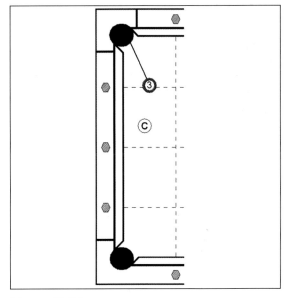

Figure 10.23
Side pocketing possibilities.

Disregard for the pocket itself and concentration on the cue ball's tangent line will help you pocket many more balls in the side. See Chapter 8 and "Plot the Cue Ball" for more.

Slip Stroke Shots

Slip shots disobey many of the rules I've outlined for stance and stroke, but for added power or spin, it's considered occasional fine form to let the body or even the cue stick slide through a stroke.

Moving the body for power during the stroke I call a *body slip stroke*. Some players allow the cue stick to glide along their hand during practice strokes until they find a final position, and these players are said to have a slip stroke. When generating extra power, some experts use a reverse slip stroke, in which the cue is nearly let go then caught again somewhere on the forward stroke!

Most players need more *accuracy*, not power, on their strokes. Keep these techniques under advisement for now—at least until we power the break shot in Chapter 14.

Around Your World Shot

Here in Figure 10.24 is a stroke every player ought to master, but I've left your diagram without too much information for exploration on your own.

Figure 10.24
Around the world in one stroke.

Shoot the 3-ball with center ball, sinking it in the left corner pocket as indicated. Send the cue ball around the entire length and width of the table with the stroke to return to visit you. Watch this shot illustration on the companion DVD for more detail.

Straight in Shots

This is a rough one. Many players go to pieces over lengthy, full hits when shot line and aim line are one. The long straight shot should be easier than the long cut, but anxiety creeps in.

I recommend you set a cue ball near one corner pocket and place an object ball near the middle of the table. Shoot the object ball into the far corner pocket ten times. This drill requires concentration and technique to sink the shot seven times or more out of ten tries. Consider using the bases or the tops of both balls to align the rare, perfectly straight shot.

Still stuck on the long straight shot? Stroke down the aim line and forget the object ball is there, and it should pocket anyway.

Tripod Bridge Shots

You may remember the raised hand bridges of Chapter 4. You want to position the balls to avoid making bizarre hand bridges in the first place, but when pressed, keep the cue as level as possible, not applying english unless absolutely necessary.

Dealing with an obstacle between the shooter and the cue ball, the goal in tripod situations is typically a little jab of a stroke taken without sidespin.

Pocket Speed Shots

TV commentators love to say about your favorite pool pro, "They are shooting well and sinking balls at pocket speed." *Pocket speed* is optimal speed, not so slow that balls roll off line on an imperfect table, nor so fast that balls hit the back of the pocket before jumping out again. And now you know.

Balls on the Rail

When an object ball is nestled on the rail, questions arise on cutting the ball to the closest corner pocket.

The best way to cut the object ball is to aim and pretend the rail is not there at all. If the cue is positioned so that the hit is exceptionally thin, by which is meant it's impossible to pocket the ball with a cut shot, shoot to *miss* the object ball by a credit card's width or two with outside english. As the cue releases from the rail it knocks the object ball in on the rebound! A beautiful shot played with a speeding cue ball.

Flipping English Mystery Shot

Balls with english sent about the table reverse english direction after striking two opposite rails (on opposite sides of the table) but retain their english on adjoining rails—until the third rail struck with inside english, when english flips to become outside english.

There are cool moments when a cue ball with inside english travels two adjacent rails, slowing down all the while, then hits a third rail and converts to outside english, widening the angle and speeding up again! It's mystery and magic applied when you tell the crowd it will happen then show the trick.

The Final Ball Shot

The 8-ball in Eight-Ball or the 9-ball in Nine-Ball, a game winner, gives people fits and starts at times. Our gang used to call this troublesome condition "ring around the 9-ball" when a player *failed* like clockwork to can a game-winning ball.

The best advice to avoid choking the *case ball*, the big winner, is to pretend there is another ball on the table still waiting following the winner. Watch the cue ball after it impacts the object ball until it comes to rest for the "next ball" you plan to shoot. In your mind's eye, this makes the last shot equivalent to all the shots taken before.

The Avoid English Shot

The skilled player, the best hustler, the pro, avoids unneeded spin and english wherever possible. I'm not referring to a tad of outside english to cinch cut shots, but the tendency of the mediocre shooter to pull out the spin fireworks for no reason. I see intermediate players resorting even to simple draw and follow too often. Shooters learn to draw, for example, and overuse this fun skill, hurting their position play.

I am extremely good at aiming "regular" cut shots as I am hitting them constantly. Competition for the big bucks or fun with pals, I am practicing cut shots always and ever. I hit center ball (or outside english) cuts thousands of times a year.

I am hitting so many cuts, remaining interested always in improving impact and accuracy, that when my opponent leaves me a terrible, deadly cut shot, they find me ready for the challenge. Shoot lots of cut shots and save the four-rail maximum left english with topspin shots for your trick shot show.

Time to Read

You may be a bit overwhelmed from all you learned in this chapter, but we need to move ahead and learn to read—reading the table as it lies.

Which ball to shoot when, why, and where is the emphasis of Chapter 11. Each illustration presents mysteries for us to solve together.

11

Draw the Map: Reading
Your Table

Making order from table chaos

WILLIE MOSCONI, the most famous and arguably the best pool shooter ever, was asked about winning a world championship zipping the cue ball *five rails* to sink an object ball. Willie said in essence, "There's *always* a shot that can be made," a sentiment he shared on many other occasions, too.

We are going to study reading the table *before* shooting to plan effective strategy. Are balls easy to sink or blocked by other balls? Are there any logical patterns to be made of balls scattered randomly across a table?

After you digest the concepts presented in this chapter, you will be able to assess patterns, thinking three to eight shots ahead or more, in a few seconds.

Survey Before Shooting

THE S.B.S. CODE FOR "Survey Before Shooting" is precious for the new pool shooter. Until one finds discipline to read the table before bending to shoot, it would be wise to bend farther and kneel for fervent prayer!

School yourself for one hour to shoot no ball before first considering at least two possible pockets, plus three routes for the cue ball. Pros and hustlers know where the balls will go and can visualize possible routes before any shot.

Sorting the Mess

You've broken the balls apart and one or two have fallen in. You wish to run the table, clearing it. You are trying to sort 13 or 14 balls in your mind and set them in sequence. What is required is reading the table and *shaping* the cue ball, positioning it at the end of every shot for the next.

Taming "Goldzila"

Remember the acronym "Gold.Zi.La," and you'll understand where to send the cue ball following impact for subsequent shots. Begin by placing the cue ball onto the *golden angle*.

Golden Angle

"Seek the golden angle!" was advice Ralph Greenleaf once shared with a young Willie Mosconi. Willie admired the tremendous cue ball skill his tour partner and rival "handsome Ralph" possessed, sending the cue ball following many

shots to within six inches from the next object ball. For comparison, today's pro is probably winning a major tournament if their cue balls come to rest a diamond's distance of about one foot from subsequent shots.

In part, Greenleaf earned great cue ball shape from his *golden angle* of about 10° off straight for cut shots. Two such angles are shown in Figure 11.1, Ten degrees or so allows for simple thick cuts without the need to often resort to strong draw or follow, as with the full hit.

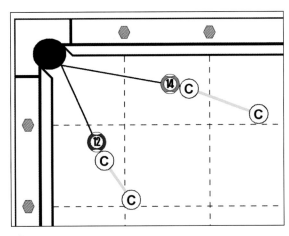

Figure 11.1
Two golden angles.

Even 15 to 40 degrees of cut is adequate for most shots, but seek for the gold, and the golden angle of Goldzila where you can.

Zone Intention

The *position zone* for most shots is roughly triangular in shape, formed by two rails of the table plus the farthest angle from where the average player is confident of sinking a given cut. This triangular zone widens as the cue ball comes to rest farther from the object ball.

In Figure 11.2, which includes seven from among the many possible cue ball positions, a cue ball entering the zone from a point near the far rail allows a two-foot margin of error. Close to the 6-ball near the pocket, however, a two-inch margin of error is available. For any shape play, the correct distance of *approach* is almost never close to the ball, but far enough to allow for wiggle room.

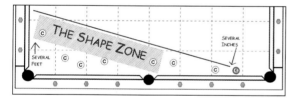

Figure 11.2
A wide and narrow zone.

By entering the wide part of the zone wherever possible, the shooter can make an error with cue ball distance but still sink the next shot, yielding the "Zi" of Goldzila.

Avoid Snookers

A ball sitting behind an interfering ball is known as *snookered*. Here, the addition of one object ball clouds the 6-ball zone to become the situation of Figure 11.3. Your position solution must now include avoiding the zone within a zone occluded by the 10-ball.

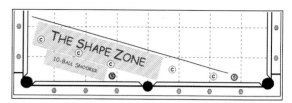

Figure 11.3
10-ball trouble.

Let Sleeping Balls Lie

Never move balls without a reason. Break apart a cluster when you choose and avoid disturbing a cluster or single ball accidentally. It's too easy otherwise to change a good ball for you to a bad one.

There's a temptation to hit the cue ball into the 10-ball for shape on the 6-ball in Figure 11.3, but a hit on the wrong side could bury the cue ball, leaving the ten between it and the six. When you plot routes avoiding obstructions, you watch your win percentage soar.

Line of Aim

A good player often targets the conclusion of the cue ball's path along the aim line for the upcoming shot. In Figure 11.4, the cue ball banks on the rail in the widest section of the zone for the 6-ball. We did not need to play a golden angle but went straight in, as in this case the 6-ball was the final ball of the game.

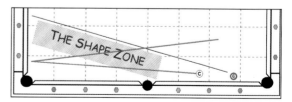

Figure 11.4
Down the line.

Here the margin of error for distance is nearly eight feet! The cue ball could come to rest many feet short of the 6-ball while leaving an easy shot. Playing down the line, even along the line moving away from the object ball, is intimidating to the opponent as the ball rolls on, always on the aim line, for the "La" of our Goldzila acronym.

TAKE A TIP

It's considering the *Gold*en Angle, the *Z*one *I*ntention, and the *L*ine of *A*im with each shot that makes the pro tougher to beat than "Goldzila." You will be able to calculate all three shape aids in seconds for any shot, soon after you take some time to practice these shape visualization skills.

Which Ball First?

It's natural to feel a little anxious for the first shot of any *inning* or turn at the table. Pick off the easiest ball first if you have a choice. Play some object ball close to a pocket or the cue ball itself, and one you can use to shape easily for the next shot with the cue ball. Do pick a second shot rather than shooting to some vague, general area.

Which Ball Last?

The last ball is often predetermined in the pool game you are playing, such as the black 8-ball in Eight-Ball or the striped 9-ball in Nine-Ball. It proceeds that the ball shot immediately before the last ball becomes critical for the player, known in pool as the *key ball*. Your key ball unlocks your winning ball.

Always plan the run in reverse, choosing the last ball first, then its key ball. The expert preserves the key at all costs and may consider a backup plan also. In Figure 11.5, the player has chosen the green 6-ball last for this game of Eight-Ball, with the maroon 7-ball held as a safety option should the 6-ball be disturbed from its present spot.

Figure 11.5
Two key ideas.

Can you see how a stop shot taken on the six into the right corner pocket will set for the win? How would you plan to shoot the 7-ball, and with what spin or english, if the 6-ball is removed early?

Speed Control

Perhaps the biggest factor for cue ball shape is speed control. Recall that a half ball hit reduces cue ball speed by about one-half, a three-quarter impact by about 75%, and so on.

Stroke the cue ball the short distance between two diamonds, about one foot, without touching any object ball. This gentle stroke will be relied on often. Less than 1 in 100 casual players can execute it when needed; can you?

Remember to bring both your shooting and bridge hands far forward along the cue stick as explained in Chapter 5. As you devote more practice to speed control and less to exotic shots and paper-thin cuts, your overall game will improve rapidly.

Play Natural Shape

Strive to find a natural position for the cue ball as much as possible. On each shot, you need to calculate the tangent line anyway (see Chapter 8), so ask yourself, "Can I shape the cue ball for the next shot with a center ball stroke (natural position) or something close to center ball?"

Side Pocket Tolerance

In these politically correct times, we must also learn *side pocket tolerance*, the steepest possible angles from where a ball may be sunk into a side pocket. Some side pockets are less vulnerable than others to your skills, especially if a side rail was misaligned during table assembly and the point of the pocket juts out.

Right and Wrong Sides

Side pocket tolerance often plays a role in considering the *right side* of an object ball, the section of table allowing shorter cue ball distance for the subsequent shot. The classic example is played near the side pockets of the table, as in Figure 11.6.

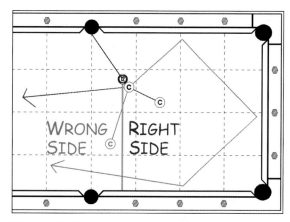

Figure 11.6
Right vs. wrong.

The shooter wants to go down table for the next shot, somewhere ahead of the arrows. Positioned on the right side of the blue line beneath the 12-ball, starting with the purple cue ball, a gentle stroke is played with a little follow spin added. Trials await the unwary from the wrong side, however, as seen with the orange cue ball and its convoluted path.

As promised in Chapter 7, I have outlined a use of topspin for shape, as in Figure 11.6. The pro chooses something like the purple shot line and the beginner the orange line, most every time.

Take time to plan, especially near the side pockets, as a matter of inches can separate a cue ball from the right to the wrong side of its object ball.

Avoid Rails and Spin

The pro wants no uncertainties in their run. Why send the cue ball three rails if it can shape with two rails or perhaps one? Or why shoot a firm draw shot, when a soft center ball stroke accomplishes as good a shape?

The easiest route typically requires the least possible speed, english, rails, and spin, as shown in Figure 11.6. Boring to watch, exciting to shoot—since one rarely misses the next shot, too, when taking the simplest position route. I *enjoy* boring my opponent who sits fast in their chair to observe me run 10 to 15 or more balls on my turn. I am always delighted to practice yet another dozen simple shots while they wait!

The amateur finds such discretion wimpy and loves to pound the cue ball around the table at all times. TV viewers at home likewise prefer the long, spectacular shots of Nine-Ball and similar games to simple position play. Pool programs are further edited to present the "most exciting" content and avoid safety play and simple cue ball position strokes.

Did you know that using wise, simple patterns, Willie Mosconi claimed he could run 100 balls in Straight Pool—without touching a rail even one time! Witnesses say no one ever paid to take Mosconi to task. Try to duplicate Willie's feat, even for five or six balls, before you rush to judge the exquisite skills you can add to gentle position play.

Get Centered

The most options for widely scattered balls find the cue ball somewhere near the center of the table, between both side pockets. There may be clear shots to all six pockets from the center. The player's reach and bridge hand will be also more

comfortable in the middle than with the cue ball near a rail. Strive to find one exact spot for the cue ball to rest after each stroke as the pros do, but when stuck for precise ideas, the center of the table is usually a safe bet.

Figure 11.7 is a good stroke I might play a half dozen times in a single pool session. Outside english, which is left english since the 3-ball will be cut to the shooter's right for Pocket "A," carries the cue ball off two rails to the center of the table.

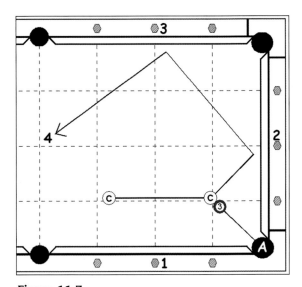

Figure 11.7
Back to center.

Use this gentle stroke and begin to teach yourself the use of the diamonds as points of reference for multi-rail play. Note that the 3-ball sits near the intersection of the first diamonds along the short and long rail, and that the cue ball's track will form three sides of a rectangle built between points 1 to 4 on the table.

Think Boxes and Parallel Lines

The parallel lines formed in Figure 11.7 yield further insight. Look for parallel lines to appear frequently as rectangles and trapezoids inside the playing area, especially the first rail line (after impact with the object ball) matching the third rail's exit path as shown.

In addition, the line taken *away* from a short rail, as with the line between points 2 and 3 in Figure 11.7, usually parallels the line taken *into* the opposite short rail (if this shot carries long enough to reach the far side of the table) making the second and fourth lines also a parallel set.

Soon, you will be able to break a cluster over a dozen feet from the first object ball with confidence and a multi-rail kick! Amaze your friends by calling such shots and rail targets in advance.

Triangles and Clumps

In Figure 11.8, there are several possible triangles of balls to center the cue ball among, opening practical shot possibilities. I might think, "Take off the triad of the 10-, 14-, and 15-balls near the side pocket before removing the triangle of the 11-, 13-, and 12-balls into both corners." A stop shot on the eleven would make for an easy three balls last. Another triangle idea might have included the 10-, 12-, and 13-balls, leaving the triangle of the 11, 14, and 15 for last. Can you see these new triangles and the possibilities for shape?

Figure 11.8
Organizing object balls.

It's imperative to switch back and forth at times to avoid leaving the table "heavy" with many balls on one side and none on the other, and forcing multiple shots taken to one pocket. If the 13-ball were quite close to the 12-ball, for example, you might want to let the 10-ball sit just in case you got stuck near the corner.

For bigger ball arrangements, the shots of choice often first include picking the corner balls first, as shown in Figure 11.9. Take the ends off the clumps and then work inward. The expert would probably remove the red 3-ball early, perhaps the 15 or 14 also, looking to shape the cue ball on the 12-ball in the corner or the 4 and 5, and whatever near the edges of the cluster looks to be troublesome ahead.

Figure 11.9
A big clump.

Use Ball in Hand

When the shooter receives the privilege of *ball in hand*, allowing him to place the cue ball where he wants, it's often best practice to sink any trouble object balls first with this immediate opportunity. If rail shots are a concern for you, shoot one off the rail first from the easiest cue ball position. If you are unhappy with a cluster, break the cluster right away. Winston Churchill's quote is appropriate here: "Things do not get better by being left alone."

Avoiding Scratches

The error of a cue ball *scratch* with cue in a pocket, ending a turn, causes concern for all players. When facing a potential scratch play, the pro avoids anxiety by acknowledging the pocket edges as two clear boundaries for where the ball can *safely* travel, rather than as a pit of terror.

The correct mindset is neutrality about the scratch pocket or even gratitude that you can see a physical pocket instead of yet another imaginary line or target to draw with your mind's eye. A change in mental attitude will enable you to bring the cue ball quite close to the pockets without fear.

Play a High Percentage Ball

In Figure 11.10, the player is confronted with two balls to choose between. Beginners routinely choose to shoot the 15-ball, yet the nearby 1-ball has a much greater margin of error. It's the backward-facing cut angle that intimidates.

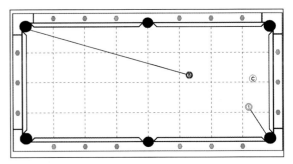

Figure 11.10
Percentage play.

Difficulty for any ball is based on two distances, the space between cue ball and object ball and the distance between the object ball and its intended pocket. The 15-ball represents triple the challenge of the 1-ball.

Practice this particular stroke on the 1-ball, and you will soon discover many such balls to be easy prey along the side or corner pocket nearest the cue ball.

Play High Percentage Sequences

The stronger shooters play every sequence they can safely make, but the weak shooters try to be heroes and fail. If you have three balls left in a game and can make two of the shots you face half the time, even with the third a sure winner, your odds of running all three remain only 1 in 4. You emerge the loser 75% of the time. Better to look before leaping and play defense with the next shot.

For another example, pretend I've broken two solids into the pockets in Eight-Ball, and I need to run just six balls with the five remaining solids, then the 8-ball to win. If I can make every shot presented 90% of the time, I still face only a 53% chance of running the entire table.

The pro reassesses the run odds following *every* shot and chooses offense or defense accordingly.

Three at a Time

Master pro Efren "The Magician" Reyes claims he looks three to eight shots ahead. That's a whole rack of Nine-Ball from the 1-ball or about half the table in Straight Pool.

Three balls at a time is simple, play the first ball for a predetermined shape on the second ball to allow for easy shape on the third ball. In other words, how will ball one be played for ball two for ball three? If you miss your shape of choice anywhere during a run, pause long enough to refocus for a new three-ball look.

Take Joy in Details

If the tangent line takes the cue ball right or left of the aim line (see Chapter 8) and topspin and draw bring the cue ball forward or backward from the tangent, where does "half topspin" or half draw (half of what you might apply regarding average speed and tip position) take a cue ball? You are correct if you assumed that for certain shots it bends the ball halfway off the tangent line or about 45° to the shot line. The 45-degree rule will assist you greatly when planning cue ball paths off rails with object balls nearby.

Not only can you bend the cue ball and object ball paths with many different degrees of throw and spin, you can be highly specific in mapping paths before the stroke. Have fun and invent new position plays for yourself.

Use Your Imagination

The most creative position player usually tops the leader board. In Figures 11.11 through 11.13, I take the cue ball to the air *after* it hits the object ball. A few minutes' practice can teach you how to have the cue ball take to the sky with what I call the *top jump* shot.

Figure 11.11
Ready, aim.

Figure 11.12
Fire a flier.

Figure 11.13
Following through.

Make a chicken wing of your shooting arm, holding it far out to the side and bringing the butt of your cue stick 30 degrees or more from level, your shooting hand turned palm down toward the floor. You can execute this shot with the cue ball much farther from the object balls than pictured.

Two more figures illustrate creativity in deciphering table layout. In Figure 11.14, when the temptation is to play follow or center ball on the 13-ball for position near the short rail, which means the shot would be hit too slowly and possibly roll off line as a result, the *draw drag* shot is used. Simply stroke the cue ball firmly with enough draw spin that underspin wears along the cloth to become natural roll.

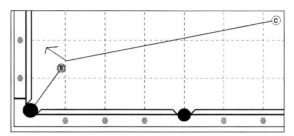

Figure 11.14
Draw drag.

Think this shot over carefully and play it several times with center, follow, and draw, as well as at different speeds, observing the results. The *draw drag shot* is the same as center ball or follow *if the cue ball was much closer to the object ball.*

In Figure 11.15, the shooter plans to play the 6- then the 7-ball sequentially. Draw action off the rail crosses the width of the table from the six after the cue ball rebounds into the rail. This is another imaginative stroke tool that can crop up many times during a session.

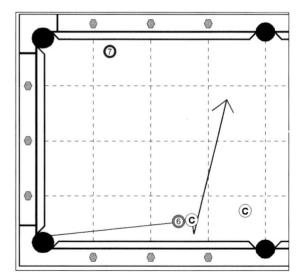

Figure 11.15
Drawing over.

Pool offers endless variety for creative players. It's not unusual for me to learn new pool techniques and position plays, even after over 30 years playing the sport. Hitting one *side* of a ball or the other or an inch here or there can change the fortunes of a game. I've even seen a top shooter intentionally bring the cue ball through the air to ride atop the rail before returning to the table where planned (*much* harder than it sounds).

A new field of billiards competition emphasizing creativity and stunning patterns has arisen in recent years, known as *artistic billiards*. Intense massé and multi-rail strokes enhance the creative and attractive shots required for artistic billiards competition. If you have the chance to watch artistic billiards online, on TV, or in person, don't miss it.

Play Your Game

MUCH OF ACHIEVING *dead stroke*, the magical mental plane where shots are mapped and played with little conscious effort or verbal thought, the kind of stroking required for artistic billiards (see above), comes from finding and maintaining one's best personal playing rhythm. In general, you should not be playing extremely fast or hitting the balls extremely hard, but if it matches your temperament, shoot a little faster and harder to work yourself into dead stroke.

Players in a rut would do well to play about 10% faster than normal, and think a bit less about technique and aiming, to get back into high swing with their game.

Let's Play Cards

Any one ball under consideration can lie on the table as one of four classifications:

▶ *Jokers* mock you as obstacle balls

▶ *Queens* rule over jokers

▶ *Kings* regally proceed into pockets but at "proper times" only

▶ *Aces* are easy to pocket and ready pool helpers

In Figure 11.16 the 6- and 7-balls are locked *jokers*, teasing us with their difficulty in pocketing. The 5-ball is freely pocketed, a *queen* of a ball that both pockets easily and allows a natural cue ball tangent for the cue ball to separate the six and seven.

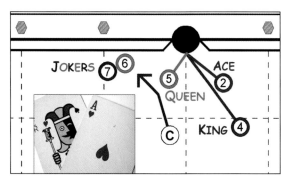

Figure 11.16
House of cards.

The *king* 4-ball will pocket in the corner but only after the *ace*, the freely pocketed 2-ball, goes in first. The king will not precede the 2-ball as long as it blocks the royal procession.

Sometimes you may reverse the order of aces and kings. Perhaps the 4-ball could be shot into a corner pocket first, playing an outside to inside pattern and making the 4-ball your ace to garner position on the king 2-ball in the side.

Play aces before kings, and use queens to lead jokers to better positions, and you will run the table more often.

Curving the Cue Ball

Infrequently, you may need to curve the path of the cue ball around an impeding ball. For the swerve shot or *semi-massé*, raise the butt of your cue above the table at between a 15- and 45-degree incline to vertical. Set your bridge hand as a tripod, as if you need to stroke over an interfering ball.

Aim through the cue ball with right or left english from above, and the ball will veer accordingly. Stroke the cue ball softly for best effect.

A *full massé* is taken at a cue stick angle close to 90 degrees, and is seen and used rarely, mostly in trick shot exhibitions. There are Hall of Fame players who have not needed the stroke for tournament competition, ever.

Many players love to see a full massé played, however. Elevate the cue stick to near vertical above the table. Hold your bridge hand against the body for added support. Stroke the cue ball anywhere but center ball, causing the cue ball to squirt from the cue tip and go forward a bit before reversing or altering direction.

This stroke is also taken softly. I recommend you practice using a house cue and not your personal cue. A poor massé (too hard a stroke, usually) can shatter a cue stick or tear a table's cloth.

Rules Are Rules

Let's pause from shotmaking to examine the rules and etiquette of the game. We will then build upon our rules knowledge to look at the battle tactics of the pool masters.

12

With Flair: Pool Rules and
Tactics

Knowing when to play by the rules

THERE'S AN OSCAR HAMMERSTEIN lyric about meeting a special stranger "across a crowded room." Unfortunately, to get a game in many poolrooms one must walk across a *cloudy* room.

I'm not exaggerating—I've opened the door to a favorite pool hall to find white, billowy clouds of cigarette smoke grazing the ceiling. Once, my children and I were inside for less than two minutes to unload a cue stick for repair. The kids smelled for days after like they had visited an opium den!

Pool etiquette and rules flex somewhat depending on the proprietor of the establishment. Obviously, it was wrong *not* to smoke in that one pool hall. I'll pick another place to shoot rather than ingest columns of smoke during play.

This chapter will describe some important rules governing pool. Behave yourself, please, and use an ashtray. Better yet, have your local room owner install added ventilation.

House Rules

SINCE LOCAL POOLROOM RULES, called *house rules*, sometimes apply to particular games or general pool practice, you should always explore the territory in an unfamiliar hall if you plan to compete there. If you don't, an argument could end with a cue stick busted over your head!

Of course, we're talking about the fighting and rowdy atmosphere that left most pool halls long ago. Hall proprietors have worked for decades to help polish up pool's tarnished image.

Smoking, Drinking, and Drugs

Even a nonsmoker could acquire lung disease playing weekly in certain pool halls. Cigarettes burn holes in pool table cloths and lungs both, so while nonsmoking halls are few, it pays to at least play where smoking is limited.

Figure 12.1
Clear minds aid pool.

Drinking is allowed at many halls. Most casual players and league players use bar and lounge tables only as their preference or with no local pool hall available. I find that in rooms where heavy drinkers play, there are arguments and violent fights, degenerate gamblers, and sexual harassment—and the male drinkers are pretty bad, too!

Whether in a clubby atmosphere with wine or a honky-tonk bar where kegs of beer overflow, play where bartenders and servers know when patrons have had enough and limit boozing before it gets out of hand.

Some pool hustlers and pros use performance-enhancing or recreational drugs at the tables. Besides the illegality of their actions, they impair rational judgment. Staying awake for days at a time, high on amphetamine, Benzedrine, or who-knows-what, eventually any money they win goes back through gambling to savvier players with more sense and more sleep.

Countless room owners are working to keep their pool parlors clean and free of drugs, but be aware whether your local owner is vigilant or not to keep street punks and drug dealers out of the picture.

Gambling Etiquette

Pool gambling where it's prohibited will get you removed from a hall—in most poolrooms nationwide, gambling is illegal per local and state regulations—but in rooms where I see everyone wielding $800 cues and changing twenty-dollar bills more casually than I change my socks, I know gambling is tolerated by the proprietor if not the law.

If you enjoy gambling, and admittedly a little money on a game can intensify your concentration and will to succeed, recognize the difference between playing a friend for a soda or table rental charges and playing "Chicago Slick" for $20 a game at Nine-Ball. One is likely to earn some laughs and perhaps a cold ginger ale, the other, big trouble.

Figure 12.2
Busted.

I've been around pool gambling enough to learn there are sometimes violent fights over money plus crosses and double-crosses as pool gamblers and those who back them with dollars conspire. Most shooters don't even pay their losses before berating the winner successfully to play still more at unfavorable odds—if they pay at all.

I like how Carl Oswald describes choosing not to gamble at pool. He states, "If you play known people, it's tough to match up for a profit. If you play strangers, it's easier to win but much tougher to stay healthy and friendly."

While entire books have been filled with humorous and exciting pool gambling stories, the sad news is gambling can quickly grow to a deadly addiction. The alcoholic may quit and find support from loved ones, friends, and coworkers, but the gambler recovers to five- or six-figure debt destroying their lives almost beyond repair. Many more gamblers commit suicide than alcoholics or other addicts.

Ask yourself a key question when considering gambling and you'll do fine. Look around the pool hall you've chosen carefully and wonder, "Would I be more likely to leave this room with cue stick in hand or broken over my head?"

More No-No's

BESIDES JUDICIOUS CONSUMPTION and curbing gambling, here are other things to do if you value your money, safety, and social standing at your local poolroom:

▶ Don't abuse pool equipment with spilled food and drink or rough play like brutal massé shots.

▶ Don't sell cue sticks and accessories to players where not permitted—often, you are competing with the room owner's wares on display.

▶ Don't shoot hazardous stunt and trick shots, smashing teeth, windows, and worse in the process.

General Pool Etiquette

Six marks of class guarantee that no matter your skill, you will always be welcomed to a friendly game at your favorite room:

1. Compliment your opponent on a fine shot, but only after their turn has ended, so they are undistracted by your comments.

2. Remain seated and silent while your opponent is at the table, because noise or distraction may be mistaken for sharking or hustling the opponent.

3. Be a gracious winner or loser; a handshake and "Nice game, pal!" is always appreciated.

4. Seek the referee's aid on any potential tournament dispute early, asking them to watch any potentially controversial shot before it is taken.

5. Do not remove any cube of chalk from the table after you miss—it's considered great disrespect for the other player who needs chalk for their upcoming turn.

6. Leave chalk cubes face-up so they don't leech chalk onto people and the table.

Call All Fouls

The temptation is to allow a slight breach of the rules to go unpunished, but too many players take advantage of such courtesy purposefully. Call foul on your opponent politely but firmly if you see them make an illegal move. Announcing a foul is courtesy to you for fair play and to them to improve their skills in the future.

Rules Infractions

Below are some of the general rules infractions that apply to most pool games and how to avoid them (or take advantage of them!) during play.

Player Fouls

A player may not touch any ball, not counting the obvious exceptions of racking to start play and returning balls to the table as required. For some competitions, even one's clothing may not touch. I ensure my clothing touches at no time, which avoids obscuring my opponent's view of the table and causing possible confusion as to the legality of my play.

To prevent player fouls caused by slipping with stick or body on the table, stretch and flex the fingers into variations of the hand bridges, and use the mechanical bridge or "rake," as described in Chapter 4. Work around table obstacles with care.

Coaching

Players may not be coached by anyone nor discuss play during competition, with the possible exception of team play, and often only the team leader is allowed to share. Penalties include forfeit of the game or match being played.

Figure 12.3
No coaching allowed.

To avoid a coaching foul, politely invite talkative bystanders to be quiet so they won't disturb your concentration or that of your opponent.

It's Over When the Fat Ball Sinks

In times past, when players kept just one personal stick at the table without specialty jump or break cues, separating your two-piece cue into sections during a match was considered refusal to play further, conceding the match.

To escape any misunderstanding or a foul ending your turn, let your opponent or referee know beforehand that you will disassemble your stick or enhance it by adding a jump shot or break shot extension. Do not assemble or dissemble equipment while your opponent is shooting—sit still and wait.

The Stick as a Sword

The cue stick may never touch any object ball during play, and the cue tip only may touch the cue ball. To evade stick fouls, pretend the cue is a sword that will cut the balls (or hapless passersby).

Towel dry your cue frequently, or have a repairman add a linen or leather wrap to its butt if people nearby open umbrellas when you perspire at the table. There's nothing like sinking a shot only to foul when the cue stick leaves your wet grip and flies across the table.

Don't Scoop the Cue Ball

A miscue taken on a draw shot struck too low may cause a cue ball to hop right off the table. The player is disallowed from lofting the cue ball in this manner, causing it to jump by digging beneath it, and lifting it with the cue stick's white ferrule section.

To bypass an illegal jump stroke, strike draw shots with a low, level shooting hand and strike all jump shots above the ball's bottom section as viewed from above. A legal jump is executed when the tip slams into the cue ball, pushing it down against the felt, before it squirts into the air.

Down the Hole, Out of Luck

The cue ball may not sink in any of the table's pockets for most games. To preclude a cue ball scratch, plot the path that the cue ball will take before taking your stance and shooting. Practice cue ball control, and then practice and practice some more.

Table Position Must Change

For a shot to be legally struck, *after* some ball is struck by the cue ball, at least one ball (cue ball included) must either strike a rail or *enter* a pocket. A ball whose base is inside the pocket opening is considered to have *entered* the pocket even if it hasn't sunk. A ball that enters the pocket but does not sink does not score a point.

In Figure 12.4, if the player shoots at the 10-ball first, the ten, the eleven, the cue ball itself, or some other ball must be driven to touch a rail. To send the 10-ball with a stop stroke toward the rail but not fully into it incurs a foul.

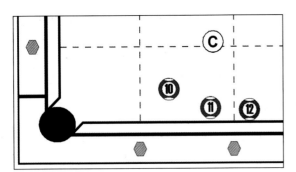

Figure 12.4
Change the table.

Consider the 11- and 12-balls, also. The difference between the two is that the 11-ball may safely touch the rail fractions of an inch away, while the 12-ball, which rests along the long rail, must be driven away to strike a *different* rail elsewhere (unless the cue ball or some other ball is driven to a rail or pocket with the same stroke).

To thwart a no-rail contact foul, check the position of any ball you plan to hit carefully if it rests close to one side of the table. Does it actually touch the rail now, or is it close but not touching? If it does touch, it must be driven to a new rail unless a different ball touches some rail after the initial impact.

A ball a tiny distance from the rail may be gently nudged to the rail for a legal play. If the ball is quite near the rail but not touching, alert your opponent beforehand if you plan to strike it softly so they do not accuse you of the no-rail foul. Technically, it is the opponent's responsibility to declare the frozen ball, but good sportsmanship avoids arguments.

PLEASE BEWARE

Beginners assume that kicking the cue ball to a rail before striking an object ball makes for a legal shot. No matter how many rails are struck first, a ball must reach a new rail or pocket after cue ball impact with an object ball.

Forward Motion

The cue stick's tip may not rest against the cue ball before the final stroke begins. Such forward cue stick motion without any backstroke is a called a *push shot*. Even on the smallest, softest strokes, a clean hit must be made from a moving stick. Also, the cue tip may not touch the cue ball for an unusual duration following impact and broom the ball along the table, which will also be called as a foul push stroke.

Close to a push stroke, though, helps on delicate strokes. Control your cue tip closely, and study players who have the touch for gentle, guided shots without pushing the cue ball in an obvious manner.

The Double Hit Foul

The *double hit* is an important and complex enough issue to warrant its own sections below. A cue's tip may strike the cue ball only once, during the final stroke taken forward. Two hits during one stroke is called a double hit foul.

One Stroke, One Touch

It should go without saying that it is illegal to hit the cue ball twice on one shot. Players agree that when the cue ball is nudged during aiming or a practice stroke, and then a full shot is taken quickly in an attempt to hide the error, this is an illegal double hit. Similarly, following through to hit the cue ball a second time on any shot is also a foul stroke.

Where arguments arise is when a cue ball rests close to an object ball, making a double hit difficult to see and a source of contention.

Understanding Double Hits

No one foul causes more headaches to a referee supervising beginning players than arguments over double hits. Players can aid the cause by better understanding how such a foul may be incurred and by calling the referee in early to judge any shot that looks to be a double hit when played.

When the cue ball rests less than $1/2$ inch from an object ball, it becomes *extremely* challenging to shoot straight through the cue ball toward the object ball without striking the cue ball a second time. Even the world's best players do not attempt the stroke other than for the occasional trick shot.

A cue ball striking an object ball on a full hit or near full hit *must* stop for fractions of a second following impact before moving away again. With a cue ball $1/2$ inch from the object ball, follow-through must be less than half an inch long to avoid a second hit.

While the pro avoids this stroke, the beginner does not know the foul incurred and plays it. The pool hustler, however, sometimes uses a double hit to gain an advantage, if they think they can sneak past the unwary.

For decades the double hit remained a subject of contention before rules were adopted by most of pool's governing bodies prohibiting the double hit.

Judging a Shot

When called to referee a possible double hit, I rely on the physical pool facts:

1. Experienced referees listen for the telltale "click" sound from the double hit, the extra loud billiard noise from two contacts made nearly simultaneously.

2. It is virtually impossible to make a cue ball follow an object ball when they rest less than an inch apart with a single hit—a longer shot would build the forward roll needed—extreme topspin was applied instead, *requiring* a double hit stroke.

3. Even simpler, any cue ball following the object ball at approximately the same speed as they "travel together" down the table is *always* proof of a double hit.

4. I place my eyes along the tangent line, and for a full or near full shot look for the "stop and go" movement of the cue ball proving one and not two cue stick hits were stroked.

Whenever your opponent is about to shoot a thick hit on an object ball close to the cue ball, call for time out, and ask a referee to observe the stroke. If there is no official referee for your competition, ask a neutral party's help, but ensure the person chosen understands how to judge a double hit.

Figure 12.5
Another double hit argument ends tragically.

Avoiding Double Hits

Trick-shot artists employ several clever techniques to avoid a double hit. One is to use a rail to curb follow-through, allowing the shooting hand to strike the table, sometimes painfully, on the table's outside edge. Another method is a tiny nip stroke (see Chapter 7) accomplished with no arm stroke at all but a minute flex of the fingers or wrist, or both, effecting the required 1/2 inch or less of follow-through. This second maneuver is so difficult it is almost never attempted in professional competition.

A more practical method the pro uses that you can learn is to raise the butt of the cue stick to at least a 45° angle with a stroke taken down toward the cloth rather than toward the object ball. Do not lower the angle with the stroke, or it will likely cause a double hit.

What if the shot may not be easily reached with an angled cue? You may be able to strike the cue ball with a nearly level cue instead, if your stroke is not aimed directly (or close to directly) through the center of both balls. In other words, rather than play a full hit, turn to the left and send the fully hit object ball to your cue stick's right or vice versa.

With raised cue or pointed away from the centers, or both, played correctly, the cue tip will never move the same direction as the cue ball travels, indicating to the referee the stroke is a legal, single hit. The companion DVD to this book illustrates both of these foul avoidance strokes.

PLEASE BEWARE

Some players think they may avoid a double hit by shooting with outside english. This generally doesn't work, since the cue tip will travel the same direction as the cue ball following impact. Use inside english instead.

Sadly, the average player and even some veterans and tournament directors do not fully understand double hits and their legal avoidance. The rule ought to be enforced in pool. Golfers incur a penalty with a second hit on any stroke, as do batters in baseball and tennis players.

Safety Play

EXPERTS ALWAYS CONSIDER defense besides an aggressive table run and use the rules of pool to their advantage accordingly. The player who calls a *safety* is announcing his intention to pocket no ball at all, but to legally drive some ball to the rail following cue ball impact. I recommend you memorize three effective uses of the safety most players don't exercise today:

▶ Clearly and loudly announce your safety only if it will be difficult to see the play, such as in Figure 12.4 above with the object ball close to a rail.

▶ Play *any* other safeties unannounced, disguising intentional defense as a mere miss—does a chess player announce, "I'll move my bishop next because I don't want you to attack it soon..."?

▶ Look for safeties often as a balanced counterpart to aggressive or risky offense.

Nice and Easy

It's the gentle safety stroke, such as in Figure 12.6, that is often the most confounding to the opponent waiting to shoot.

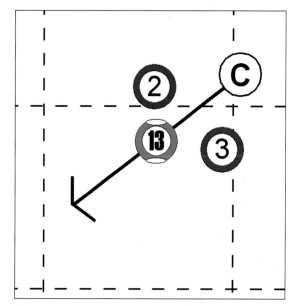

Figure 12.6
Simple but devastating.

In Figure 12.6, the player has ball in hand, playing as stripes in a game of Eight-Ball. The run for the win will be difficult with the 13-ball where it rests now.

Simply playing the cue ball as indicated with a full hit stop stroke, driving the 13-ball to a rail for a legal stroke, leaves the cue ball deep in no man's land, wedged between the 2- and 3-balls. The incoming player will be able to do little with either solid and can't see the rest of the table from behind the cue ball.

TAKE A TIP

If you are like most pool shooters, you dislike playing the cue ball when it is touching other balls or quite close to them or to a rail—so plan your defense and stick your opponent with such a cue ball as often as you can. A few such shots can halt your opponent's playing rhythm.

The Power of Safeties

It seems unheroic to play many defensive safeties until you realize how often the pros and hustlers play safe. Hustlers have pocketed millions in cash playing defense only until the last few balls of Nine-Ball and other games. You might not know how often pros play defense, because TV pool is edited for action with defensive jousting mostly eliminated from your screen.

Think "Two Way"

Not only does the pool expert consider whether to pursue offense or a defensive safety before every stroke, he is overjoyed if he can pursue both at one time.

When facing a low percentage shot, work to leave the cue ball in a position to make it difficult for your opponent should you miss. Such *two-way* shots include a safety option with offense. It's fine to leave your opponent a possible shot if you miss. Making it difficult, not impossible, for your opponent is often enough to win.

For example, in Figure 12.6, we might have driven the 13-ball to a rail and close to a pocket, ready to play with the next stroke after solids misses.

TAKE A TIP

Think when pocketing a ball, "If I sink this shot, where do I want the cue ball and objects to land, but if I miss, where does my opponent *not* want them when I'm done?" Asking that question before every stroke will cause the average player to win perhaps 50% more games than he does now.

More Timeless Tactics

AS YOU LEARN THE RULES of pool, use your creative problem-solving skills to thwart your opponents and win games. Below are more options a clever player keeps close to his heart for emergency needs.

The Intentional Scratch

Figure 12.7 presents a problem to the solids player in Eight-Ball. Left with only the 8-ball to win, his opponent has only the two stripes surrounding the 8-ball still remaining to be pocketed.

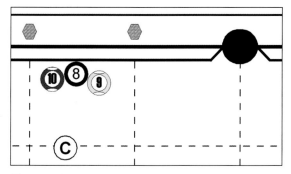

Figure 12.7
No way out?

Most leagues and tournaments no longer rule a scratch on the 8-ball as loss of game. One of the best options solids has, therefore, is to shoot the cue ball straight into the nearest pocket rather than the 8-ball (or touch the cue ball to hand it to your opponent politely) for an intentional scratch and loss of turn.

Any stroke played into the 8-ball will surely move the 9-ball or 10-ball. Let stripes sort the mess instead—if he can. If he plays an intentional scratch next (most players won't think to return your scratch with their scratch), you can stick to your guns and scratch a second time. At some point, the referee could even declare a drawn game. Better to play the percentages by not playing the 8-ball at all.

Consider that a wise play would be to shoot gently to freeze the cue ball to the 8-ball. The stripes might move a little, freeing the 8-ball, and stripes will often further disturb the balls and help.

Set the balls as diagrammed and try it both ways several times. Many beginners are unable to freeze the cue ball as they should atop the eight, especially if the cue ball is farther away than indicated in Figure 12.7. The intentional scratch lends itself to the need.

Time the Rush

The mature player will rarely disturb the balls in Eight-Ball, Nine-Ball, and other pool games, unless he is confident he can run the table for the win. He will instead jockey balls for position, nursing them gently around the table as he waits to spring his ambush.

One important example lies in the speed at which balls are shot, which is somewhat contextual to the game being played. If I am playing Eight-Ball, my opponent is potentially blocked by my object balls, and I will shoot shots accordingly slowly to leave balls resting in the pocket openings if I miss. The same tactic, however, would be foolhardy in a game like Nine-Ball, when both players share every ball. A missed ball shot too slowly would be easy for the incoming player to pocket.

Play a Big Ball

You might recall our exploration of margin error on the object ball from Chapter 8. Balls near a corner are great to kick at with the cue ball when you are desperate for a hit to complete a legal shot. Practice kick shots of varying speeds and distances to learn how to keep the cue ball on the table.

Any ball near a corner pocket is effectively a target three balls wide or more. You might hit either the short or long rail and still touch either edge of the cue ball to the object ball, as shown in Figure 12.8.

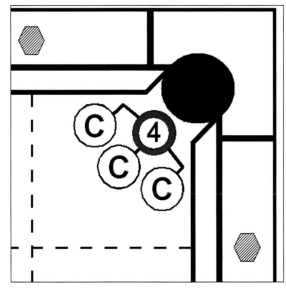

Figure 12.8
The 4-ball is a big target to kick toward.

Games and Tests

Time-honored and popular pool games, Eight-Ball and Nine-Ball, await you in the next chapter, including the chance to test and measure the skills you've learned so far. Let's go!

13

Compete and Enjoy: Popular
Pool Games

Eight-Ball and Nine-Ball make a quick blast anytime

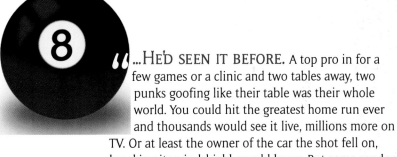

"...He'd seen it before. A top pro in for a few games or a clinic and two tables away, two punks goofing like their table was their whole world. You could hit the greatest home run ever and thousands would see it live, millions more on TV. Or at least the owner of the car the shot fell on, breaking its windshield, would know. But some random person could play the greatest rack of 9-ball or 8-ball with nothing but shadows over the table and two mosquitoes to mark the passing of the time."

—From the novel *Killer Pool* by "Quick Draw"

The little arena we call a pool or billiards table can provide high drama any time you play. Let's examine the two most popular pool games of Eight-Ball and Nine-Ball and discover basic play and strategy.

Popular Games

WE'LL EXPLORE FIRST the popular games of Eight-Ball and Nine-Ball to discover what the pros think, before we review (and hopefully, revive) some of the classic games. Some innovative games are presented in Chapter 15 for you to enjoy.

The most popular games come with their own dossier so you can gauge how likely you are to get a game of its kind or watch the action of the pros, hustlers, and gamblers at your local hall or billiards club.

Eight-Ball

Eight-Ball or "8-ball" is one of the oldest-known pool games, and certainly the most popular in the U.S. It's a chief pursuit of 40 million American players and millions more in Europe and Asia, where its variety adapts easily to every size pool table and pool league. Eight-Ball is dramatically different from Nine-Ball, the other popular game among players of all skill levels. Eight-Ball leagues host millions of players, and giant open tournaments take on thousands, even tens of thousands of entrants, for a single event.

The rules are simple, the game colorful. Bust the rack with an open break, choose solids or stripes and fire away, pocketing the 8-ball last for the win. This outer simplicity, however, belies sublime strategy. Top Eight-Ball play demands more in-depth planning than rotation games like Nine-Ball.

Figure 13.1
Readying for fun.

Eight-Ball also appears most frequently for play on coin-operated tables and in bars and lounges with only one or a few pool tables—the game provides a medium-length challenge neither long and boring nor short enough to have not been worth the wait.

Table 13.1 Eight-Ball Dossier

Distinction	You Bet!	Often	Not Often	Forget About It!
Played at pool halls	X			
Easily learned strategy			X	
Good for you (not pool junk food)		X		
Practiced by pool professionals			X	
Played by gamblers		X		
Hustler's favorite against you				X
Televised on sports channels			X	
Seen in movies and on TV today			X	

▶ Eight-Ball style—easy to watch and understand, a colorful game with an exciting break shot

▶ Handicapping for skill level—take several balls off the table following the break from the weaker player's set (okay, this is more like a hustle, as it mostly frees space on the table for the better player's run) or award points per ball sunk and extra points to the weaker player

▶ In a nutshell—a fantastic game with the complexity of chess for those who care to study deeper

Basic Rules

Following an *open break*, where any ball sunk with the first stroke continues your turn at the table, you are to pocket your half of the object balls numbered 1 through 15 before pocketing the 8-ball to win. The *solids*, numbers 1 through 7, are also called "low balls" or "spots" as distinct from the opponent's *stripes*, numbers 9 through 15, also known as "highs."

Four object balls are to be driven to the rails on the break, affording the player who wishes it a *safe break* where the balls are not widely scattered. In contrast, a powerful break could bring seven or eight balls past the side pockets toward the head of the table! Set the cue ball *near* the middle of the table for the break as the cloth along the exact middle may be worn from other players' frequent use; also, you do not want the cue ball to rebound far up table from direct impact.

Calling pockets, naming the ball and intended pocket for the next shot, allows some flexibility. The ball can go directly inside to the pocket or race around the table, off ball caroms or through the air before sinking for a legal stroke.

Pocketing the 8-ball in the wrong pocket (different than the called pocket) or on any stroke following the break before your set is cleared from the table is an immediate loss of game.

Racking for Eight-Ball

Only three balls are set for a rack of Eight-Ball in specific positions. The 8-ball must go in the center of the third row to protect it from pocketing easily with the break stroke, and a stripe and a solid ball should go to the corners along the fifth row of the rack. Those two corner balls tend to roll to land near the corner pockets, making for a more equal game if one is high and one is low.

I further set the 1-ball to the head of the rack for courtesy. Players are used to seeing it there from Nine-Ball and other rotation games where the balls are struck in number order. I also alternate stripes and solids along the sides of the rack. They will tend to scatter evenly, not offering my opponent an easy out on one set and perhaps a nasty cluster for my half of the balls (see Figure 13.2 for such an alternating rack).

Figure 13.2
Set for Eight-Ball.

Common Rule Variations

The table is *open* following the break, meaning the first called shot following the break determines your set. If you sink two solids and no stripes with the break but prefer stripes, for example, you may attempt a stripe following the break. The opposite rule variation declares the set by break unless there is a tie, such as two stripes and two solids sunk.

Many play *slop pool*, with its carefree attitude toward pocketed object balls. Make any of your solids or stripes in any pocket, even by luck, and retain your turn.

The fairest way to play Eight-Ball is with ball in hand awarded following any foul (some still play that the cue ball must be returned behind the head string for play following a scratch). With this rule, once your set is determined, you must "play clean" on each stroke by impacting one of the balls from your set first on any shot. Yet many leagues and rooms use a local convention allowing a hit on either stripes or solids first, greatly expanding shot possibilities.

Failure to strike one of your striped or solid set first (or striking one cleanly followed by subsequent failure to drive at least one ball into a pocket or rail) yields ball in hand to your opponent.

Ball in hand is also awarded following any scratch. With ball in hand, one measure designed to speed play, a second measure is that object balls illegally pocketed stay down and are not returned to the table. Technically, a player could use his turn to push an opponent's ball straight into a pocket.

Pushing or cueing an object ball illegally without using the cue ball results in a loss of game (or at the minimum, a stern warning for improper conduct).

Force your opponent to break up clusters and positions that deny you success. Control of the table, including your choice of stripes or solids, is key.

Billiard Congress of America (BCA) rules, which pave the way for enjoyable play, stipulate that scratching the cue ball while playing for the 8-ball is not a loss of game unless the 8-ball pockets on the same shot. This rule ends long defensive struggles with players afraid to move an 8-ball sitting

close to a pocket or behind the head string. Again, these rules vary for local rooms, so always determine rules in effect before beginning play and keep both your pool friends and unbroken thumbs.

TAKE A TIP

Try this game variation for fun. *Last Pocket Eights* includes the added difficulty that the 8-ball must be pocketed in the same pocket where the final ball of your set has sunk, demanding thoughtful key ball selection and often, much jockeying of the 8-ball.

Nine-Ball, King of Action

"NINE-BALL IS ROTATION POOL. The balls are pocketed in numbered order. The only ball that means anything, that wins it, is the nine. The player can shoot eight trick shots in a row, blow the nine, and lose.

On the other hand, the player can get the nine in on the break, if the balls spread right, and win. Which is to say that luck plays a part in 9-ball.

But for some players... luck itself is an art."

—From *The Color of Money* (1986), starring Paul Newman and Tom Cruise

For decades now, *Nine-Ball* or "9-ball" has been a media darling featuring a sudden, bombshell break and lengthy, dramatic shots.

Figure 13.3
Busting a rack of Nine-Ball.

Nine-Ball is a *rotation game*, where the cue ball must impact the lowest numbered ball on the table first. The 9-ball may fall on any legal stroke when the lowest numbered ball is hit, even on the break shot following the cue ball's impact with the 1-ball, and the game is over with the shooter winning. Little compares with watching a player break the 9-ball in for the win three times in a row!

▶ Nine-Ball style—easy to watch if the television can render the colors accurately (the balls may be hard to differentiate on a small screen), with an always exciting break shot

▶ Handicapping for skill level—the weaker player might be allowed to win by sinking not only the 9-ball but some other ball(s) that progress in order before it; or in a multi-game match, games might be awarded in advance to the less skilled competitor

▶ In a nutshell—the amateur wants to run Nine-Ball racks often as on TV, but it's harder than it looks

Table 13.2 Nine-Ball Dossier

Distinction	You Bet!	Often	Not Often	Forget About It!
Played at pool halls	X			
Easily learned strategy	X			
Good for you (not pool junk food)				X
Practiced by pool professionals	X			
Played by gamblers		X		
Hustler's favorite against you		X		
Televised on sports channels	X			
Seen in movies and on TV today		X		

Basic Nine-Ball Rules

The 1- through 9-balls are racked in a diamond-shaped pattern, as shown in Figure 13.3. The yellow 1-ball must go in front allowing it to be struck with the first shot without added difficulty. The 9-ball must go in the center for added safety from sinking with the break stroke. It is not necessary to apportion the rest of the balls as shown, the traditional rack with even balls to the left and odd numbers to the right. Racking this way consistently, however, will help you discern general breaking patterns.

Figure 13.4
The balls in Nine-Ball.

As mentioned, the lowest numbered ball must always be the first cue ball impact, following which anything goes. Good players have an eye to pocket the 9-ball as early as possible. Hustlers work to *ride* the 9-ball, some kind of incidental carom to set it to motion, to make some long and lucky looking win by "accident."

Nine-Ball Blues

It can be tortuous to watch a player with "9-ball blues" or "ring around the 9-ball" bat away at the last ball of the game without success. In large part

a psychological phenomenon, otherwise fine players who can run the other eight object balls cannot seem to can the 9-ball for the win.

The best solution I know to end the struggle is to leave one's head and body down to the table following cue ball impact with the 9-ball, waiting to rise until both balls have come to rest. Pretend there is a 10-ball on the table and the 9-ball is just another ball to be played in sequence, not for the win.

Pick the specific cue ball shape for that imagined 10-ball and commit to it. This focus will allow you the freedom to pocket the 9-ball "with a good or poor shape on the 10" rather than obsess over taking some stroke of perfection for the game win.

Breaking a Rack

What is not luck to a pro is the Nine-Ball break. Think of this shot as skillfully determined rather than the product of chance. The hustler can pop the 1-ball in the side, and on a poor table the two rear balls in the corners, fairly regularly.

Think, "I'll pocket a ball and leave the cue ball in the middle of the table" rather than hacking away at the rack with all your might. Set the cue ball nearby the right-hand long rail if you're right-handed or vice versa for the left-handed player. Strike the cue ball on the break with a bit of inside english and a little draw, aiming to impact about one tip's width to the near side of the 1-ball.

If you're playing Nine-Ball at length on one table, look for patterns in the break. You may find a certain ball pockets easily in the corner, or the 1-ball sinks in the side, when breaking from a specific position. Sometimes the 2- or 3-ball travels three rails to a pocket.

If you scratch in the side often, aim a little more to one side of the 1-ball in an attempt to deflect the cue off the rack, into the side rail, and out again into the middle of the table. Pros otherwise move the cue ball. Placing it an inch or two, back or forward, can help manage the ball's bouncing movement.

TAKE A TIP

Nine-Ball becomes a multiplayer game as a ring game with shooters taking turns in order and points or wagers affecting balls in addition to the 9-ball. Typical is to assign a value to the 5-ball and to spot it and the 9-ball if sunk out of numerical order. The skilled player can thus sink the 5- and 9-balls several times within one rack.

Common Rule Variations

The *push out rule* allows the stroke following the break to send the cue ball anywhere you wish, not requiring that a rail or object ball be struck at all. Your opponent may accept the new position or force you to shoot again. Play a push to somewhere, therefore, that you'd like to play from but your opponent would probably dislike.

Here the hustler is well placed to start hiding the cue ball immediately. Do not confuse the push out opportunity with the foul taken for playing a push stroke (see "Forward Motion" in Chapter 12).

The *three fouls rule* has three successive fouls or scratches by the same player or team end the game with a loss. The referee or opposing player must have verbally announced when two fouls have been taken, making such announcement between the second and third fouls. Yet another device for the skilled hustler who can make your safety balls appear to have taken "lucky rolls."

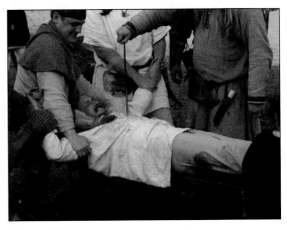

Figure 13.5
Punishment for hustling pool has long been torturous.

Amateur and professional tournaments waver on occasion between calling all shots taken, calling the 9-ball for its intended pocket only or slop pool. It's almost insulting for a top professional to be able to continue their turn after a ball goes in the wrong pocket, but luck adds a little dash to the proceedings. Certainly, the more I practice, the luckier I get.

TAKE A TIP

The game of Nine-Ball readily lends itself to *Stunt Pool* where anything goes except a simple ball in pocket stroke—you must play a carom, a bank, a combination, a massé, something fancy on each and every legal shot taken. Providing much merriment, Stunt Pool helps players learn to think creatively at the table.

Eight-Ball Versus Nine-Ball

AMERICA'S TWO MOST popular games both have a strong fan base, with action fans giving the nod to Nine-Ball and strategic thinkers enjoying Eight-Ball more. What are some of the other differences that make for an exciting choice for beginners and experts alike?

Figure 13.6
Which game to play next?

In Nine-Ball, running racks brings the player with the better break an important advantage. In Eight-Ball, the break is not as clear an advantage, being more difficult to predict and master. In Nine-Ball it is often easy to play a safety after the break, but Eight-Ball's opening shot is generally more critical because it establishes the choice of solids or stripes. If the first shot is made but the second missed, the opponent does not have choice and might have a low chance of running from the incoming position.

Nine-Ball demands a finely tuned stroke and the ability to control the cue ball over long distances. Eight-Ball requires more thinking, planning, and the precision cue ball control needed to deal with 15 potential obstacles. Whereas Nine-Ball requires defense against one ball, Eight-Ball may require defense against as many as seven balls at once.

Strategically, Eight-Ball probably has more in common with chess than it does with Nine-Ball and often demands solid defensive play. At the professional level, perhaps half of the games of Nine-Ball are won without a defensive maneuver. This is not the case with Eight-Ball. The top Eight-Ball players are masters of defensive strategy. This is not to infer that they are better players—but it is no secret that the two games require different skills. The great shotmaker tends to win Nine-Ball, the great thinker Eight-Ball. Of course, possessing all the various skills makes you a winner at any pool game.

Many players should shoot Eight-Ball more than they do to build their skills, but they dislike having beginners play poor position with the cue ball yet luckily find another stripe or solid to shoot toward. The hustler knows a lucky player can still run the table and usually avoids betting *his* mortgage on the game.

Eight-Ball and Nine-Ball Defense

Another key to Eight-Ball and Nine-Ball, one ignored by most, is to plan ahead for safety shots. Instead of waiting until you are in a difficult situation to start thinking about a safety, learn to predict and avoid tough situations. Rather than going for a difficult break shot and the chance for a run, play position for a safety. Let your opponent take the foolish chances. In Nine-Ball, where only two object balls need to be driven to the rail on the break, it is possible to play safely even on the opening shot of the game with a gentle stroke.

You will use balls in contention for both players for Nine-Ball safeties. Eight-Ball allows you to use your balls as sheer obstacles for the opponent though he can only hit them indirectly.

For either game, when playing defense look for *lock safes*, where the opponent has scant chance to succeed, instead of opting for the first safety that comes to mind. Put yourself in your opponent's shoes and search for the worst place for the cue ball for them to use next. What might they do with that shot? Leave them in position to play a better safety to you, and you've failed.

You can hamper an opponent's chances on the Nine-Ball break by setting the 3- and 5-balls behind the 1-ball and the 2- and 4-balls above the 8-ball in their rack, scattering as widely as possible the early balls in the run.

Running Racks

Plan any runs backward from the 8-ball and a key ball or two to get close to it (or ensure the last few and 9-ball are clear in Nine-Ball). An easy run still demands careful shot selection.

Figure 13.7
Get to running.

Eight-Ball and Nine-Ball are less often won by great shots than lost by poor choices. The expert earns ball in hand for sure wins more often than their opponents and avoids performing difficult shots.

Eight-Ball and Nine-Ball champs bypass unsure runs for defense instead. Only run if you are relatively sure of success, with no jacks or troubling balls on the table, and aces and queens on opened firing lines to the pockets (see Chapter 11 and "Let's Play Cards"). Never save your toughest positioned balls for last. But avoid breaking jacks apart in Eight-Ball unless there is *another* ball close by whose position is resting secure. Leave an exit ball, what author George Fels has called a pool "safety valve," to continue the run if the cluster break fails.

Shot Selection

Look for at least three ways to accomplish any given task to expand your possibilities. Options should include multiple ways to pocket an object ball, play offensive position, and play safeties for defense.

Walk around the table to view the run (or safety play) from multiple angles. If I had a nickel for every pool shooter who said after the play, *"I didn't see that the [problem or solution] was to simply...."* I have earned far more than nickels from some of these nearsighted folks!

Is there an ideal shot choice for any given Eight-Ball or Nine-Ball shot? Usually, there is, by playing position on your next ball plus an eye to defense against your opponent's run in case you miss. Thinking this way provides the luxury of never being forced to make a difficult shot to win.

Don't give in to a tempting but difficult offensive shot. There are always defensive options.

Never move any balls without a specific reason. Accidental nudging of object balls is a common error made by novices. The flip side, skillful ball work, is maintenance of all nine or 15 balls in correct positions, maneuvering your winners to good spots and your opponents into trouble.

Physical pool skill is finite and so is your practice time. Mental skill is potentially unlimited. Challenge your imagination to constantly seek better shot selection.

Powerful Open Breaks

THE AVERAGE PRO breaks with the cue ball at around 25 miles per hour. Women professionals range from around 16 to 25 m.p.h., the men 20 to 30 m.p.h., although female pros are growing in their knowledge and application of strength training for the break.

Break Rumors and Myths

It used to be rumored that a good pool break shot could fly at 100 miles per hour or more, at least until author Robert Byrne and physics expert Bob Jewett, Byrne's frequent pool project collaborator, pulled a short rail from the foot of a pool table and measured cue ball breaking speed, derived from

flight distance as the balls left the table (and rolled from the pool garage down the driveway and at passersby on the sidewalk). Thanks to Byrne and Jewett's (literally) groundbreaking efforts, we've since learned that controlled power, not wild gyrations with the body and cue stick, is the hallmark of successfully harnessing break energy.

The average pool shooter mistakenly believes that outside english can aid the open break stroke, another myth. Outside english will not help separate a rack or cluster better but will have the cue ball travel farther and escape impact better—leading to a careless scratch on many breaks. *Inside* english kills the action of the cue ball following impact.

I've seen players injure themselves and others by adding topspin to the break. Although topspin may help a cue ball burrow a second time through the cluster following impact, the unpredictable results attained can include sending the cue ball high into the air rather than dispersing energy through the racked balls. Follow spin can even jump the cue ball clean off the table following impact with the rail. The pros use a bit of *draw* and inside english on most breaks instead.

More Break Tips

Enjoy this digest of breaking tips to aid your powerful opener for Eight-Ball and Nine-Ball:

▶ Practice slamming the cue ball with all your might into the far corner pocket—players otherwise afraid of the break collision tend to shoot at the corners as they ought to at the rack, bearing down a bit and vigorously moving the shooting arm. Take a little might off the stroke if the room owner suggests you are abusing the pocket.

▶ Insist on a tight racking of the balls from your opponent and get a re-rack if you are dissatisfied with his efforts. You can also suggest racking your own balls where local rules allow, although I am sure to inspect my opponent's racks most carefully if I think they are on the hustle.

▶ Experiment with grip, holding the stick so loosely that it might clatter to the floor with a slightly looser hold on the break.

▶ Set your shooting hand about three inches back from where you normally grip the cue and the bridge hand about two inches to the rear for added speed without sacrificing control.

▶ In contrast to the above tip, you might want to try choking far forward on the cue instead, pressing the muscles of the shooting arm into the compressed position used for weightlifting.

▶ Use a far lighter cue stick than you think you need—I've broken in many, many balls using a 15-ounce break stick, as net force equals mass times acceleration—you can accelerate a light cue more easily than a heavy one.

▶ Pivot your shooting side foot to stand higher to the table than normal, a foot higher for your shoulder and head frees your shooting arm to move powerfully through the stroke and creates a longer distance for the lower arm to travel.

▶ Take the final backstroke slowly, feeling as though you are drawing a bow back and storing energy for the final thrust forward—the beginner rushes the backstroke and wastes energy in the direction opposite the break.

▶ Make a smooth breaking motion—smooth is not "slow"—the break can be fast and smooth.

▶ Add some ulnar deviation (see Chapter 4) to the shooting hand's wrist on the last backstroke, allowing for an extra flex of speed coming forward again.

▶ Pause with the final backstroke, stepping toward the shot and slightly upward, forcing your muscles to tense with contraction and press forward.

▶ Quick hands are all you truly need for a mighty break stroke—fast-moving hands and fingers will do more for the player than other body parts, and fast hands with slight body movement equate to a power break controlled with ease.

▶ Feel as though you are dancing or gliding through the break; muscle tension will tighten and choke the power stroke.

▶ Strike near the head of the apex ball of the rack, but if you find your concentration wanes, try the second row of balls instead (for Eight-Ball and other games).

▶ Lightly apply chalk before the break stroke—the added friction of chalk forces the cue tip to adhere to the ball longer, but you want the cue ball to rebound faster on the break—a thin, hard tip helps also.

▶ Add minimum spin and english to the break—a cue ball that skids into the rack will rebound at impact and stop somewhere near the middle of the table where you want it for the next shot.

▶ See if you can find a crooked cue to break with; a twisted cue can provide the feel of a pro break stroke where the stick twists, flexing at impact—please don't bend a friend's cue for this reason.

▶ Practice the break stroke without racked balls by sending the cue ball to strike as many rails as possible on an otherwise empty table.

▶ Move the body a bit forward before the final forward stroke, bringing the large and *then* the small muscles of the body into play for maximum power.

▶ Have the follow-through come so far forward that the stick tip comes close to touching the rack area going forward.

Wrap Up

Understanding the theory and strategies of the most popular games, with an eye to improving your practice and wins in competition. That's what this chapter is all about.

A look at *Straight Pool* and its family of games and the battle known as *One Pocket* come next.

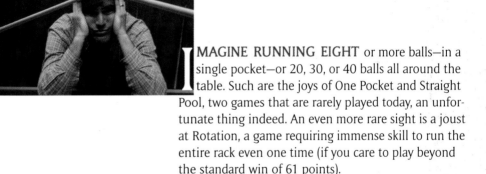

Strengthen Your Skills: Classic
Pool Games

How pros test themselves

IMAGINE RUNNING EIGHT or more balls—in a single pocket—or 20, 30, or 40 balls all around the table. Such are the joys of One Pocket and Straight Pool, two games that are rarely played today, an unfortunate thing indeed. An even more rare sight is a joust at Rotation, a game requiring immense skill to run the entire rack even one time (if you care to play beyond the standard win of 61 points).

You can learn from these games the pros and hustlers play "for fun." Start playing them at your local poolroom, and you can help me revive these games for all to enjoy.

14

Classics to Remember

WHILE EIGHT-BALL and Nine-Ball occupy most of the tables in the Western world, there are other classic tests of skill that make for a fabulous game and strengthen your skills to practice them also. Pocket Billiards, Straight Pool, Rotation, and One Pocket are not seen often enough today. Adopt them and make them your own, and pool will thank you for it.

Pocket Billiards

Pocket Billiards is both the official name of the sport of pool and a game that is simple and enjoyable. Its official name is *Fifteen Ball Pocket Billiards*. Rack all 15 balls together, break 'em up, and then shoot them in as best you can. Be the first to reach eight balls sunk (more than half of 15) before your opponent and win.

Pocket Billiards is a good challenge for the intermediate and offers many run possibilities following the break. A newer player can learn to run from the break frequently to win in an inning or two. I'd like to see this game played far more often by beginners, limiting their pool frustration and heightening the basic fun of pool.

Figure 14.1
Breaking Fifteen Ball Pocket Billiards.

TAKE A TIP

For a clear exposition on all the general rules affecting Pocket Billiards, plus game-specific rules not covered here, I recommend the Billiard Congress of America (BCA) rules listed at www.bca-pool.com.

Rotation

Combine the scoring of Fifteen Ball Pocket Billiards with many of the rules of Nine-Ball, and you have the challenging skill game of *Rotation*.

Play as in Pocket Billiards, but count each ball's number as the number of points it scores—the 15-ball is worth 15 points, the 8-ball eight points, etc. With 120 points available in the rack, 61 points or more wins between two players.

Rotation, also known as *Chicago*, was extremely popular in the World War II era, and it provided servicemen and women overseas plenty of entertainment, as it would make for a longer game on a coin-operated table where sunk object balls may not be retrieved until the next rack. The game faded into near obscurity as bachelor soldiers returned home from theatres of war and pool halls to marriage and family.

Rotation is a good game to have in your repertoire with its reliance on kicks and safety play with the early balls in the rack, plus possibilities for running the last balls or even perhaps battling to the final 15-ball for the win. Running all the balls from the break, whether as combinations, caroms, or singly, is so difficult that it is considered a once-in-a-lifetime achievement to run three racks of Rotation or more in a row.

The skill game Rotation is popular along with the challenging game of Straight Pool (see below) in the Philippines, another reason why top professionals from that country are dominating the sport in the U.S. today.

Mr. & Mrs. Billiards

The chauvinistically named *Mr. & Mrs. Billiards* recalls the days when men would carouse, gamble, and smoke at the pool hall with a seldom pool visit from a spouse.

The stronger male player would need to run the balls in rotation order, and his wife could shoot any ball she wished, possibly putting the fellow away with the shortest possible 61-point win of five balls, such as the 12-13-14-15 and any other ball numbered seven or more.

Rotation versus Pocket Billiards seems a fair handicap for the author of a pool book to tackle, but Janine Sherman has often doused my hopes in similar prompt fashion. Mr. & Mrs. is great for introducing your friends to pool and you to occasional humiliation.

Straight Pool

MORE THAN A CENTURY AGO, Pocket Billiards and other games were considered far too simple for the experts; therefore, *14.1 Continuous* or *Straight Pool* was devised.

▶ Straight Pool style—a lengthy game if played for more than a few points and requiring some of everything, including banks, combinations, and caroms, defense, offense, and thoughtful strategy

▶ Handicapping for skill level—the stronger player typically awards points in advance to the weaker shooter, or limits are placed on maximum ball runs

▶ In a nutshell—the king and queen of pool games, worth exploring if you want to improve your skills and walk in the steps of pool's greatest champions

Table 14.1 Straight Pool Dossier

Distinction	You Bet!	Often	Not Often	Forget About It!
Played at pool halls			X	
Easily learned strategy			X	
Good for you (not pool junk food)	X			
Practiced by pool professionals		X		
Played by gamblers			X	
Hustler's favorite against you			X	
Televised on sports channels			X	
Seen in movies and on TV today				X

Basic 14.1 Rules

Call every shot taken to an intended pocket, including the break, which makes for an often gentle break designed to thwart the incoming player's chances.

Each ball pocketed is worth one point, with any bonus balls falling on a called shot counting toward the player's score. Balls sunk illegally are returned to the table in a line along the *center string* of the table, an imaginary line dividing the table in half along its length. Beginning with the foot spot, balls returned to play could ruin a player's day. You can see three balls strung together in Figure 14.2 and inviting shots to be taken only at the player's peril.

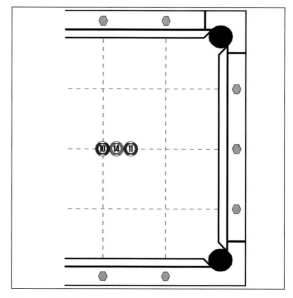

Figure 14.2
Stringing balls in Straight Pool.

The first scratch costs the player a point, the second successive scratch a point and a declaration warning of two successive fouls, and a third turn's scratch costs one point for the foul, 15 points added penalty, and a full re-rack of all 15 balls. Ouch! Cue balls sunk in the pockets are returned to behind the head string for the next shot.

TAKE A TIP

A common break is to drive the two rear corner balls of the rack to the rails, returning the cue ball three rails to the head of the table for the incoming player. It is possible to drive two and only two balls to the rail and have them roll back exactly into place, leaving a perfect rack once again! Find witnesses who will testify to this rare feat, and take a few photos if you perform it someday.

Break or Pay

The rule that sets the challenge of Straight Pool above all others is this—following the pocketing of the 14th ball of the rack, the 15th ball and the cue ball must rest in position while the rest of the balls are racked before play continues. A break on the pack with the 15th shot each time would thus continue the player's term indefinitely.

As shown in Figure 14.3, the intention would be to pocket the yellow 1-ball in the corner plus send the cue ball into the pack of 14 balls, scattering at least some of them in a controlled fashion. Note the foot spot remains empty while the other 14 balls are re-racked.

Figure 14.3
Break shot below the rack.

Straight Pool rack shots require skill and care, especially in the selection of key balls and positioning the cue ball. What if following the stroke of Figure 14.3, the cue ball remains hopelessly buried in the mass of balls? What if some ball set loose knocks the cue ball into a pocket for a scratch? Perhaps worst of all, what if the rack is scattered beautifully, allowing for easy pocketing everywhere, but the 1-ball fails to sink, giving the incoming player an entire table of shots?

Sorting the Pack

Soon you will be able to plan the sequence of 15 balls in a few seconds. You can follow the guidelines outlined in Chapter 11 for sequencing. Try to leave two to four loose balls near the center cluster. All 15 do not group easily, with usually three to five balls somewhere representing single plays. I like to leave one ball loose below the rack for later, perhaps as a backup break shot, besides at least two possible break balls near the rack's sides.

Champs at 14.1 strive to keep each cue ball path away from reaching a second rail. Gentle position shots are the rule. Look for as many stop and limited cue ball movement shots as possible.

Straight Strategy and Records

Unlike seven balls in Eight-Ball or one or two in Nine-Ball, defense at Straight Pool is against an entire rack of balls, though they are generally found clustered together for defense.

The expert can separate clusters of balls during one or more cluster shots per rack and continue to pile on the offense. While Willie Mosconi and Ralph Greenleaf relished separating all the balls fast in one go, most of us other mortals gently separate the rack across several cluster shots, reserving balls near the pack each time for this purpose.

A handful of elite players have run 400 or more balls in Straight Pool practice or competition without a miss, a feat that typically requires three hours to complete. Strong players sometimes play *ten or no count*, meaning that any run of less than ten balls counts as no points scored, giving rise to the expression, *"This shooter is so bad they can't run [even] ten balls."*

It's just a hard game for scoring many long runs. A 9-ball or 8-ball run is usually made easier as the rack progresses and the table's empty space widens. Straight Pool gets tougher with fewer options as the rack thins. Pressure mounts as a run gets higher and the odds tighten, plus balls can't slop in with luck to count.

Willie Mosconi's official high run of 526 balls in Straight Pool may never be equaled. Mike Eufemia's run of 625 has not been accepted as official because no one other than Eufemia witnessed the whole run. There are likewise rumors of Arthur "Babe" Cranfield and Mosconi running over 700 in practice sessions.

Scary good of Mosconi, is it not? Leave the 15th ball and the cue ball where they come to rest, and then sink this lone ball while breaking the other 14 again. Scoring 526 straight is 37 re-racks without a single miss!

Break Shots

Set the three break shots, as shown in Figure 14.4, for practice. These diagrams are not to scale, but the general principles apply even if you do not shoot the same precise shot on the table. The angle off the 2-ball into the pack is a good shot to play for a safety also, as a gentle stroke will leave the cue snug against the group, though if the ball hits much farther from the center of the two head balls, it can scratch. You have the option in Straight Pool of calling safe and sinking a ball like the 2-ball with the stroke.

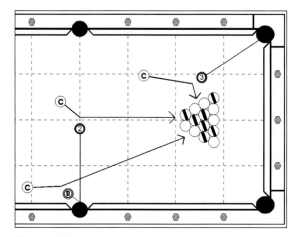

Figure 14.4
Break opportunities.

The cue ball tends to be more effectual at splitting the pack when not striking the corners as with the 2-ball but along the second row along any of its three sides.

If you play the 13-ball with some draw, it won't wander into a scratch following rack impact. The 3-ball is played with topspin and perhaps a bit of right english to get the cue ball off the pack again.

Practicing 15th ball break shots will save you years of play in improving at Straight Pool and waiting for appropriate shots to arise. The pros like to run four to eight or nine balls to a key ball for the break for practice. On the final stroke of each set, they focus on moving the cue ball from the rack impact toward the center of the table, sometimes drawing off the rack but on other strokes, rolling through an edge of the rack.

PLEASE BEWARE

The sides of the rack are likely places to have the cue ball stick unless speed and spin are strong. In contrast, hitting the corner balls may separate fewer balls at a time from the pack but release the cue ball back into play better.

Opening Lag

Lagging for the break in Straight Pool requires both players to hit a ball from the head of the table to its foot and back, with the closest to the return rail winning the lag and choosing who breaks.

An old story has Mike Eufemia (see "Straight Strategy and Records" above) preparing vigorously for months for a rival match against Willie Mosconi. For months, Eufemia labored over all his

skills, honing them to a knife's edge: banks, kicks, break shots, running tens of thousands of balls, and much more.

The big day came and the two pool giants lagged for the break. Eufemia's ball came to rest fractions of an inch from the rail, a few credit card widths away from perfection. Mosconi's ball came to rest upon the rail itself for the win. "Break 'em," followed Mosconi's barked order.

Eufemia's near perfect break left an edge of one object ball visible behind the rack. Mosconi called the ball and made it, going on to sink 125 balls without a miss to end the match. Eufemia had taken but one shot.

"Mosconi, I was ready for you! I practiced and practiced, and I could have beaten you!" exclaimed the distraught Eufemia. "You should have practiced your lag also," quipped Mosconi.

My lag is usually a winner. Here are some tips:

1. Strike the cue ball 7/10 up its vertical axis for immediate true roll at impact.

2. Use a bridge distance of about four to six inches for control.

3. Look at the cue tip last rather than the rail target at the head of the table—hit the cue ball precisely for *distance*, it need not meet the rail precisely opposite you to succeed.

The Workout

Straight Pool is good for you to practice, requiring concentration and skill in all its aspects. Set one of the strokes of Figure 14.2 on the table or your favorite break shot and see how many you can run without a miss following the cluster break. If you can get through 14 balls and into a second rack with a second successful break shot, you are truly coming along to be a fine player.

Indeed, Straight Pool is the sole game to practice short of repetitive ball drills if you want to enhance your overall pool skill. It's been frustrating to watch new and average players hack at Nine-Ball or Eight-Ball for years without ever bettering their game.

Equal Offense

I like the game Equal Offense, a slightly modified version of Straight Pool, invented by Jerry Briesath, which may be used to build a practice log to score results over time. One of its highlights is an open break rather than the more delicate break that Straight Pool demands.

Player rankings, score sheets, and much more are available online at www.ieotour.com.

One Pocket

IF EIGHT-BALL and Straight Pool approach or exceed chess in complexity when played by experts, One Pocket is the pool equivalent of World War II. Jockey the balls for position for up to an hour before the final assault is launched!

▶ One Pocket style—it is war, and the winning side can change in a moment; patience and skill are required in equal measure

▶ Handicapping for skill level—the weaker player will need to pocket fewer balls than his opponent and is often awarded the opening break

▶ In a nutshell—banks, kicks, and exotic safety play mark this game relished by hustlers and pros

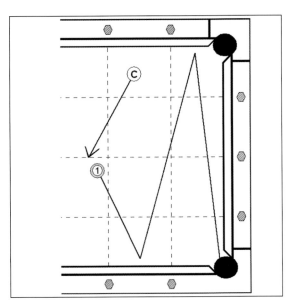

Figure 14.5
Bottom outside english One Pocket bank.

Table 14.2 One Pocket Dossier

Distinction	You Bet!	Often	Not Often	Forget About It!
Played at pool halls				X
Easily learned strategy				X
Good for you (not pool junk food)			X	
Practiced by pool professionals		X		
Played by gamblers		X		
Hustler's favorite against you		X		
Televised on sports channels				X
Seen in movies and on TV today				X

Basic One Pocket Rules

Rack the balls and sink half plus one (or eight balls) in either corner pocket close to the rack to win. The breaking player announces his choice of pocket beforehand, his opponent is awarded the other pocket, and the breaker designs to send much of the rack toward his own pocket.

Balls pocketed in any of the other four pockets are returned to play after the inning ends, along the center string starting from the foot spot as in Straight Pool.

Spotting a ball punishes scratches. The player's score is lowered by one point, also. A player counted to have sunk five balls in his pocket is scored as four following a scratch. A player with zero balls sunk who scratches owes a ball to the game and is scored as minus one point.

Banks and Bunts

The easiest way to defend in One Pocket is to send the cue ball to near the opponent's pocket following a miss. If the cue ball is within a diamond's length along the rails, as shown in Figure 14.6 where the opponent's corner is Pocket A, it will usually be difficult to score a ball back in that same pocket.

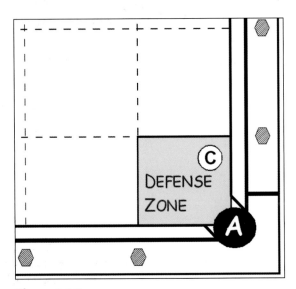

Figure 14.6
One Pocket's defensive zone.

Cue ball control is one name of the game in One Pocket, the other being spectacular bank and kick shots. The expert varies between running eight-and-out in the same pocket, requiring top cue ball positioning, or sending the cue and object balls on long tours around the table to finish in or near their corner following multi-rail shots.

Mind the Score

A key determinant setting One Pocket offense or defense is the current score. With a big lead of six balls scored to only two for your opponent, for example, you might send balls away from your key pockets to the head of the table. If you leave your opponent an open shot, he can't run many balls and get back into the lead. You are attempting to reduce the game into mini-games of one or two balls per turn. You need only one or two of these small games. Your opponent would need to succeed as many as six times in sinking a ball and leaving you without an easy ball to pocket.

You might otherwise play more aggressively, leaving the balls at the foot of the table if you are trailing far in score.

Get Sleep Beforehand?

Knowing that a good One Pocket player can sink many balls in a row given a chance, there can be a long defensive struggle with players waiting a half-hour or more to gather balls to their liking before running much offense. I often take a foul and owe a ball rather than give up the whole game on a risky stroke.

One Pocket can produce exquisite shotmaking, if sometimes only after a long war campaign of balls juggling without many balls sunk at all.

TAKE A TIP

A faster game of One Pocket is made by racking nine balls in the diamond shape of Nine-Ball instead of the full rack of 15 balls. Five balls sunk in one pocket wins the game and the added space around the table allows freedom for offense to be played early on.

Patents Ahead

Read on for some out-of-the-box innovative (and fun!) games you can use to dazzle your pals and learn a few more pool angles.

Turn Practice to Pleasure: Innovative
Pool Games

Games to tempt you

"**I** TAUGHT YOU EVERYTHING you know, kid. But I didn't teach you everything I know."

—James Coburn as pool hustler "Nick Casey" in *The Baltimore Bullet*

Pool holds few measuring standards to look to with comfort. I can tell any golfer that I hit my drive 280 yards down the middle and he assesses my skill instantly. I can tell a soccer fan that I've scored a hat trick or a basketball player that I can make 9 of 10 foul shots and they understand my ranking.

The following games, besides being more fun than a dozen barrels of monkeys, allow you to better assess and refine your skill levels at pool.

Gopher Eight-Ball

SOME TIME AGO, I was seeking to create a new pool game to add value to my students' practice, including some of the best that Eight-Ball, Nine-Ball, and Straight Pool has to offer without their game complexity. *Gopher Eight-Ball* lets the player run a string of shots together easily while still requiring caring about the consequences of a miss.

Simply rack the balls and play as in Eight-Ball (see Chapter 13) with a key difference—any and all balls may be played before the 8-ball is sunk for the win. You can add ball in hand for any *miss*, let alone a foul, for a more action-packed game.

Gopher Eight-Ball forces the player to consider the key ball concept by saving good opportunities for a sequence immediately before the 8-ball. You can also consider your opponent's skill level and play safe or hide balls accordingly. Failure to do so by clearing most but not all the balls makes you a gopher, fetching help for the incoming player!

For example, you have five balls left besides the 8-ball, and with more options than in a rotation-style game (the lowest numbered ball must be struck first), you decide to attempt to run the table. If you make four balls and then miss, you leave your opponent only two balls, having done the work of the game for them as in Nine-Ball.

Game variations players enjoy include:

▶ Gopher Hunt—The opponent is forced by the player's declaration to shoot the last ball missed, first, with two such declarations allowed per game per player.

▶ Keyed Up Gopher-Eight—The key ball the player plans to shoot before the 8-ball must be declared to start any turn, when five or fewer balls remain on the table.

▶ Eight Gopher-Eight—All the stripes (or solids) then the other set are to be cleared from the table, with the player able to change sets at the beginning of their turn by declaration.

Bank Pool

RACK ALL 15 BALLS (or nine in the diamond shaped rack of Nine-Ball), and you have set the table for *Bank Pool.* Following the open break, when any balls pocketed are returned to the table but the shooter retains his turn, each and every legally pocketed ball must bank at least one rail.

A confidence-building game for many, although one should generally avoid bank shots during competition (why take a chance with unpredictable rail action?) running five-and-out or eight-and-out in bank pool is a memorable thrill.

Sharkers!

WHEN JACK NICKLAUS was a teen golfer, his father admonished him that a temper outburst would be punishable by his leaving the golf course. Once and only once did young Jack break his dad's rule and walk home, ashamed, the lesson learned to control his emotions during competition. Earl Woods went one step further with son Tiger, who was only nine years old when Earl said, "No matter what I do, Tiger, no matter what you hear or see from me, you may not respond to me or the game ends now." Tiger soon developed nerves of steel as dad taunted and cajoled him, locking out all distractions.

Sharkers! is a laugh-inducing riot of a game inspired by these great athletes' unusual training sessions against uncontrolled emotion and distractions. Pick your favorite pool game and set an added rule that short of physically touching the shooting player or the equipment on the table, any and all devices may be employed to get the player at the table to miss. In other words, go wild!

Shouting out loud, disco music, dropped sticks clattering to the poolroom floor, funny faces and gestures, bizarre voice intonations while disrobing, gross bodily functions, you name it—anything you wish or imagine can be done, although the player is often less disturbed by the unusual behavior than their opponent and the onlookers.

Sharkers! may enhance a pool friendship or end it, so get agreement from all around before playing. Be prepared to laugh until you cry.

Seven-Ball

*S*EVEN-BALL IS A FINE GAME that has stepped into prominence in recent years on sports channel television. Rack as in Figure 15.2 by circling the number one through six balls around the maroon seven. The wooden rack is angled to one side to set the yellow 1-ball on the spot in a secure cluster of balls. Shoot in rotation order using the rules of Nine-Ball (refer to Chapter 14).

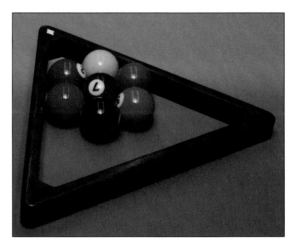

Figure 15.2
Racking Seven-Ball.

The pros add a bit more skill to the game by shooting the 7-ball into the side and by awarding ball in hand following any miss, not just any scratch or foul stroke.

I heartily recommend Seven-Ball. It is far easier to run a rack than in Nine-Ball. The ball in hand rule keeps folks on their toes at most times. As an addition, players can by agreement reserve a safety call or two per game, so they can play a defensive shot without yielding ball in hand for a missed pocket.

They can further call the 7-ball to an intended pocket *and* a safety for the same shot, giving them a shot at the game winner with a safety possibility rather than handing the opponent ball in hand on the 7-ball. Being the first to call safety or forgetting to call safety on the final shot can have losing consequences.

Figure 15.1
A powerful Seven-Ball break.

Try Seven-Ball soon; it's *the* game of the future, in my opinion.

Six-Ball

*S*IX-*BALL* SHOULD seemingly be easier to run than Seven-Ball. Again, the game ball is in the middle (see Figure 15.4) and there is one less object ball in Six-Ball than Seven-Ball. The reality is that no ball of the six easily yields on the break, and fewer balls positioned around the table make for a sometimes more difficult run.

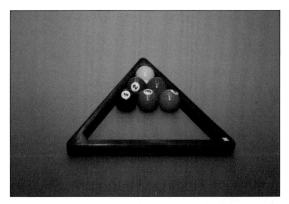

Figure 15.4
Ready for 6-ball.

Six-Ball and Seven-Ball are still in their infancy as far as play in professional tournaments. The pros are debating currently whether it is to one's advantage or disadvantage to play the opening break and take the first try at the rack!

Either game is good for the newer player who might have trouble running even one rack out of 40 or 50 games of Nine-Ball.

Figure 15.3
Breaking six object balls apart.

Cutthroat Billiards

AN ELIMINATION BILLIARDS game, *Cutthroat Billiards* is popular in social settings such as collegiate poolrooms where multiple players wish to share one table together. For three players, assign the 1 through 5 balls to Player A, the 6 through 10 balls to Player B, and the 11 through 15 balls to Player C, or leave an open table until shots are taken to determine sets following the break. Shoot until your balls have been removed from the table. The last pool shooter standing wins.

Rule variations are unlimited and add to the social nature of the game. For example, I like to stipulate that the player may shoot any balls including their own set, but if they personally sink the last of their set, they may continue that turn in an effort to run the table and defeat their opponents. Another rule punishes a scratch by spotting one of each set from the opponents but not the player, possibly resurrecting an eliminated player to the rack once again.

Cut Matt's Throat

Cut Matt's Throat was created after I was counted too great a threat by playing pals. (Thanks, guys.) Winning a rack of Cutthroat removes a ball from the player's set for subsequent racks until the player is ultimately crowned champ after winning five racks. The weaker players receive an automated handicap to aid them—the more one wins, the easier it is to knock them out from subsequent racks until only one ball needs to be removed to take them out of competition. The other players tend to gang up against the player in the lead and are allowed to plan strategy, making for a social game.

Stick to one set of balls as lows, highs, or "mids" across the multiple racks of this game to avoid confusion. Mids are often a winning position, fooling the other players who carelessly forget that you carry solids, stripes, and the 8-ball all in your set.

Three Minutes and Counting

HERE'S ANOTHER CONTROVERSIAL game. Will *Speed Pool* ultimately help or hurt the amateur who needs to take enough time over each aim played, or does rushing through a rack build vital elements of tempo and trust in one's stroke?

Rack all 15 balls as for Pocket Billiards and break them apart. Give yourself three minutes to shoot them all in. When you can get the job done in a timely fashion, restrict yourself to two minutes or even one.

Speed Pool pros can run a rack of 15 balls in 45 seconds or less. Although entertaining to watch, I am uncertain whether a game that is played faster than the TV commercials block following it is a good or bad product of our busy consumer culture. The popular and charming "Machine Gun Lou" Butera, who once ran 150-and-out in Straight Pool against Allen Hopkins in 18 minutes, would not mind. Willie Mosconi, known for running 125 in less than 30 minutes, and especially if he held a ticket to a local baseball game starting within the hour, might have also approved.

Some hustlers reveal their skill at fast play in a unique way. Preying on the unwary late at night in a pool hall, these sharks duel with their fish over a few "friendly" money games. The hustler remains nearly even in victories with their opponent until closing time is announced, "That's it, folks! Last drink of the night, please!"

The speed hustler then runs four or five racks without a miss fast while the snails in the room finish their last game. The hapless mark, of course, must pay losses in full without a chance for reprisal that night. The hustler hits the road until they go fishing once more in a new location.

Bowliards

WHEN DIRECTING A POOL league, I enjoy mixing the regular work of Nine-Ball, Eight-Ball, or Straight Pool with social events filled with games like Seven-Ball or *Bowliards*, a fast favorite of many players.

Bowliards combines a simple pool game with the bonus scoring of spares and strikes from bowling. Rack any ten balls, as shown in Figure 15.5. Shoot an open break. Balls pocketed on the break stay down. You now have two successive innings to attempt to pocket all balls.

Figure 15.5
Time for bowling.

All ten balls made with the break and first inning are scored as a strike as in bowling (the player's next two innings' scores are added to the strike's inning score of ten points). Use the second turn to finish, and you have a spare (adding one bonus inning's score to the spare of ten). Scoring is easy if you cannot complete all ten balls in two turns with one point awarded per ball sunk.

Ten frames of bowliards (ten to 22 innings at the table) provide a score up to 300 points for a perfect game of 12 strikes (ten strikes plus two strikes in the bonus innings following the tenth frame). If you can score 150 points or more at bowliards on any size of pool table, your game is growing healthy and strong.

I like Bowliards and Fargo (see below) to help the newer player work on his break shot. I recommend that players try different breaking speeds with the cue ball. Work on feel to scatter the rack of ten balls well across the table.

Fargo

Fargo is a clever game derivative of Bowliards, named after Fargo, North Dakota, hometown of Mike Page, the game's creator. As with Bowliards, ten frames are played. Break all 15 balls, spotting any balls that sink and taking cue ball in hand to begin the frame.

Again, a single frame is worth up to 30 points. Balls shot in rotation order score 2 points each or else count only 1 point.

If you shoot the balls in rotation order (as in Nine-Ball or Rotation), they score 2 points each. Otherwise, they count as 1 point each. You must declare during the frame when and if you switch from one-point shots to a rotation attempt to run the table, at which time it is advisable to mark your score to that point of the frame. You may declare for rotation one time only—it's a commitment to finish the table or else garner a few two-point strokes that are simple for you before a miss.

For example, Billy and Nancy are playing Fargo competitively, alternating frames at the table. Billy runs five balls for 5 points before calling rotation and sinking three more balls for 6 points, for a total of 11 points. Nancy runs ten balls for 10 points before switching to rotation and runs three more balls but forgets to declare her choice until the last ball sunk. She earns 1 point for each of the two undeclared rotation balls and 2 points for the final ball as declared, giving her a total score of 14 points (she would have had 16 points if she declared at the correct time).

Fargo provides balance between aggressive greed and a realistic assessment of the table and your skill. Consistency in the break and placing the number 2 through 5 balls in the rack to advantageous rack positions (experiment with ball placement, the 1-ball must go to the apex for the break) will help your scores greatly.

Scoring 100 points would be a solid score for an intermediate player. 150 points is an outstanding achievement. 250 and up would be world-class, with 300 being considered impossible as Rotation is already a difficult game indeed. Then there is the Fargo restriction limiting balls to be pocketed in order without the possibility of shooting scoring combinations using the lowest ball.

Q-Skill Scoring

Top pro Allen "Young Hoppe" Hopkins created another scoring tool similar to Fargo and Bowliards that you can use to assess your skill level. This game is also fun to play. For Q-Skill, rack all 15 object balls and break by shooting from the head spot.

Figure 15.6
Bank pool break.

A scratch on the break scores minus 1 unless the cue ball is jumped off table for a minus 2. Balls scored on a non-scratch break count for one point apiece.

After the break, shoot using the cue ball as it lies or 1) shoot from behind the head string, 2) shoot from your choice of head or foot spot at any ball, or 3) place the cue ball anywhere within the rack area. Moving the cue ball following the break, however, is subject to a penalty of minus 1.

Following the break, whether a ball has sunk or not, try to run the table calling all shots. The last five balls remaining are shot in rotation. Again, non-sequence balls are worth a point and the rotation balls 2 points apiece, for a maximum 20 points per inning.

Ten frames are scored as with Fargo or Bowliards to comprise a session. The total score from ten sessions, 100 racks, determines your official rating as follows:

Table 15.1 Q-Skill Scoring

Score Across Ten Sessions	Official Skill Rating
0 – 300	Recreational Player
301 – 600	Intermediate Player
601 – 900	Advanced Player
901 – 1200	Developing Pro
1201 – 1600	Semi-Pro
1601 – 1800	Professional
1801 – 2000	Touring Professional

Three-Ball

*T*HREE-BALL, WHICH MAY BE racked as shown in Figure 15.7 or Figure 15.8 (see below), still challenges one's skill with the balls separating to perhaps much poorer spots than in Six-Ball or Seven-Ball.

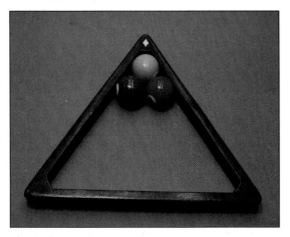

Figure 15.7
Three-Ball.

Take any three balls you wish, as this is not a rotation game but a golf-like game, where the player seeks to make the lowest score possible by taking the fewest strokes. Break the balls hard or softly, your choice, but any scratch with the cue ball in the pocket ends your turn.

Any non-pocketing cue ball stroke is accepted. In other words, the cue ball need not hit any object ball or even a rail to make a legal shot. The player may jostle the cue ball into position as needed. You

have four strokes including the break shot to sink all three balls or else end your turn at the table.

The Wrinkle

Three-Ball takes off in high gear when it is opened as a multiplayer gambling or social game. It's my preference of game for large groups of seven players or more while not running a formal tournament. Everyone antes one monetary unit or one point per round. Ties carry over for every player to ante and increase the pot for the next round.

For example, eight beginning players each put a dollar in for a turn at Three-Ball. With a pot of $8 on the line, five of the players scratch the cue or fail to run the rack in four strokes. One player shoots a 4, but the remaining two shooters score 3, one having broken in a ball on the break before sinking the next two balls on subsequent strokes and the other breaking in two and taking two more strokes to sink the final ball. Since the lowest scores were tied, the money carries over to the next round. Everyone puts in an additional dollar and has a chance now to win $16. A dozen players can enjoy an hour of entertainment for a few dollars apiece.

The real fun begins somewhere after each round begins as scores are posted. Let's say the first player of the round scores a 4. The second player knows a tie is useless for a payout, and breaks the balls hard, attempting to score a 1, 2, or 3 without scratching the cue ball. The remaining players are allowed to coach the second player, giving advice—after all, they want a tie to occur and make their money safe for now. In other words, everyone is excitedly chattering away from one of three perspectives, player one wanting player two to fail in four tries, player two wanting a low number score for himself, and the other six players rooting and advising for a tie score of 4.

The fun can get a little sour or strange when serious (degenerate) gamblers are involved. An old trick is to help a two tie another two for score by racking the rear balls spaced apart carefully and illegally—so they tend to fly as combination shots straight into the corners on the break! I've even had the displeasure of seeing cheaters bend a player's break cue. More often than not, this seems to result in unusual spin imparted to the balls, and a 1 scored when all three balls sink on the break. Cheaters never win.

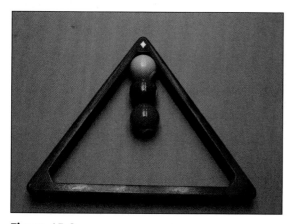

Figure 15.8
Alternate rack for Three-Ball.

Judge of Character

I find this gambling game provides an accurate portrait of a player's determination and table knowledge. The Three-Ball intermediate will score many fours, the expert many threes, especially when the balls are racked in a triangle pack, sending the rear balls around the table into the corner or side pockets with the break.

When balls are missed on the break and on subsequent shots, I can quickly appraise how a player comprehends and strokes various caroms, kicks, and banks. Following two misses, the player is forced to attempt to sink more than one ball on a single shot. A player has reasonably strong skills if he can get both balls in motion consistently, let alone sink them with a stroke. And whether the player quits the game or makes an attempt at all three balls on one stroke as need arises is also telling.

As a Practice Game

As with Straight Pool, Three-Ball makes for a reasonable practice game. Running three balls in some planned sequence is at the heart of solid pool.

For an added challenge, break the balls before pocketing them in numerical rotation order. Can you run the balls seven of ten times from the break? It's time to add a fourth ball to the rack. When and if you are ready, add a fifth ball to your practice challenge.

If you can consistently run five balls from the break in order 90% of the time or more, you are ready to earn money in your local pool tournaments and perhaps bigger challenges, too!

Card-Based Games

YEARS AGO, *SHAKE BOTTLE* pool games were popular, requiring that random numbers were drawn from a specially made plastic bottle to determine key object balls, team affiliation, and more—even the bottle itself became a target for the cue ball in the game of *Bottle Pocket Billiards.*

You can simulate these exciting games using one suit from among a deck of cards. Each card represents a numbered ball from the rack of 15, the ace the 1-ball, the two the 2-ball, up to the jack as 11-ball, queen as 12-ball, king as 13-ball, and two additional cards or jokers to represent the 14- and 15-balls. Two or more players may draw cards and hide them to everyone except themselves. Shoot the balls in rotation order. If a player sinks the object ball appearing on their card, they reveal the card to declare the win (or points scored or whatever you choose by agreement).

The playing cards, lying face up on the cloth, can also make handy targets for the cue ball or object balls to rest upon for score. For example, the player may choose to declare their object ball before the stroke is taken and rest the card on the table where they plan to land the cue ball with the stroke for a bonus point. You are limited only by your imagination.

Drill Games

ANYTHING ONE CAN DO to turn drill practice to fun can only aid your game. *Daddy's On One* is a little game the kids invented for me when they were young. They would roll a ball onto the table and say, "Daddy's On One." If I could sink the ball immediately on the next stroke, they would place two balls on the table and say, "Daddy's On Two." We all looked forward to see how far Dad could get before a miss. "Daddy's On Fifteen" required 105 shots made just to see the layout.

This practice game was always a delight for us all until the children realized where Dad's weak spots lay on the table and placed all the balls there, for example, in pretty, symmetrical patterns, such as all balls touching one another or all balls on the rails, or both!

Another charming drill game involves placing the cue ball alone with the stroke. Besides requiring a table and rail in good condition, driving the cue ball five times from the foot spot to the head rail and back to touch your cue tip with a straight stroke requires nearly perfect stroke technique. A top pro can send the ball away and back to them again 20 out of 20 times.

You can make a healthy practice game from any favorite shot or a shot that has caused you issues in the past. Simply bring the cue ball close to the object ball and, after you have some success with the shot, remove the cue ball farther and farther back along the shot line for increasing difficulty.

One of the best of these drills is shown in Figure 15.9. The 8-ball is off the long rail, however slightly. Sink the 8-ball in the corner with a straight stroke. Any deviation at all from a straight stroke, and the cue ball will move a small distance following impact. Strive for a perfectly still cue ball at impact.

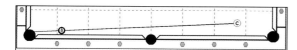

Figure 15.9
Super drill.

Ten to twenty of these shots just before competition will strongly enhance your stroke and your confidence and concentration at the table.

Golf pool games involve setting a "course" of predetermined shots to be made successfully in as few strokes as possible. Classic golf drives an object ball into each of the six pockets of the table.

Beginners can place a ball at the mouth of each of the pockets on the table, as shown in Figure 15.10, and start with the cue ball behind the head string before working to make all the shots without a scratch in less than six strokes.

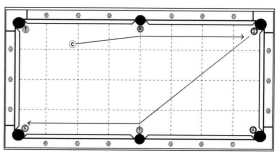

Figure 15.10
The first two of a golfing three.

My suggestion for the first two strokes for a simple three is shown in Figure 15.10. I'll leave it to you to discover how to pocket the 9- and 4-balls with the third stroke. Finally, a practical use for the common scratch in the corner taken from near the side pockets!

Scoring Your Personal Best

YOU MAY WANT TO KEEP a record of your personal bests in pool, giving you marks to shoot for (pun intended) at the game. For example, a professional shooter's best might read like the following chart. I added a sample intermediate player's score next to the pro's records for comparison.

Table 15.2 Player's Record Card

Measure	Sample Pro's Score	Intermediate's Score
Straight Pool Hi-Run	110	23
One Pocket	15 balls and out	8 and out
Rotation	Break and run (120)	Break and run of 30 points
Bank Pool	8 and out (rack of 15)	5 and out (rack of 9)
Nine-Ball Racks Run from the Break in a Row	10 racks	2 racks
Most Balls Sunk on Nine-Ball Break	6 balls	4 balls
Eight-Ball Games Run from the Break	6 racks	1 rack
Most Balls Sunk on Eight-Ball Break	5 balls	3 balls
Bowliards	300 points	126 points
Fargo	205 points	90 points
Q-Skill	1,750 points	547 points
Three-Ball Racks Run	Five 3s and 2s	Four scores of 4
Longest Pool Session	30 hours	5 hours
Fastest Speed Pool Run of 15 Balls	45 seconds	2 minutes, including three missed shots
Most Balls Sunk on Trick Shot	13 balls	4 balls

Player Ratings

THERE ARE A VARIETY of rating and ranking systems in use for various tournaments, leagues, and pool games. The A-B-C system is a general rating of overall skill. *C players* frequently miss simple, routine shots, can run three balls in rotation order about a third of the time, and make significant judgment and position errors.

B players comprehend most of the shots available in pool, have a working knowledge of spin and english, and are skillful with cue ball shape, banking, kicking, and defensive safeties. They run the table often, especially if the lay of the table looks to be easy.

A players run many tables from the break and frequently extricate their cue ball from difficult positions. They hardly ever fluff a basic stroke or shot.

A+ players are commonly called *shortstops*, beneath the professional level they will be stopped in their tracks by a pro, although they defeat A players routinely.

These informal ratings fluctuate depending on the local hall and region and what games are played most there.

Edu-Tricks

What I call *edu-tricks* for educational trick shots are listed in a bonus section on the *Picture Yourself Playing Pool* companion DVD and will add to the skills presented with these innovative games. Check out the DVD for the *three go down shot, one hand magic*, the confidence enhancing *wing shot*, and more fun at pool.

Build Your Game: Buying and Maintaining a Personal Cue Stick and
Table

Swing with zing

"IT'S A BALABUSHKA.

It's beautiful. It makes the others look like stickball bats. This yours?

You want it?

No. This isn't for me. I don't know who this is for. No, this isn't for me. John Wayne would carry something like this... if he played pool. Babe Ruth."

—From *The Color of Money* (1986), starring Paul Newman and Tom Cruise

I've enjoyed owning different cue sticks and playing with trusted pals' cues, as well. A favorite cue in my collection, once owned by fine shortstop player (see "Player Ratings" in Chapter 15) and Broadway, movie, and TV star, the late Jerry Orbach, was handmade by the legendary Frank Paradise

Learning from Paradise and going one better was George Balabushka, creator of perhaps the finest cue sticks ever. Balabushka's wood craftsmanship was so extraordinary that he once lost a finger in an industrial accident and crafted a replacement of wood. Few people ever noticed the substitution.

Go and Buy

A T SOME POINT in your pool career, hopefully soon after you've completed the exercises in this book as a beginning player, you will purchase your own cue stick to enjoy for years to come.

Invest an appropriate amount in your first pool purchase. Cheaply made sticks available at wholesale department stores are usually poor buys. Plan to spend around $100 for a quality cue stick (less if you can find one new on eBay.com or perhaps a still straight, used cue stick). Avoid ostentatious decoration on your first cue—at least until you are more comfortable with personal weight and balance specifications before committing to a fancy cue. Decorations add to the price but little to the playability of the cue.

Consider a "cheap" cue ($100) that you can abuse without much risk and learn pool with, breaking, jumping, and shooting massé with it. Many beginners play for several years with such a cue until they discover the stick qualities they want to make a larger investment in.

Used Values

Consider a new tip, ferrule, or an entire shaft for a cue, if existing damage means you'll get a substantial discount on a broken cue you like. Tips and ferrules are between $3 and $10 apiece, and a cue maker can provide a second shaft (ferrule and tip included) for between $35 and $150, even for a stick costing many times more than that.

Some players carry a second shaft in their case, like tennis pros who bring multiple rackets to a tournament. Many dealers provide a second or even third shaft for their new cues, including them in the price of their merchandise.

Appearance is also a factor, if a modest one, as some design will fit you personally; and to feel confident at the table is to play confidently.

Take a Test Drive

Billiard parlors featuring cue rentals are helpful and often have several different brands you can try. Good brands for a beginner and up include McDermott, Meucci, Mali, and Adam (maker of Balabushka mass-manufactured cues, Adam cues, and Helmstetter cues).

A cue with a weight or tip much different from what you're used to playing with can lead you to form a false opinion of a cue. I like to heft the cue in a hand or two first to get a general feel for the balance and weight of the cue. The feel of the weight can differ from the actual weight due to an insert sunk inside the butt of the cue, materials and tapers used, and other factors.

Perhaps a friend will let you play with one of their cues for a few games. Most of my students are shocked at the quality differences between even a modest personal cue and a typical house cue. Often, the seller of a used cue will let you play test the cue for an hour or two.

Figure 16.1
Tranquility on the blue felt.

General checklist for a stick you are considering for purchase:

- ▶ roll the cue, assembled and both halves separately, to check for warp and set it on edge as described in Chapter 3

- ▶ no visible gaps or glue marks between any two parts

- ▶ should have a rounded leather or fiber tip, carefully applied (no screw-on tips; they are poor indeed for play)

- ▶ look at and feel the ferrule for discoloring and scratching

- ▶ look and feel for nicks on the shaft

- ▶ examine the joint for signs of excessive wear

- ▶ check the wrap for signs of wear

- ▶ look for a name embossed on the butt, verifying the manufacturer (some custom cues do not have this feature)

- ▶ of greatest importance—shoot with the cue to see if you will enjoy it

Lots of Money for One Tip

IN ONE OF POOL'S IRONIES, the player is spending money on a cue mostly for the action provided by a tip worth a few dollars. By having the same cue at the table each session, the player ensures the tip width and shape remain consistent, making aim and stroke repeatable.

You are also paying for a one-piece cue feel when purchasing a two-piece cue stick. It's simply too difficult to lug a 57-inch or longer cue around town. Cue innovator Herman Rambow perfected a counter-recessed joint, making for a two-piece cue assembled at the poolroom and feeling solid as one unit, earning a cue maker's spot in the Billiards Hall of Fame.

Tip Care Tips

Most players from amateurs to pros appreciate a cue tip 13 millimeters in diameter, and this is standard in cue construction. Some prefer closer to 12 mm. or 11mm. for their style of play or to accommodate smaller hands.

Figure 16.2
When tips come together, the game is great.

The best tips *mushroom* little, maintaining an even circumference. Water buffalo tips or a Triangle or Le Pro hard leather tip are adequate for a cue. A softer tip may be more forgiving, but it requires far more maintenance to stay round and will likely harden quickly with play anyway.

Some cue repairmen will add fiber or a material pad of some type between a new tip and your cue ferrule. The pad helps absorb the shock of ball impact and helps keep the tip in shape longer in my experience. Certainly worth the few dollars charged for the service.

The pros like to fine-tune the height of a tip, where the crown of the tip is in semi-circle standing above the rest of the leather. A crown of about an eighth to a sixteenth of an inch is preferred.

You can use a black, magic marker to color the edge of a tip for a consistent, crisp look that is darker than the natural brown leather. Rotate the tip beneath the marker and possibly add some masking tape first to the white ferrule to avoid discoloring it with a stray mark.

Tip Care Tools

Most tip shaping tools you'll ever need are provided in an all-in-one unit available for a few dollars called the Ulti-Mate Cue Tip Tool, made by APT Industries. The tool includes two *shapers* in the form of sandpaper, molded to a dime's circumference and a nickel's, a *tip tapper* for slightly pricking the cue tip at the beginning of a playing session to best adhere chalk, *trimmers* for removing the mushroomed edges of a tip and a *compressor* for keeping the tip tight and avoiding mushrooms in the first place. These tools are available separately from other manufacturers also.

Before play begins, I give my cue a few taps with the tapper to better hold chalk. When a new tip is in use, I shape it carefully over several sessions to round it to a nickel's edge (a dime's edge goes out of round faster), and that's about it for maintenance.

Players who tend to play close to the center develop a flatter tip, and those who enjoy playing with a lot of draw and spin have a more rounded tip from play.

Weighty Words

Cues are getting lighter as the professionals play on fast cloth more often. Pros tend to use 19 to 19 1/2 cues for most shots, but if slower cloth is unveiled for the pro ranks, weights will change again in the sport. As mentioned in Chapter 3, a slightly heavier cue will aid the beginner, 20 or 21 ounces, and the lighter cue is more easily manipulated with the hands by the intermediate.

If you aren't a pro, you will probably want a softer tip, a short stroke, and a flexible cue. People see the top pros with ultra-stiff cues and three-foot long strokes and mistakenly feel that's what they need for their game.

Rock Bottom

The *butt* of the cue is often of sturdier wood than the shaft, providing a solid, weighty grip for the player's use. Its thickness lets the average person wrap his hand around it, touching his fingertips together around the other side.

The area where the player grips the cue with the shooting hand is the *wrap*, where leather or fabric promotes a better grip than bare wood for perspiring hands.

Nylon is the standard wrap for most cues priced around $100. A little more buys linen, often a cloth known as "Irish linen." Both are cool to the touch and adhere to the fingers well. A leather wrap is the most expensive type available, and it comes as a standard item with only the finest cues.

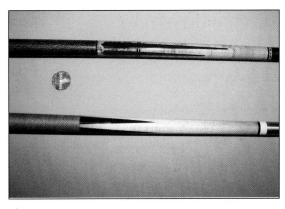

Figure 16.3
A Frank Paradise masterwork and a modern cue by Quest.

Another option is a polyurethane coating, a finish, over the fabric or the wood itself, making a sure grip and an attractive, glossy-looking cue.

Except for leather, which requires delicate care, clean the butt of a cue with a little soap and small amounts of water. Take care not to bleach the color out of a fabric wrap.

Rubber Bumpers

The bumper is the rubber protuberance at the back of a cue that protects it from being chipped on its bottom. It is another aid in reducing the vibrations that pass through a cue stick, keeping the tip from prying loose from the cue. A bumper can also be a blessing to your walls and furniture!

Rapping one's cue stick against the floor, in a sort of pool player's salute, is the traditional way to applaud an especially skillful or clever shot. Today, you can be a purist and remove the bumper from your stick to make an extra loud noise.

Wood for Purists

Although graphite cues are readily available, these should be used for breaking only. Wood is the last word for the pool purist. Don't leave your cue in the trunk of your car overnight. Extreme changes in temperature can warp the wood of the stick.

The butt including the nylon or linen wrap needs to be wiped down on occasion with a dry soft towel. Avoid wetting the wrap or tugging at it, fraying it. A soft cotton cloth is fine for wiping debris from shaft and butt alike.

Cues have lengthened since the 1950s from 56 or 57 inches in length toward 58 inches, saving the player the use of the mechanical bridge. Manufacturers are getting requests for 59 and even snooker-length cues of 60 inches. Be warned that you might wait a long time if requesting a longer custom cue. Properly prepared, it's something you have to plan for a year or more in advance. The blank cue sections must be cut longer and then allowed to age over time before the cue is finished.

Make Your Own Cue

LIKE ROBERT REDFORD fashioning a magical baseball bat from a tree struck by lightning in *The Natural*, many pool players have been bitten by the desire to create unique cue sticks.

Hundreds of new cue craftsmen have sprung up in recent years, opening cue shops with varying degrees of success. Many of the more successful at this endeavor already worked in a wood shop or industrial manufacturing before entering the trade. Locally near my home, Chris Nitti's fame has been growing for handcrafted cues mastered at his Orlando shop, and his cues are fetching handsome prices today. I have also enjoyed working with Russ Sill of Gainesville, Florida, who honed his woodworking craft for decades as a yacht and boating architect and repairer.

Sill's story is like many new to the cue industry. He once told me, "When my son hooked me into playing pool again several years ago, I wanted to use my talent in wood and inlays to produce beautiful cues for pool players to enjoy." Sill has trademarked his innovative Q4 Shaft and other pool inventions. Searching for just the right shades of orange and blue for Gator cues celebrating the University of Florida, Sill uses a semi-transparent orange material for ring decorations, and has even made an entire cue butt from the material. When sunlight streams across the cue, you can see through it.

There is a danger in treading new cue waters, however. Over the years, countless cue pioneers have poisoned themselves breathing in varnish, wood dust, and other byproducts of cue manufacturing. It's best to apprentice another craftsman first and use all appropriate safety devices when crafting homemade cue designs.

Down to Cases

THE BEST PROTECTION for your new cue stick is a fine case. Spend enough money on a case to guarantee that random bumps and jostles will not damage the stick. A carrying case conveniently holds one cue or more and accessories. Fabric cases, with a shoulder strap and soft lined pockets, are available for less than $25, and one is necessary if you plan to leave home with your cue.

Figure 16.4
Setting for the break.

More expensive are fancy leather cases, or hard cases with fitted compartments, resembling the type used to transport musical instruments. Heavier than the soft, nylon varieties, they give the cue added layers of protection from collision and the elements. At a higher price range, Whitten Cases at www.whittencases.com makes astonishingly attractive cue cases in a wide range of styles and designs to your personal specifications.

The beginner will want a "2 by 1 case," designed to carry one butt and two shafts (you can experiment and have two shafts for a cue stick with different tips, tapers, or other specifications). Pros will carry up to a "6 by 3 case" and beyond for multiple break and jump cues, favorite cues, hustling cues, and more. A micro-weave rag may be used to wipe down the shaft and butt following play.

I wipe the chalk fully off my cue tips with a rag or a wet fingertip before returning the shafts to the case, preventing stray chalk bits from sliding along the case to scratch and discolor the cue inside. The Cue-Z protects a cue from stray chalk also and is available direct from its inventor, Nancy Cote, at her website at www.cuezcuetipcover.blogspot.com. Cote also sells finger slides, billiard gloves to aid a smooth stroke that cover only the fingers needed for the stroke, a technique she calls "UnGloves."

Consider buying a personal cue clip to hold your cue upright and out of harm's way at the local pool hall. These clips instantly snap on to the side of the table for your convenience. Keeping a cue vertical is also the best way to prevent warping.

A Clean, Smooth Cue Shaft

A SMOOTH SHAFT enhances a gliding, oily stroke. Fast Orange hand cleaner may be used to remove chalk stain from a shaft. I also like Cue Doctor's Cleaner & Conditioner, a formula that tends to slick the shaft as well as clean it.

Grime deeper inside the wood can be carefully removed with fine grain sandpaper of at least 600 grit grade. Rub down the shaft and then use a damp towel to lightly rub the shaft. After it dries, go over it again with 600 sandpaper and after that apply a good wood wax to seal the pores of the shaft. 800 to 1200 grit sandpaper may be used after to remove the excess sealer from the surface.

A light rub with fine sandpaper before play will not thin the shaft noticeably for many years. Bear in mind that some shafts receive a coating of varnish by the stick manufacturer and removing the varnish could reduce the look and resale value of a collectible cue stick. Sandpaper and wax or not, most players would benefit from a quick cue rubdown with a dry towel.

An old trick but one not well known is to *glass* the cue stick with silica. Take a smooth tumbler or glass with no decals or straight edges on it. Place the cue stick tip on the floor and hold or rest the cue at a 45° angle to vertical. Vigorously rub the glass as fast as you can up and down along the cue shaft, fast enough so that the cue stick becomes warm to the touch.

Microscopic amounts of silica from the glass will bond with the cue shaft's wood, to slick its length. Great exercise for the arms and hands, as it takes 5 to 10 minutes to coat a shaft length well. Interestingly, no harm will come to the glass from the microscopic particles released. You may use and safely return a favorite drinking glass to your cabinet.

Do not clean a sticky cue shortly before an important match, unless you are ready to shoot with a suddenly changed slick and quick cue.

Shaft Variations

SHAFT TAPER, FERRULE MATERIAL to absorb vibration, and tip hardness and shape make the most noticeable differences in cue playability. A shaft may have a *gradual taper* along its length, forming a conical-shaped cue half that

thins from a foot or so ahead of the joint separating its two sections down to the ferrule. This sort of taper will have the stick grow along the bridge hand during the forward stroke until the cue sticks inside the hand, helping end the follow-through.

A *pro taper*, where the shaft maintains an even thickness from the ferrule for about a foot going back, is nothing special. It is called "pro taper" to help sell the stick. This taper is usually found on less expensive models, but if you like it, it's for you.

A *double taper* has the shaft narrow at first, starting a few inches behind the tip, then widening again, making the shaft thinnest near its middle, a boon if you have arthritic or small fingers. The expert's delicate touch benefits from this thin shaft. The extra lathe work required to produce this type of stick tends to raise the price.

Repairing Dents

THERE ARE CERTAIN CLEVER WAYS a dented shaft may be repaired to create a conical, smooth surface again. They are best left to a repair professional, who can be found through your local pool hall. Be sure to get references from satisfied customers, also.

For a gentle dent, a few drops of water applied to the stick and soaked in will tend to swell the wood to fill in the gap. The water soaks into the shaft, fixing any nicks and cracks by swelling the wood, or at least reducing them in size. Wood shafts scar easily, but anything less than a large, deep gouge should not affect play.

Figure 16.5
Six balls, endless possibilities.

Gauging Deflection

HOW DO YOU TEST a new or used cue for its playability? There is a simple test for straightness as outlined in Chapter 3 under "Looks Cool and Works," but how can you determine how much undesirable deflection (see "Deflection a.k.a. Squirt" in Chapter 9) a cue stick or replacement shaft for a stick might provide?

A quick test will reveal if a cue stick is worth the money, and many expensive sticks fail this test. The test movement is similar to the application of pivot english in Chapter 9.

Line straight on a cue ball to strike a nearby object ball (perhaps one diamond length distant) with a full hit. Pivot your shooting hand using the forearm so that the cue runs crooked through your bridge hand. Shoot straight through this new shot line, hitting the object ball full, and observe the action of the cue ball. Shoot firmly enough that the cue ball will not have time to curve off line.

The cue ball should sit in place spinning like a top after hitting the object ball. Each cue stick will have a precise bridge length that makes this test possible. Experiment to play as much english as possible without a miscue. The shorter the bridge length you may use safely, the more deflection the cue will generate, forcing conscious or unconscious compensation on many strokes.

Much deflection is undesirable in a cue stick, especially if you use parallel rather than carabao english strokes. You might be fortunate enough to have a deflection bridge length equal to your typical bridge length, which could help you compensate for any swerve motion off line of a straight stroke. In other words, the cue's squirt factor is adjusted to your game.

Designing a Pool Room

REMEMBER RUMPUS ROOMS, the party atmosphere, a place to goof off a few hours in solitude or with close friends? What was once a party room or garage has made way for an all-entertainment room filled with computers and a gaming console, large screen televisions, fabulous stereo speakers, and on occasion, a beautiful pool table. Here are some elements of design if you wish to create a room to enhance your pool experience.

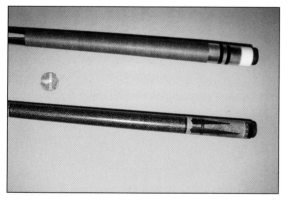

Figure 16.6
Butt end designs, then and now.

Consider the installation of media batts or noise block. I remember waking my family to the click-clack sounds of billiards from downstairs—and so do they, not fondly. If building a new room or home, sound baffles can go inside the walls, fitted between the lining and drywall of the building. Uninterruptible Power Supply (UPS) units will cut down on electronic noise from high-consuming large televisions and equipment.

Heavy room curtains will curb screen glare and absorb noise, and thick carpeting will do the same. Neutral shades of blue-gray, gray, or light brown will also provide a welcoming, cozy atmosphere.

Pool tables require direct lighting above their surface, few shadows thrown across the balls. Antique lighting, replica antiques, or modern recessed lighting add to the atmosphere.

Although tables of about eight feet in length are the most popular, if you can afford the space, get a nine-foot table—your game will thank you for it.

Make Room

Art and Dana Rogers, who designed Gainesville, Florida's Art of Billiards where many of the photos for this book were produced, started with the correct mindset for their hall. Dana explained their room philosophy: "Gainesville is a central location for our APA Pool League, plus we wanted to bring what we hope is a full-service poolroom to the area. The rooms were designed so players wouldn't bump into each other while playing, and colors were used that would be calming and serene."

Much more than those sentiments for room to stretch and feel serene, a player cannot ask for reasonably. When installing a table in your home, plan to leave five feet clear surrounding each side of the table, so players do not strike walls or furniture with cue sticks.

Clean the Table

ALWAYS VACUUM THE FELT on pool tables with a gentle, dustbuster-type vacuum. Don't use the whisk brush that usually comes with a table, as it just brushes the chalk into the felt. Dry Cleaner's Secret cloths (available at drug stores and supermarkets) are moist enough so that three or four cloths applied will clean your table easily.

Keep food and beverages from the table, and the cloth should last for many years if it was installed tightly beneath the rails to begin with.

Figure 16.7
Taking to flight at Art of Billiards.

Poolroom Checklist

YOU NEED THE FOLLOWING ITEMS for your personal poolroom.

▶ a 4 1/2 x 9 foot or 4' x 8' table from a reputable dealer or a used table in good shape

▶ a set of 15 balls plus a cue ball

▶ at least one triangular ball rack and perhaps a diamond or specialty rack

▶ chalk cubes, preferably Master brand blue

▶ your personal cues, if you have any, plus three or four extra house cues for visitors' use

▶ a storage rack for equipment not in use

▶ a gentle vacuum for cleaning the felt

▶ a mechanical bridge for hard-to-reach shots

Note to Potential Investors

SAVVY BUSINESSPEOPLE and the media are discovering America's adoration of a hot trend— "cool pool." New rooms are opening weekly, offering great pool and other diversions, hundreds each year in the United States and Canada alone. The number of small-to-corporate sized pool manufacturers working to meet demand is increasing exponentially.

Figure 16.8
Soaring, flying.

Equipment sales, league memberships, etc., however, have barely begun to reach the millions of potential aficionados of the game. This powerful profit base is still mostly untapped, and should last for decades.

Ninety percent of pool table manufacturers' *tenfold* sales increase during the late '80s, following the small rush provided by the pool movie *The Color of Money*, came from homeowner purchases. Each home's new "play-furniture" carried a life expectancy of 20 to 40 years or more—and each home's "pool hall" can receive new cloth, cues, balls, posters, furniture, music equipment, etc., more than once. There is much advertising to be done.

The ranks will continue to swell, doubling and tripling over the next few decades, if pool's potential growth pans out. Top echelon marketing can do it, if pool is managed on the massive scale that corporations like Nike and stars like Tiger Woods and Shaquille O'Neal have created for golf and basketball.

Pool has quickly grown beyond its humble origins, fallen away, and grown again. Where it's going is up to you.

Continue the Epic

POOL IS AT ONCE A GAME, a hobby, and a sport (making pool books sometimes hard to find in a bookstore). Pool has a rich history, a tapestry of colorful characters and international events. And it is the game of a lifetime. You will still be learning new strokes and new strategies many years from today.

If you've had half the fun reading this book as I've had writing it, you are probably anxious to get to your local pool hall right now for some Eight-Ball or Straight Pool, maybe even a few trick shots. Take this book with you and set up sample shots as illustrated for practice.

I salute you and wish you well on your pool journey, and I hope you will find time to correspond with me to let me know how you enjoyed *Picture Yourself Shooting Pool* and to share your suggestions for future editions.

Appendix

Selected Bibliography

Here's my list of standout books to complement *Picture Yourself Shooting Pool* and allow the reader a glimpse of pool's rich history and fiction. Pool has had more than its share of fabulous writers, including Tevis, Byrne, Stein and Rubino, Dyer, Fels, and many more. They make pool almost as much fun to read about as it is to play.

The 99 Critical Shots in Pool by Ray "Cool Cat" Martin

Clear and classic in its presentation, Ray Martin's study is worth reading for its information on Straight Pool alone.

Answers to a Pool Player's Prayers by Richard Kranicki

Featuring his collaboration with Willie Mosconi, Kranicki's title is an interesting exposition of the role of the eyes in pool aiming and unraveling the complexity of taking aim effectively at faraway, indistinct spheres on the table.

The Billiard Encyclopedia: An Illustrated History of the Sport by Victor Stein and Paul Rubino

One of the most impressive books published on any subject, *The Encyclopedia* is monumental in its scholarship, presentation, and illustrations. A gorgeous book and the result of over six years' dedicated research, in one volume is the complete history of pool, the art of the great cue makers and table craftsmen, and much more.

Billiards by John Grissim

The subtitle says it all: "Hustlers & Heroes, Legends & Lies, and The Search of Higher Truth on the Green Felt." Out of print but worth looking for, Grissim's book is an exploration of all things pool, told in an entertaining style from bar fight pool to playing opposite a young Efren "The Magician" Reyes in the Philippines.

Blue Book of Pool Cues by Brad Simpson

Illustrations and prices for thousands of custom and mass-manufactured cues. A must have for the cue aficionado.

Byrne's Book of Great Pool Stories by Robert Byrne

Entertaining compendium of billiards short stories old and new.

The Color of Money by Walter Tevis

Significantly different than the movie of the same name and worth the read. Includes a moving description of "Fast Eddie" receiving an 8-ball education—a literary look at true Eight-Ball.

The Eight Ball Bible by R. Givens

Eight-Ball concepts that apply to any game situation and in-depth study on how to play with over-sized or overweight cue balls on bar tables.

Encyclopedia of Pocket Billiards by John "Johnny Holiday" Deamato

Johnny Holiday's three books lack some clarity but are a treasure trove of knowledge for serious students of Straight Pool and cue ball positioning.

The Hustler by Walter Tevis

The novel that started it all. Fast Eddie meets Minnesota Fats, loses Fats, meets girl, loses girl, loses himself, meets Fats again. You'll weep and cheer as you read this book, on occasion at the same time.

The Hustler & The Champ: Willie Mosconi, Minnesota Fats, and the Rivalry that Defined Pool by R. A. Dyer

The revealed story of pool's greatest rivalry. The real-life Minnesota Fats taunted Mosconi until one day, Mosconi showed the world what eight hours of daily practice for 30 years adds when you're already the best pool shooter who ever lived.

Mastering Pool by George Fels

Stories of Eight-Ball, Nine-Ball, One Pocket, and Straight Pool tables told in photos and text. A seminal pool book that grows more enjoyable with each read.

McGoorty: A Billiard Hustler's Life by Danny McGoorty and Robert Byrne

Danny McGoorty drank, gambled, womanized, and rode trains like a hobo, and was one of the gentler, funnier people you'll ever meet. Byrne captures McGoorty's joy and anguish at discovering Cushion Billiards and taming it even as the sport was on the decline in America.

Playing Off the Rail: A Pool Hustler's Journey by David Mccumber

At once travelogue and pool romance, *Off The Rail* takes a pool fan across the nation to watch hustlers and gamblers in action. It only adds to my satisfaction that book protagonist, Tony Annigoni, meets some of the characters I've played on the road and beats them as they so richly deserved!

Pool Tables 101 by Doug Walters

This slim volume can be read in an hour but will save the reader thousands of dollars if they are serious about owning a quality pool table. After 20 years managing two antique and modern pool table retailers, Walters retired to become a whistle-blower on the pool table industry. Filled with tips on how to inspect, install, and maintain a quality pool table.

The Science of Pocket Billiards by Jack H. Koehler

Koehler has been a leader in the movement to quantify pool physics through experimentation and clinical observation. The mix has resulted in helping many players shoot better pool.

Index

What do you PICTURE YOURSELF Learning?

Picture Yourself Felting Your Knitting
Sarah E. White
1-59863-485-2 ■ U.S. $24.99

Picture Yourself Creating Digital Scrapbooks
Lori J. Davis and Sally Beacham
1-59863-488-7 ■ U.S. $29.99

Picture Yourself as a Magician
Wayne N. Kawamoto
1-59863-499-2 ■ U.S. $29.99

Picture Yourself Learning American Sign Language, Level 1
Janna M. Sweenie and David W. Boles
1-59863-516-6 ■ U.S. $34.99

Picture Yourself Playing Violin
Bridgette Seidel
1-59863-448-8 ■ U.S. $34.99

Picture Yourself Planning Your Perfect Wedding
Sandy Doell
1-59863-439-9 ■ U.S. $19.99

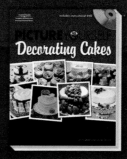

Picture Yourself Decorating Cakes
Sandy Doell and Linda Shonk
1-59863-440-2 ■ U.S. $24.99

Also Available

Picture Yourself
Creating Metal Clay Jewelry
1-59863-506-9 ■ U.S. $29.99

Picture Yourself Dancing
1-59863-246-9 ■ U.S. $34.99

Picture Yourself
Learning Mac OS X 10.5 Leopard
1-59863-514-X ■ U.S. $24.99

Picture Yourself
Creating Video Games
1-59863-551-4 ■ U.S. $34.99

Picture Yourself Directing a Movie
1-59863-489-5 ■ U.S. $29.99

Picture Yourself Learning
Corel Paint Shop Pro Photo X2
1-59863-425-9 ■ U.S. $29.99

Picture Yourself Creating
with Photoshop® Elements 5.0
1-59863-350-3 ■ U.S. $34.99

Picture Yourself Drumming
1-59863-330-9 ■ U.S. $34.99

Picture Yourself
Making Jewelry and Beading
1-59863-450-X ■ U.S. $19.99

COURSE TECHNOLOGY
CENGAGE Learning™
Professional • Technical • Reference

Visit us at www.courseptr.com
To order: 1.800.354.9706

License Agreement/Notice of Limited Warranty

By opening the sealed disc container in this book, you agree to the following terms and conditions. If, upon reading the following license agreement and notice of limited warranty, you cannot agree to the terms and conditions set forth, return the unused book with unopened disc to the place where you purchased it for a refund.

License:
The enclosed software is copyrighted by the copyright holder(s) indicated on the software disc. You are licensed to copy the software onto a single computer for use by a single user and to a backup disc. You may not reproduce, make copies, or distribute copies or rent or lease the software in whole or in part, except with written permission of the copyright holder(s). You may transfer the enclosed disc only together with this license, and only if you destroy all other copies of the software and the transferee agrees to the terms of the license. You may not decompile, reverse assemble, or reverse engineer the software.

Notice of Limited Warranty:
The enclosed disc is warranted by Course Technology to be free of physical defects in materials and workmanship for a period of sixty (60) days from end user's purchase of the book/disc combination. During the sixty-day term of the limited warranty, Course Technology will provide a replacement disc upon the return of a defective disc.

Limited Liability:
THE SOLE REMEDY FOR BREACH OF THIS LIMITED WARRANTY SHALL CONSIST ENTIRELY OF REPLACEMENT OF THE DEFECTIVE DISC. IN NO EVENT SHALL COURSE TECHNOLOGY OR THE AUTHOR BE LIABLE FOR ANY OTHER DAMAGES, INCLUDING LOSS OR CORRUPTION OF DATA, CHANGES IN THE FUNCTIONAL CHARACTERISTICS OF THE HARDWARE OR OPERATING SYSTEM, DELETERIOUS INTERACTION WITH OTHER SOFTWARE, OR ANY OTHER SPECIAL, INCI̶ ̶ ̶ ̶ ̶ ̶T MAY ARISE, EVEN IF COURSE TECHNOLO(̶ ̶ ̶ ̶ ̶ NOTIFIED THAT THE POSSIBILITY OF SUCḨ

Disclaimer of War̶
COURSE TECHNOL̶ ̶ ̶ ̶Y AND ALL OTHER WARRANTIES, EI̶ ̶ ̶ ̶ANTIES OF MERCHANTABILITY, SU̶ ̶ ̶R FREEDOM FROM ERRORS. SOME S̶ ̶ ̶D WARRANTIES OR LIMITATION OF I̶ ̶ ̶HESE LIMITATIONS MIGHT NOT APPLY̶

Other:
This Agreement is g̶ ̶ ̶ ̶t regard to choice of law principles. The ̶ ̶ ̶ ̶le of Goods is specifically disclaimed. Thi̶ ̶ ̶ ̶ou and Course Technology regarding us̶

SARATOGA SPRINGS PUBLIC LIBRARY.

CD

SARATOGA SPRINGS PUBLIC LIBRARY, NY

0 00 02 0433905 5